# ADMINISTERING THE NEW FEDERALISM

edited by
LEWIS G. BENDER
AND JAMES A. STEVER

 Westview Special Studies
in Public Policy and Public Systems Management

# Administering
# the New Federalism

# About the Book and Editors

With the passage of the Reagan Block Grants in 1981 and other subsequent policies and programs designed to reduce federal control over domestic programs, state and local governments began adjusting to a significant series of changes in the intergovernmental system, especially in the management role subnational governments play within the federal system. The "New Federalism" is likely to have a lasting impact on the way programs are managed in the federal system. In order to understand these changes more completely, Drs. Bender and Stever use a management focus rather than a narrow fiscal focus that measures impact in monetary terms. They use the most comprehensive survey and case research available on the administrative and subnational policy aspects of the New Federalism and present readers with both summary and critical analyses of the management responses and adjustments now taking place throughout the fifty states and their governmental sub-units.

Lewis G. Bender is director of the Center for Governmental Research at Central Michigan University. James A. Stever is director of the Graduate Program in Public Affairs at the University of Cincinnati.

# Administering
# the New Federalism

### edited by Lewis G. Bender
### and James A. Stever

Westview Press / Boulder and London

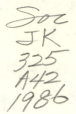

*Westview Special Studies in Public Policy and Public Systems Management*

----------------------------------------------------------------------------
This Westview softcover edition was manufactured on our own premises using
equipment and methods that allow us to keep even specialized books in stock.
It is printed on acid-free paper and bound in softcovers that carry the
highest rating of the National Association of State Textbook Administrators,
in consultation with the Association of American Publishers and the Book
Manufacturers' Institute.
----------------------------------------------------------------------------

Chapters 2 and 4 reprinted with permission from Publius: The Journal of
Federalism. Chapter 2 originally appeared as "Out with the Old, in with the
New": The New Federalism, Intergovernmental Coordination, and Executive
Order 12372" in volume 14 (Summer, 1984), pp. 31-48. Chapter 4 originally
appeared as "Federalism and Competing Values in the Reagan Administration"
in volume 16 (Winter 1986), pp. 29-47.

Published in 1986 in the United States of America by Westview Press, Inc.;
Frederick A. Praeger, Publisher; 5500 Central Avenue, Boulder, Colorado 80301

Library of Congress Cataloging in Publication Data
Administering the new federalism.
  (Westview special studies in public policy and public systems management)
  Includes index.
  1. Federal government--United States--Addresses, essays, lectures.
2. Administrative agencies--United States--Management--Addresses, essays,
lectures. I. Bender, Lewis G. II. Stever, James A., 1943-    . III.
Series.
JK325.A42    1986        321.02'0973         85-26626
ISBN 0-8133-7153-8

Composition for this book was provided by the editors.

Printed and bound in the United States of America

 The paper used in this publication meets the requirements of the
American National Standard for Permanence of Paper for Printed
Library Materials Z39.48-1984.

6  5  4  3  2  1

# Contents

viii

# Acknowledgments

The authors are very grateful for the hard work, skill, and care of four very special people. We thank Bea Windgaston for her skill and diligence in typing the manuscript and for understanding complicated instructions that we didn't fully comprehend. We thank Sandy Kline and Susan Keilitz for many hours of translating our material to the word processor and for applying consistency to our inconsistent styles.

We are also very grateful to Linda Perry for her willingness to help and for her kindness in distinguishing between a book and a V.L.D.

Any errors in this volume belong to the authors and not to the generous people who have assisted us.

*Lewis G. Bender*
*James A. Stever*

# PART ONE

# Overview of the New Federalism

Defining the parameters and the nature of specific interrelationships in any federal system can be a very difficult task. Correspondingly, the series of complex intergovernmental arrangements, programs and agreements that permeate the U.S. federation are not easily reduced to clear and cogent definitions. Terms and concepts such as centralization and decentralization fail to capture the wide variety of programmatic and institutional arrangements that are established in a federation involving over seventy-eight thousand governments and hundreds of thousands of elected and appointed public officials. The problem of providing a cogent definition is further complicated by the realities of sudden as well as evolutionary change that historically affect U.S. intergovernmental relations.

Rather than establishing hard and fast definitions of federalism, the three chapters in this section provide differing perspectives for viewing and explaining the programs and processes involved in President Reagan's New Federalism. In Chapter 1 Bender and Stever present an organizational and administrative view of the U.S. federal system. Essentially, they assert that the past and present changes in U.S. intergovernmental relations can be understood and explained through the application of traditional organizational and management concepts.

Timothy J. Conlan, in Chapter 2, analyzes President Reagan's New Federalism by pointing out that it is permeated with competing political values. Conlan asserts that conflicting values within the Reagan administration have often resulted in policies that centralize programmatic control in the national government. This tendency is contrary to the president's expressed goal of locating greater policy and programmatic control over domestic programs in the hands of state-level policy makers.

Finally, in Chapter 3, Richard Williamson presents the goals and objectives of the Reagan administration in regard to New Federalism programs and policies. Williamson provides an "insider's" perspective on the ideological, political, and practical considerations that went into the formation of President Reagan's New Federalism.

# 1

# An Organizational-Administrative View of Federalism

*James A. Stever*
*and Lewis G. Bender*

The two-hundred-year process of adaptation and evolutionary change within the U.S. federal system has been well documented and analyzed by numerous scholars of varying academic disciplines. The everchanging and emerging patterns of interrelationships within the federal system have been variously described and characterized as old and new, as adversarial and accommodating, as dual and cooperative, as decentralized and centralized, as a legal concept and a process of negotiation, and as a constitutional structure versus a series of pragmatic arrangements. Various metaphors have been applied to the federal system, such as layer and marble cakes, surging waters, picket fence. Though they have added color, these metaphors and their cumulative effect have added to our internally inconsistent stock of knowledge on the federal system.

It is not our desire to duplicate or reformulate the sometimes confusing array of explanations and descriptions that have been used to depict the major and subtle changes during the past two hundred years. Nor is it our intention to add another set of methaphors to the lexicon of federalism. Rather, it is the goal of the following chapter to provide a taxonomy for viewing and under- standing some of the managerial and administrative aspects of the federal system. In this system, there are ongoing intricate administrative processes where multiple governmental entities, some with constitutional authority, implement programs that are national in scope.

There is an inevitable relationship between federalism and administration. The interdependency of units in a modern federal system contributes to this

3

relationship. The very proximity of one unit to another necessitates that they interact administratively to implement projects and resolve disputes. The administrative relationships that develop with a federal system are not unique to federal systems. Thus administrative models and theories can be used to elucidate the structure and interactions between the central government and various member units of the system.

In drawing parallels between the U.S. federal system and large organizations, we are aware of the unique aspects of federalism--aspects that prevent us from claiming that the federal system is a large, integrated organizational structure. Factors such as electoral politics and constitutionally sovereign states add dimensions to the federal system not found in most large organizations. Nonetheless, it is evident that the federal system has evolved into a highly interdependent and integrated set of administrative arrangements quite similar to the arrangements for managing large organizations. The constitutional independence and autonomy of the subordinate federal units has been moderated, even eroded, by the economic, social, and political realities of a highly complex and interdependent society.

The following sections of this chapter elucidate some of the parallels between evolving U.S. federalism and large organizations. We explain how some typical organizational and administrative processes apply to the evolution of federalism. We then discuss how some typical administrative functions such as leadership, coordination, efficiency, and accountability are performed within the U.S. federal structure. The remaining chapters in this book examine the impacts of the policy and administrative changes of the Reagan administration on the operation of subnational units.

## AN ORGANIZATIONAL VIEW OF FEDERALISM

In spite of some of the political rhetoric surrounding President Reagan's New Federalism, the relationships between federal, state, and local governments were not eliminated. Rather, they were changed. In the new environment, state and local governments still participate in programs and functions that are national in scope. The New Federalism, however, has altered and rearranged many of the administrative and policy roles of subnational governments in regard to the implementation of these nationwide programs and functions.

The periodic rearrangement of administrative and policy roles and the reorganization of bureaucracy is common to both large organizations and the U.S. federal system. Frequently, real and/or perceived crisis is the catalyst for rearrangement and reorganization. Examples abound of large public and private organizations that institute massive reorganization in response to the impacts of internal and external crises. A recent example is the response of the U.S. automobile industry to the combined threat of competition from abroad and expanded demand of consumers for well-built, fuel-efficient automobiles. The crisis brought on by plummeting profits and worker layoffs created an environment that not only allowed for but demanded significant changes in the market strategies, organizational structures, and management philosophies of the big three automobile companies. As a result, these corporations decentralized certain critical functions relating to production processes, and product quality control. These corporations also centralized other functions relating to market targeting and financial planning.

Historically, significant changes in the U.S. federal system have also been the result of reactions to crises that have affected the entire political and economic system. Indeed, the very creation of the U.S. federation was the result of a series of military and economic crises. Later crises centered around the Civil War, the inability of the states to control the impact of industrialization, World War I, the Great Depression, and World War II. Each of these crises contributed to a series of administrative rearrangements between the units of the federal system. The reorganization resulted in greater centralization of power and authority within the system. Most scholars agree that these centralizing tendencies reached their apex with the development of the Great Society programs during the 1960s.

The federal administrative processes and arrangements during the Great Society era were similar to those found in highly centralized, yet geographically extensive corporations. The central government attempted to exercise tight policy and programming control over the development and implementation of programs and projects. With the expansion of categorical grants, emphasis was placed on accountability and extensive reporting of programmatic expenditures. Categorical grants restricted the discretion available to subnational units of the system.  Communication within the system was increasingly characterized by top-down directives and bottom-up informational reporting.  Power and prestige gravitated to the federal government at the expense of state and local administrators.

The real and/or perceived failure of the Great Society programs to win the war on poverty coupled with criticisms of growing federal power led to a series of rearrangements aimed at decentralizing federal administrative power and authority.  Nixon's New Federalism which included expanded use of block grants, and the passage in 1972 of general revenue-sharing legislation began a trend toward loosening central control over subunits within the federal system.  Subsequent actions during the Ford and Carter administrations, including further expansion of block grant programs, continuation of revenue sharing, and the advent of deregulation phenomena, sustained the decentralizing trend.

The federal government's movement toward decentralization, furthered by many of the policies and programs of the Reagan administration, has paralleled changes in numerous organizations in the private sector.  Currently, popular approaches to management, such as Theory Z and other participative management efforts, signal a general trend toward reorganizing and decentralizing organizational decision-making authority and responsibility.

The relationship between federalism and administration can be further illustrated by considering how typical administrative functions operate within federal systems.  Though hardly exhaustive, the following five administrative functions are essential to the performance of organizations:  leadership, coordination, regulation and accountability, efficiency, and discretion to subordinate units.  If any of these elements are missing or performed out of synchronization with other elements, the organization suffers.  When each of these operations is synchronized with the others, the system is administratively integrated.

Though we commonly associate these five administrative functions with the operation of organizations, it is also appropriate to apply these concepts to the operation of federal systems.  Like private organizations, contemporary federal systems require under certain conditions that certain system-wide administrative functions be performed.  These administrative functions have become important in the federal system for a variety of reasons.[1] Two primary reasons, though, concern the effects of technology and industrialization on the system; they have thrust the units of the system into an interdependent relationship. The integrity of the overall system has become increasingly important. Thus, in critically evaluating U.S. federalism, administrative issues and the performance of system-wide administrative functions are as important as classical constitutional issues. The emerging importance of administrative issues to U.S. federalism can be illustrated by discussing how the above five administrative functions are performed within the U.S. federal system.

## ADMINISTRATIVE FUNCTIONS IN FEDERAL SYSTEMS

### Leadership

According to Philip Selznick, the institutional leader is "primarily an expert in the promotion and protection of values."[2] Selznick goes on to argue that the leader is concerned with more than efficiency. He is concerned with relating in the most effective way the organization that he heads to the surrounding environment. Thus, the successful leader structures the organization so that it serves the values of people inside and outside the organization.

Constitutionally speaking, the federal system does not have a leader. Yet, since the presidency of Franklin D. Roosevelt, it has become increasingly apparent that the president is the leader of the federal system and performs a role similar to that of the institutional leader Selznick describes. Finding the capitalist economy in chaos, the banking system inoperable, and an unacceptable percentage of the citizenry unemployed, Roosevelt proposed a restructuring of the traditional relationships between the states and the federal government. This restructuring was not only political but administrative as well. Fulfilling the role of an institutional leader, President Roosevelt altered administrative relationships to serve democratic and capitalistic values. Put differently, the New Deal was an administrative restructuring of the federal system designed to preserve and protect democracy and capitalism.

Since Roosevelt's times, successive presidents have, as part of their political campaigns, proposed various administrative restructurings of the federal system. Presidents Johnson and Nixon advocated two very different administrative relationships between state, federal, and local governments. The point, though, is not the content of their respective proposed changes, but rather is the fact that presidents now routinely regard it as their responsibility to change the system so as to enhance their political values. Both President Johnson and President Nixon were able to effectively introduce congressional legislation to secure these changes.

Changing the federal system was a central, major theme in President Reagan's 1980 campaign. Once states were restored to their constitutionally guaranteed place in the system, Reagan argued vital American values (for example, self sufficiency, popular control over government, experimentation) would again emerge. Like his predecessor, Jimmy Carter, President Reagan declared that his election would signify a popular mandate to initiate major restructurings within the system. However, unlike his predecessor, Reagan has enjoyed Congressional support sufficient to accomplish the alterations he promised.

## Coordination

Intraorganizational coordination is an ongoing concern of administered organizations. In private sector organizations, coordination of diverse organizational tasks toward a single goal can frequently be accomplished by the supervision exercised by a single organizational authority. Nonetheless, several factors often inhibit, even prevent, functional coordination in large hierarchical organizations. Private and public sector managers, for example, must frequently contend with subunit desires to protect organizational turf and to undermine overriding organizational goals. Attempts to promote coordination through negotiation, planning, or rigid hierarchical control are sometimes subverted by the narrowly defined interest of organizational subunits.

The task of coordinating the actions of member governments in the federal system surpasses in complexity even the task of coordinating large multinational corporations. In addition to the fifty state governments and over 78,000 local governments, numerous federal agencies, interest groups, and quasi-public organizations are often involved in implementing the policies of national programs. Given this complexity, it is not surprising that coordination problems accompanied the New

Deal, the first presidential attempt to manage the U.S. federal system.

To coordinate New Deal policy, Roosevelt delegated authority to staff members such as Harold Ickes. Roosevelt observed, "A very long experience convinces me of two things. If forty states go along with adequate legislation and eight do not ... we get nowhere."[3] When staff members proved incapable of generating a working consensus among the states, Roosevelt formed the National Emergency Council, an organization of federal bureaucrats and state directors. The performance of this organization also proved unsatisfactory.[4]

Since the New Deal, the intergovernmental landscape has become littered with a raft of solutions to the coordination problem: Annual Arrangements, Model Cities, Councils of Governments, A-95, Integrated Grant Projects, Capacity Building Projects, Planned Variations, Pilot Neighborhood Centers, Interagency Coordinating Councils, and Joint Funding Projects. The need to continually propose new solutions to replace ineffective ones indicates that the barriers to effective coordination within large organizations and the federal system are many, and the rewards are few.

During the Reagan administration, numerous changes reversing previous coordination measures have been implemented. However, the effectiveness of these new measures has yet to be determined. Of the thirty-nine federal programs that provided funds for regional agencies, twelve have been eliminated. Federal Regional Councils have been eliminated. Planning funds have been severely curtailed in many policy areas. The A-95 review process has been eliminated. The Reagan philosophy is that the primary onus for administrative coordination should be placed on the states. To accomplish this, Executive Order 12372 requires local governments to funnel their requests through state agencies and thus rely on state governments to coordinate local programs with others throughout each state.

## Regulation and Accountability

Within any large organization, political relationships develop between constituent units. The differences among staff and line units on matters such as personnel policy and budgeting are legend. Regulations set the limits within which political and administrative action occur. Regulations are also designed to insure that units within a system can be held accountable to organizational norms.

Within the federal system, two major types of regulations can be found: regulations designed to insure certain conformity levels within a specific policy area, such as health or transportation, and regulations that extend over numerous policy areas. The regulations affecting specific policies seek to insure that policy goals and approaches to implementation are relatively consistent in all subunits. Crosscutting regulations have goals that transcend the concerns of any specific policy area: for example, the Davis Bacon Act or the Civil Rights Act of 1964. In either case, the federal government is the major source of regulation, though each state regulates its own local governments.

The issues of regulation and accountability arise both in large organizations and in the U.S. federal system. Proponents of expanded regulation within large organizations want bureaucratic subunits to be held accountable to the goals and directives of centralized organizational authority. Proponents of added regulations within the federal system want subnational governments to be held accountable to national norms. Recently, it has become obvious that the federal government's attempt to regulate the actions of states and localities frequently exceeds its ability to enforce these regulations. Furthermore, advocates of more state and local freedom from federal regulation charge that excessive regulation inhibits the operation of the system.

Under the Reagan administration, major changes are occurring in the way that the federal government regulates subnational entities. First, there has been a dramatic reduction in the quantity of regulations. For example, the Department of Education reduced its regulations to the point that they required only 20 pages of space in the Federal Register as opposed to 667. Second, there has been a reduction in the substance of federal regulation: the federal government has narrowed the range of requirements that it imposes on subnational entities within the system. Third, there has been a reduction in the reporting requirements (red tape) that the federal government has traditionally imposed on subnational entities.

## Authority and Discretion of Units

Specialization is an inherent feature of large,

bureaucratic organizations. When organizations specialize, they create smaller, subordinate organizations to perform specialized functions. These subordinate organizations, as noted previously, not only create coordination problems for their host, but also with their creation bring up the question of their autonomy: that is, how much freedom they should be allowed. Organizational managers routinely confront this question in all phases of organizational operation. Hence, when top organizational managers make personnel decisions, establish budgetary targets, and set policy, they must continually determine how much authority and discretion to allow subordinate units.

The issue of authority and discretion has always been an issue within the context of federalism. In the nineteenth century, debates about the appropriate degree of authority for states and localities were based almost exclusively on constitutional grounds. Nineteenth century scholars of federalism such as Lord Bryce argued that the consititution should be repeatedly updated in order to precisely delimit the authority of all member governments in the system.

As national programs developed in response to technological and economic interdependency, administrative criteria became a factor in determining state and local authority and discretion. Thus, authority was parceled out to subnational governments based not on their legal entitlement, but on administrative feasibility. For example, the New Deal forced many states to chose between their legal right to provide welfare versus the administrative expediency of participating in the national welfare programs conceived by the federal government.

When states and localities are drawn into an administrative relationship with the federal government, neatly fixed legal parameters for subnational authority and discretion are sometimes difficult to establish. In order to accomplish programmatic goals, subnational governments are often asked to accept plans, budgetary limits, personnel decisions, and policy goals that jeopardize their traditional legal rights. As Marshall Dimock points out, administration tends to be more dynamic than law.[5] Thus, as authority and discretion of subnational governments are increasingly determined by administrative criteria, we can assume that there will be dramatic shifts in the administrative freedom allowed these governments. This freedom will vary from policy area to policy area, as the federal government changes the latitude of freedom allowed.

Under the Reagan administration, there has been a determined, though sometimes inconsistent, attempt to shift the locus of decision-making authority to the states. One evidence of this determination is the renewed emphasis given to block as opposed to categorical grants. The argument is that block grants allow greater state discretion. Another tangible expression of the Reagan administration's intent to shift the locus of authority can be found in Executive Order 12291. It states: "Federal regulations should not preempt state laws or regulations except to guarantee rights of national citizenship or to avoid significant burdens on interstate commerce." Nonetheless, in certain policy areas such as environmental policy and nuclear policy, the Reagan administration retains close, centralized federal control.

## Efficiency

Efficiency questions are at the heart of management. To be concerned about efficiency is to be concerned about maximal effect from minimal investment of resources. Hence, organizations continually attempt to reduce the amount of time, tooling, personnel, and raw materials necessary to produce a given item.

As American federal relations have become more administrative, concerns about efficiency have increased. Many of the criticisms leveled against President Johnson's Great Society programs were based on alleged inefficiencies. Efficiency-minded critics targeted categorical grants with such narrow purposes as to: 1) encourage subnational governments to spend money on unnecessary projects and 2) distort the budgets of subnational governments and cause subnational governments to increase their personnel investment in order to comply with excessive federal regulations. Critics also cited the Great Society's emphasis on involving often untrained personnel in governmental decisionmaking. This involvement, they charged, contributed to the inefficiencies in the system.

This concern for administrative efficiency also extends to the Reagan administration. Thus, this administration not only justifies the changes it seeks on constitutional grounds but also by pragmatic arguments for efficiency within the federal system. The Reagan administration amplified a theme that began to emerge during the Nixon Administration--that the federal government was hyper-centralized. Consequently, President Reagan argued that in the interest of efficiency, selected programs and responsibilities should be returned to the states. The president's Executive Order 12291 echoed this concern for efficiency by requiring that all federal regulations be scrutinized to insure that the benefits outweighed the costs of implementing the regulation.

CONCLUSION

Taken collectively, both the organizational dynamics and the five administrative functions discussed above offer us a starting point from which to begin to appreciate the administrative features of the modern federal system. Contemporary federal systems have become so administratively oriented that numerous other parallels beyond those mentioned here could be drawn. To further illustrate this relationship, we have chosen to focus on President Reagan's New Federalism. We have selected thirteen articles that assess from differing perspectives four of the administrative features of the New Federalism: 1) the goals and values that the leaders of the New Federalism reforms intended to accomplish, 2) the administrative impacts of the New Federalism on state and local governments, 3) the New Federalism's effectiveness in implementing certain nationwide programs, and 4) further administrative reforms suggested by the New Federalism.

These articles raise a series of questions regarding the New Federalism. First, in the midst of substantial shifts in the administrative philosophy of the federal government, how are state and local governments reacting to these changes? Second, what are the broad policy objectives running throughout the federal system and how are they being accomplished? Third, do state and local governments have the capacity to implement programs that are national in scope? Do they have the budgetary capability, the organizational networks, and the expertise to implement policy? Finally, does the New Federalism improve or detract from the entire federal system's administrative ability to support a national economy, deliver social welfare, maintain a national transportation network, protect the environment, and accomplish a series of other national goals that we have come to expect will be accomplished?

14

## NOTES

1. We recognize here the difficult task of determining what historical factors have changed the American federal system. Our purpose is not to settle that issue but rather to simply suggest that historical changes have necessitated attention to administrative relations between the federal government and other units within the system. Our point is that administrative issues and problems have become more important. We are not prescribing any particular administrative configuration among the units of the system.

2. Philip Selznick, Leadership in Administration (Berkeley: University of California Press, 1957), p. 28.

3. Cited in James Patterson, The New Deal And the States (Princeton, N.J.: Princeton University Press, 1969), p. 102.

4. Ibid., pp. 107-111.

5. Marshall E. Dimock, Law and Dynamic Administration (New York: Praeger Publishers, 1980).

6. Executive Order 12291, 46 Federal Register 13193, February 19, 1981.

# 2

# Ambivalent Federalism: Intergovernmental Policy in the Reagan Administration

*Timothy J. Conlan*

To a remarkable extent, President Reagan has made federalism a central concern in his administration. He speaks frequently of his deep commitment to revitalizing the federal system and of his desire to return government responsibilities to states and localities. As he told a conference of state legislators in 1981, "My administration is committed--heart and soul--to the broad principles of American Federalism."[1]  Indeed, Richard S. Williamson, the president's former assistant for intergovernmental affairs, has argued that federalism stands at the very top of the president's policy agenda-- higher than tax or budget cuts and higher than regulatory relief:

President Ronald Reagan has a dream. His dream is not to cut the bloated federal budget ... His dream is not about tax cuts ...  His dream is not about regulatory relief ...  Rather, the President's dream is to change how America is governed ...  He is seeking a "quiet revolution," a new federalism which is a meaningful American partnership.[2]

The administration has taken major strides to translate such intentions into tangible results. With the passage of the Omnibus Reconciliation Act in 1981, the Reagan administration achieved the creation of nine new, or substantially revised, block grants and produced the first absolute decline in funding for federal grants to states and localities since the 1950s.[3]  The Reagan administration also became the first to make inter- governmental regulations--those requirements that directly

15

or indirectly affect state and local governments rather than the private sector--a major target of regulatory reform.[4] Most importantly, the president placed a sweeping New Federalism initiative at the center of his 1982 legislative agenda.

In measuring the true depth of Reagan's commitment to strengthening federalism, however, it is instructive to examine his administration's record on those occasions when the goal of rebalancing federalism, as the president defines it, conflicts with other deeply held values. How high does federalism rank on the president's scale of priorities when truly difficult decisions must be made? When judged by this standard, federalism has not fared as well as one might expect under this administration. Devolutionary policies consistent with the president's definition of federalism reform have repeatedly lost out in the Reagan administration when they have conflicted with the goals of reducing the federal budget, deregulating the private sector, and advancing the conservative social agenda. A full listing would embody administration policies and actions across the broad expanse of federal activities, from restricting local regulation of cable television, to preempting state usery laws. Some of the most prominent examples include policies urging reduced appropriations for most block grant programs, opposing the expansion of General Revenue Sharing, supporting national product liability legislation, advocating elimination of the deduction for state and local taxes, preempting state laws regulating double-trailer trucks and establishing minimum drinking ages, overriding state objections to increased off-shore oil drilling and expanded use of nuclear power, requiring states to establish workfare programs; and suing localities that seek to retain aggressive affirmative action hiring plans. Each of these policies is briefly described in the following sections.

## BUDGETARY POLICY AND REAGAN FEDERALISM

Domestic program budget cuts have long been an intergral part of President Reagan's approach to federalism because they help to reduce the relative fiscal profile of the federal government while encouraging greater financial independence among state and local governments. All federal programs are not identical in their effects, however, and an intergovernmentally sensitive program of budget cuts could be expected to affect certain federal grants far more than others. In particular, narrowly prescriptive and intrusive categorical grants might be expected to bear the brunt of federal budget cuts, allowing more flexible programs, such as block grants and general revenue sharing, to be touched more lightly or not at all. Because they can be readily adapted to meet a range of diverse local needs, block grants and revenue sharing formed the core of Richard Nixon's New Federalism agenda, and they have remained a top priority of state and local governments. Although they were also a major policy goal of his administration, block grants received very different budgetary treatment under Ronald Reagan.

In 1981, the President proposed seven sweeping new block grants intended to consolidate eighty-five federal aid programs for state and local governments. Although most of these proposals were significantly modified by Congress, nine new or substantially revised block grants were created as part of the Omnibus Reconciliation Act of 1981. This historic legislation consolidated more federal grant programs in one stroke than all previous block grants combined.

Yet consolidation, with its attendant cuts in application, reporting, and paperwork requirements, was not the only important feature of these legislative changes. The new block grants also embodied large reductions in spending. In his initial block grant proposals, the president had requested reductions averaging almost 25 percent less than fiscal year (FY) 1981 spending on the programs suggested for merger, far below the modest 10 percent reductions in federal aid the governors had offered to accept in exchange for broader program authority. In fact, the president recommended block grants for some of the deepest spending cuts of any segment of the federal budget--deeper than total cuts in federal aid--while entitlements and defense actually increased over 1981 spending levels (see Table 2.1). Although less severe, a similar pattern was evident in the block grants enacted in FY 1982 (see Table 2.2).

This spending approach marked a dramatic shift in federalism strategy from the Nixon and Ford adminis- trations. These administrations had demonstrated a consistent willingness to accept higher spending levels for block grant programs in order to enhance political support for them in Congress.[5] As a result, much of the political debate about the Reagan block grant proposals focused on their budgetary features rather than on the

TABLE 2.1
Comparison of Reagan Budget Requests For FY 1982 With Actual FY 1981
Expenditures on Comparable Programs
(Budget Authority, in billions)

| Program Category | FY 1981 Expenditures | Reagan FY 1982 Request | Percentage Change FY 1981-FY 1982 |
|---|---|---|---|
| Total Block Grants | 18.7 | 14.8 | -21% |
| New block grant proposals/ prior categorical spending | 12.8 | 9.7 | -24% |
| Existing block grants a/ | 5.9 | 5.1 | -14% |
| Total Federal Aid | 105.8 | 86.2 | -19% |
| Major Entitlements b/ | 311.4 | 335.3 | +8% |
| Total Domestic Spending c/ | 511.2 | 546.1 | +7% |
| National Defense | 182.4 | 226.3 | +24% |
| Total Federal Spending | 718.4 | 772.4 | +8% |

SOURCE: <u>Budget of the United States</u>, <u>Budget Appendix</u>, and <u>Special Analyses</u> for appropriate years.

a/ Not including public service employment programs

b/ Including social security

c/ Total federal spending minus defense and international affairs.

TABLE 2.2
Comparison of Actual FY 1982 Expenditures With FY 1981 Expenditures
on Comparable Programs (in billions)

| Program Category | FY 1981 Expenditures | FY 1982 Expenditures | Percentage Change FY 1981-FY 1982 |
|---|---|---|---|
| Total Block Grants | 13.6 | 11.6 | -15% |
| New block grants established/ prior categorical programs | 7.7 | 7.1 | -8% |
| Existing block grants a/ | 5.9 | 4.5 | -24% |
| Total Federal Aid | 105.8 | 91.9 | -13% |
| Major Entitlements b/ | 311.4 | 323.7 | +4% |
| Total Domestic Spending c/ | 511.2 | 545.9 | +7% |
| National Defense | 182.4 | 218.7 | +20% |
| Total Federal Spending | 718.4 | 779.9 | +9% |

SOURCE: Budget of the United States, Budget Appendix, and Special Analyses for appropriate years.

a/ Not including public service employment.

b/ Including social security.

c/ Total federal spending minus defense and international affairs.

merits or demerits of grant consolidation. Most liberals in Congress, and even many mayors and governors, viewed the block grant proposals mainly as a "Trojan horse" for cutting social program budgets. As former Carter aide Eugene Eidenberg expressed it:

The driving force behind the Administration's decisions about federalism is primarily a concern with the federal deficit ... At the bottom of the New Federalism is, I believe, the Administration's belief that the best way to cut spending is to eliminate the substantial support that the federal government currently provides for a variety of programs administerd by state and local governments[6]

Though significant, such political concerns about the budgetary impacts of the 1981 block grants were not sufficient to prevent their enactment, principally because the normal patterns of block grant politics in Congress were temporarily overwhelmed by broader political and economic forces. Since that time, however, the administration has made twenty-three additional proposals to expand existing block grants or to enact new ones. It succeeded only once, replacing the CETA program with the Job Training Partnership Act in 1982. In most cases, the administration advocated further budget reductions in connection with its new consolidation proposals, and rarely did it subsequently signal a willingness to sacrifice these budgetary goals in order to secure block grant enactments. On the contrary, as part of its FY 1986 budget, the administration proposed terminating one block grant and cutting another by 10 percent. Thus, the message to state and local governments remained consistent and clear: the president would continue to support the general goal of grant reform, but--in contrast to other objectives such as national defense, tuition tax credits, and urban enterprise zones--he would not adjust his fiscal priorities to advance this cause.

A similar situation existed with respect to General Revenue Sharing (GRS). General Revenue Sharing was the crown jewel of Nixon's New Federalism and the federal program most dear to state and local governments. President Reagan has not shared this affection, however. He holds a far more skeptical view of efforts to harness the federal tax apparatus to provide funds for state and local governments. Accordingly, the president on several occasions has proposed terminating or severely modifying the program or reducing its budget. In 1975 and again in

1982, Reagan advocated folding the GRS program into a broad package of federal program and revenue turnbacks to the states. In late 1981, he proposed a 12 percent cut in GRS spending as part of a planned across-the-board reduction in federal domestic expenditures. The president returned to more drastic solutions in his FY 1986 budget, which proposed terminating GRS in October 1985, one year before its authorization expires.

Such proposals have stirred great concern and significant lobbying by mayors and other local government officials anxious to maintain their favorite program. In 1983, their efforts succeeded in obtaining administration agreement to retain GRS at existing funding levels when the program was renewed. Continued large deficits since that time led the administration to argue once again that "the Federal Government can no longer afford general revenue sharing."[8] In 1985, this argument carried the day in Congress, which, after exploring various options, agreed to let the program expire in October, 1986.

Perhaps the sharpest conflict between the administration's federalism and its budget priorities occurred in the context of the president's 1982 federalism initiative. Although the president's sweeping initiative served to underscore his extraordinary interest in intergovernmental reform, its ultimate failure to advance beyond discussions with state and local officials was due in large part to the president's unwillingness to make fiscal concessions sufficient to gain gubernatorial backing for the plan.

The structure of the federalism initiative was complex, but in essence it had two parts: (1) a "swap" component in which the federal government would acquire full financial responsibility for the Medicaid program in exchange for state assumption of the Aid to Families with Dependent Children (AFDC) and Food Stamp programs; and (2) a "turnback" component in which the federal government would return to states full responsibility for approximately forty federal programs, along with a variety of tax resources to pay for them. The administration claimed that the ultimate fiscal tradeoffs between the federal government and the states would be neutral or even slightly beneficial to states, and it went to great lengths in the initial phases of its program to avoid economic winners and losers among the states. Nevertheless, this fiscal neutrality was contingent on having Congress make a series of budget cuts in the affected programs prior to putting the federalism initiative into

effect. Without such cuts, the Congressional Budget
Office estimated that the turned back programs would cost
$34 billion to continue, rather than the $30 billion
estimated by the White House or the $28 billion provided
for in the trust fund.[9] Similar budget cuts were
anticipated in the AFDC and Food Stamp programs. Such
actions tended to reinforce earlier perceptions that the
New Federalism was mainly a vehicle for shifting budget
cuts to the states, an interpretation seemingly supported
by some officials'attempts--most notably David Stockman's-
-to utilize the federalism package to help address the
federal government's growing deficit problem.[10] As
Richard S. Williamson later acknowledged, such attempts to
use the federalism initiative for short-term budgetary
gains undercut political support for the proposal:

In retrospect, the administration could have taken steps
that might have enhanced the prospects of reaching final
agreement in sorting out ... First, and most importantly,
we allowed ourselves as an Administration to be trapped
into an obsession over short-term budget considerations.
The budget was allowed to dominate internal Administration
machinery and crowd out the Federalism initiative.[11]

   Moreover, such actions heightened governors' concerns
about the long-term fiscal and policy impacts of the
federalism proposal. The administration argued that, in
the long run, states would benefit financially from the
swap portion of the initiative because the federalized
Medicaid program was growing much faster than AFDC and
Food Stamp programs, which were slated for devolution.
But many state officials worried that Medicaid benefits
and eligibility in a nationalized program would be set so
low that they would feel compelled to supplement the
federal program in their states. Governors were equally
concerned with establishing a viable benefit floor in the
income maintenance programs. Although the administration
agreed in negotiations to retain federal funding for Food
Stamps, it refused to decouple Food Stamp benefits from
AFDC payments. As a result, states would confront a
federal disincentive to establish higher AFDC allowances
because such payments would reduce food stamp benefits to
their citizens.
   Despite these difficulties, negotiations on the
federalism initiative made substantial progress during
early 1982, and some participants believed that they came
close to an agreement.[12] Agreement with the governors

almost certainly could have been achieved if Reagan had been willing to devote additional federal resources to ease their concerns, just as Nixon had done before him. This would not have guaranteed enactment by Congress, but such fiscal accommodation would have given the plan a fighting chance by securing strong gubernatorial support for the package and undercutting charges that the initiative was merely a cloak for further budget cuts. In the final analysis, however, the president was unwilling to make such adjustments. As Williamson observed, Reagan simply could not bring himself to sacrifice his budgetary goals for the sake of federalism:

As much as the President wanted to strike a deal with the governors, and walk in step with them to Capitol Hill, the philosophical gap proved to be too wide. To more state and local officials, the President needed a bigger carrot than in good faith he felt he could offer.[13]

## TAXING CHOICE: FEDERALISM AND TAX REFORM

The sacrifice of federalist reform to budgetary considerations has a fiscal parallel in President Reagan's ambitious tax reform plan of 1985. In order to finance the overall goal of significant tax rate reductions, the plan proposes to eliminate the federal income tax deduction for state and local tax payments and to place severe restrictions on tax-exempt bonds.

In deference to federalism, deductibility has been part of the federal revenue code since the income tax was first enacted in 1913. Today, it constitutes one of the largest federal subsidies to state and local governments. However, the $33 billion annual cost to the federal treasury also makes it an inviting source of funds to tax reformers. As Mitchell Daniels, White House Director of Intergovernmental Affairs, explained to the U.S. Conference of Mayors shortly after the tax plan was announced: "Lower rates,... special relief for the poor, economic growth--none of these goals can be reached without the revenue ... recaptured by repeal of deductibility."[14]

For fiscal conservatives, eliminating deductibility has the added appeal of increasing the marginal price of-- and thereby constraining--state and local government revenues. Although estimates vary widely, the Congressional Research Service estimated that, over the long run, eliminating deductibility would reduce state and

local revenues by 20.5 percent.[15] This fact has raised
suspicions by congressional Democrats and many state and
local government officials that eliminating deductibility
is part of a two-pronged administration strategy (along
with federal budget cuts) to "'dismantle state and local
government' by shrinking its revenue base."[16]

Regardless of the motives, the president's tax plan
appears to place disproportionate burdens on state and
local governments. Although deductibility constitutes
only 11 percent of all federal tax expenditures to
individuals, it makes up 67 percent of the tax
expenditures eliminated to finance tax reform.[17]
Moreover, the administration proposes to raise an
additional $5.7 billion a year by 1990 by placing new
restrictions on state and local tax-exempt bonds. It is
estimated that these restrictions will remove tax-exempt
status--and thus eliminate or substantially raise the
cost--of 62 to 80 percent of all currently exempt bonds.[18]

In stark contrast, numerous other tax expenditures in
the present revenue code are left wholly or largely intact
in the president's reform plan, even though they enjoy no
stronger economic rationale than do intergovernmental
subsidies. These expenditures include deductions for
charitable donations for interest on residential mort-
gages, and for oil and gas drilling expenses. For a
variety of philosophical and political reasons, several
broad areas of the tax code were granted favored treatment
by the president. Provisions encouraging strong and well-
balanced fiscal systems at other levels of government were
not among them, however, leading some observers to
question the president's commitment to federalism:

The principled point is the need to guard the vitality of
state and local government, not to impair it by hogging
still more traditionally local tax sources for the federal
treasury. In a better hour you can imagine Ronald Reagan,
who sometimes poses as a federalist, voicing these
sentiments.[19]

DEREGULATION AND THE NEW FEDERALISM

Deregulation, like federalism, has been major policy
focus of the Reagan administration. In many instances,
the two goals have tended to complement each other.
Although significant regulatory reform initiatives were
begun under presidents Ford and Carter, Reagan's
administration was the first to recognize and seek to

reduce the distinctive regulatory burdens imposed on state and local governments over the past twenty years. The president's Task Force on Regulatory Relief, the new regulatory review procedures established in the Office of Management and Budget (OMB), and individual departmental paperwork reduction efforts have all been employed at various times to help redress problems stemming from intergovernmental regulation.

Yet, as in the past, most deregulation efforts in the Reagan administration continued to focus predominantly on government regulation of the private sector. Most responsible officials continued to frame regulatory issues almost exclusively in such terms. Moreover, it readily became apparent that deregulating the private sector can easily conflict with deregulating states and localities. When it comes to regulation, business generally prefers, not only fewer requirements to more, but uniformity to diversity. Yet states, like the federal government, have become increasingly active regulators in recent years in more and more policy areas--from consumer and environmental protection to occupational and product safety. Such activity is often built upon federal regulatory foundations, as in the case of environmental programs where states are required or strongly encouraged to enforce federal minimum regulatory standards but are permitted to supplement or exceed them.[20] In other cases, states have chosen to develop their own regulatory activities beyond minimum national standards or to preempt state regulatory authority in a given field entirely. As one business spokesman observed of such actions when it comes to regulation, the "national interest cannot be subjected to the parochial interests of localities."[21]

Such concerns have not been ignored by the Reagan administration. As increasing conflicts have arisen between deregulation and intergovernmental deference, the Administration has sided repeatedly with business interests. According to one recent study of proposed federal preemptions, for example, the administration "supported moves to take regulatory powers from the states" in nine out of twelve cases studied.[22] Similarly, an analysis of Reagan administration briefs to the U.S. Supreme Court concluded that:

The Administration ... does not hesitate to give states' rights a back seat ... In each instance (examined), the issue, broadly framed, concerned states' rights, and... the Administration argued that Federal regulation should

prevail ... Cynics might suggest that ... the Administration preference for big business is so strong that it
will override conflicting concerns for federalism.[23]

Whatever the merits of this view, several cases
involving transportation, energy, and product liability
regulation illustrate the conflicts that have arisen in
this area.

## Product Liability

Administration support for national product liability
legislation has been described as a case in which "result
oriented reformers (in the Administration) won out over
those who would have adhered to ... the (federalist)
principles of the framers."[24]  Historically, manufacturers' liability for injuries resulting from defective
products has been governed by state laws.  In recent
years, however, mounting concern has been voiced by
business spokesmen about the difficulties resulting from
differing and often increasingly stringent state laws in
this area, and many have called for preemptive federal
legislation.

Backed by the Product Liability Alliance--a coalition
of over 200 trade and business organizations--legislation
to this effect was introduced in Congress in 1982 by
Senator Robert Kasten (R-WI).  The Kasten bill would
supersede state product liability laws but, in order to
avoid overloading already crowded federal court dockets,
would retain state court jurisdiction to try liability
cases and interpret federal law.  Thus, in the words of
one analyst, the bill "represents a new approach to
centralization that borders on state conscription."[25]

Confronted with a difficult choice between the
concerns of manufacturing interests and its own federalism
proclivities, the Reagan administration "agonized" for
several months over whether to support national product
liability legislation.  Strongest support for endorsing
national legislation came from Commerce Secretary Malcolm
Baldridge and from regulatory reform advocates in the
administration.  As one administration supporter of
preemption wrote, conflicting state liability laws have
created "significant burdens on interstate commerce" and
"tremendous uncertainty for manufacturers."[26]  Others in
the administration, however, including Attorney General
William French Smith and Labor Secretary Raymond Donovan,
argued that such a position was hardly consistent with the

president's recently announced federalism initiative. Moreover, opponents pointed to practical difficulties in the Kasten approach. For example, denying federal courts jurisdiction to resolve likely differences of statutory interpretation by fifty state judicial systems was hardly a format designed to guarantee uniformity in the product liability domain. Nevertheless, when the issue was put to the president for resolution, "Reagan overrode the objections ... that endorsement of federal legislation would run counter to the Administration's 'federalism' drive" and agreed to support the preemptive Kasten bill.[27]

## Two for the Road: Regulation of Trucking and Drinking-Age Standards

In the last three years, two new and highly visible federal regulations have been enacted in the transportation field with the support and encouragement of the Reagan Administration. Like several other pioneering intergovernmental regulations enacted in the 1960s and 1970s, both requirements threaten reductions in federal highway aid as levers to force state adoption of federal uniform standards on truck size and a twenty-one-year-old drinking age.

Preemption of varying state restrictions on truck length, width, and weight has long been a goal of the trucking industry, which has sought by this means to expand the use of highly efficient double trailer trucks. Although such trucks were permitted in most areas of the country by 1982, they were still prohibited by fourteen states and the District of Columbia because of concerns about their safety and their destructive effects on highways.[28] Against a backdrop of concerns about crumbling infrastructure and deteriorating highway conditions, the Reagan administration launched an initiative to alter this situation in May 1982. To help fund additional highway renovation, Secretary of Transportation Drew Lewis proposed increasing the federal gasoline tax and raising truckers' fees, but he combined these new levies with provisions to establish higher, uniform truck size-and-weight requirements to appease truckers unhappy about the new rates. Under this proposal, states that refused to comply with the new standards would lose federal highway funds.[29] Shortly after it was announced, however, the president began to back away from the Lewis initiative, primarily because of his uneasiness with the sizable tax increase it contained, but also because of opposition expressed by many truckers and several state governments. When the president again endorsed the need for new transportation revenues following the November 1982 elections, a lame-duck session of Congress enacted legislation along the lines of Lewis' proposal in the waning days of the 97th Congress.[30]

Having helped write uniform truck standards into law, the administration pushed preemption to its limits in subsequent regulations. The administration decided to permit the large new trucks not only on interstate highways, but on an additional 140,000 miles of primary and access highways—38,000 miles more than state highway departments had designated as suitable for large trucks. This action infuriated officials in many states, including those in some states that had long permitted double-trailer trucks on their major highways. In response to state criticism, the Federal Highway Administration eventually removed 17,000 miles of roads from its initial designation, but it added another 19,000 miles of highways to its list and moved to quash outstanding lawsuits against its actions.[31]

In 1984, the administration reversed an earlier position and, in the face of rapidly spreading popular pressure, endorsed a second major highway-related regulatory expansion. On 17 July 1984, President Reagan signed legislation designed to compel all states to adopt a minimum drinking age of 21 or face reductions by 1987 of 10 percent in federal highway aid. Initially, the president had been reluctant to support such a heavy-handed approach to changing state drinking laws, preferring instead to continue an existing program of incentives for state actions against drunk driving. Indeed, stronger federal action on this issue appeared to be unnecessary because twenty states had raised their drinking age since 1980 and only eight still permitted alcohol consumption at age 18.[32] Moreover, legislation in this area seemed firmly fixed within the sphere of state responsibilities—a tradition strongly reaffirmed by the wording of the Twenty-First Amendment.

Yet, if raising the drinking age proved to be a popular cause in most state legislatures, it became almost irresistible in Congress. In the wake of emotional publicity and effective lobbying by families victimized by drunk drivers, strong support emerged in Congress for an immediate uniform approach to the problem. Faced with the prospect that Congress might enact preemptive legislation despite his own misgivings about it and urged to change his mind by Transportation Secretary Elizabeth Dole, the president reversed his position on 13 June 1984, and came out strongly for federal sanctions to enforce a national drinking age.[33] With this policy reversal, the legislation sailed through Congress and was signed by the president a month later. "The problem is bigger than the individual states," he proclaimed at the signing ceremony. "With the problem so clear-cut and the proven solution at hand, we have no misgiving about this judicious use of Federal power."[34]

## Fueling Conflicts over Energy

Two prominent controversies over energy policy illustrate the conflicts that have arisen when the administration's goal of expanding domestic energy production has clashed with state environmental policies and concerns. In seeking to accelerate off-shore oil drilling and nuclear power production, the Reagan administration has faced a series of lawsuits and congressional action inspired by the affected states. In both cases, long-running disputes have ensued as deference to state concerns has been sacrificed to other policy objectives.

Both controversies began early in the president's first term. Indeed, one of James Watt's first actions as secretary of Interior was to open bidding on new off-shore oil and gas drilling leases. By this action, the administration sought to expand domestic energy production rapidly, to reduce federal restraints on oil and gas exploration, and to utilize the proceeds from stepped-up sales to diminish federal deficits. But Interior's February 1981 sale of leases off the California coast was quickly challenged by the state in federal court. State officials were concerned about environmental effects and successfully challenged the federal government's lack of consultation as required by the Coastal Zone Management Act of 1972 (CZMA).

Faced with this reversal in the courts but still determined to expand the sale of off-shore leases, the administration undertook to rewrite the regulations. According to one report, officials from Interior--with the president's support--overcame objections by the Commerce Department to altering the regulations and played a major role in rewriting the rules, even though they were legally under Commerce's jurisdiction.[35] Critics charged that the resulting regulations "virtually eliminated(d) state participation in decisions concerning their coasts" and made "a mockery of Reagan's 'new federalism'."[36]

Having laid the necessary legal groundwork, Secretary Watt subsequently announced a massive new leasing plan. Again ignoring state objections, the administration proposed to make a billion additional acres available for gas and oil exploration--forty times more than all the acreage leased during the previous thirty years. Once again, several of the affected states went to court in an attempt to block the longterm leasing plan. They also took their case to Congress where, over administration opposition, they won legislative changes that for the first time gave coastal states a portion of the proceeds from federal off-shore lease sales.[37] Congress also limited the sale of leases off the coasts of several of the most severely affected states. However, the administration has consistently threatened to veto bills requiring that leases conform to state coastal management plans, and thus has blocked such legislation.[38]

A similar pattern of intergovernmental conflict emerged over administration policies supporting the construction of nuclear power plants. In 1976, California enacted a moratorium on the licensing of new nuclear power plants until an adequate method for disposing long-term nuclear wastes has been developed. Two California utilities subsequently challenged the state's moratorium in federal court, arguing that state action in this field had been preempted by federal law. Having lost the decision in circuit court in 1982, the utilities appealed the decision to the U.S. Supreme Court. Their appeal was supported by the Reagan administration, which asserted a broad interpretation of federal powers in this field and sought to overturn the moratorium as part of a broader policy of promoting nuclear power.[39] Despite the administration's arguments, however, the Court upheld the ban as an expression of the states' historic function of regulating the economic activities of public utilities.[40]

NATIONALIZING CURRENTS IN SOCIAL POLICY

Social policy historically has offered fertile terrain for intergovernmental conflict, and the Reagan administration has not entirely escaped such frictions. Although most fields of social policy traditionally have come under state and local jurisdiction--thus permitting adaptations to the cultural and social diversity of the nation--issues that arise in this arena also tend to evoke fundamental principles and values. This linkage not only tends to make compromise difficult, but it also creates strong temptations for policy advocates to seek a single national solution--a temptation that afflicts conservatives and liberals alike.

Both implicit and explicit tensions between its social policy and federalist objectives have arisen in the Reagan administration. Implicit conflicts have been most evident in education policy. President Reagan generally shares the view of many state and local advocates that the federal role in education has grown unnecessarily large and intrusive and that the federal government should focus its resources more carefully on areas of clear national responsibility, leaving most aspects of education to states and localities. Yet despite the recent flurry of state activity to reform and upgrade educational programs, the president has found it hard to resist using his office as a "bully pulpit" for advocating his own vision of educational reform, legitimizing in the process the basic concept of national strategies for educational improvement. Thus, the president has appointed and called attention to his own reform commission on education, has proposed and lobbied for the passage of tuition tax-credit legislation, and, in a move that harkens back to the Sputnik era, has proposed new federal legislation for enhancing mathematics and science instruction.

There have also been explicit conflicts between the administration's social policies and its federalist objectives. Two cases illustrate the tensions in this arena: the administration's efforts to mandate state-implemented workfare programs for welfare recipients and its attempt to regulate medical care for handicapped infants.

Many governors, economists, and welfare reformers have long urged that funding for the nation's income maintenance programs be nationalized in order to promote greater equity and rationality in benefit levels. Reagan has never shared this view, believing instead that welfare programs should be shaped by community standards and carefully monitored by each locality. As he remarked in a 1975 speech: "If there is one area of social policy that should be at the most local level of government possible, it is welfare. It should not be nationalized--it should be localized."[41]

Yet the president also believes that the current welfare system should be trimmed back and that anyone who is able to work should be required to do so. Hence, his administration has sought repeatedly to require that states establish "workfare" programs for able-bodied welfare recipients. It helped get workfare provisions covering AFDC and Food Stamps written into law in 1981, at which time Congress authorized--but did not require--state utilization of three workfare approaches: community service in compensation for welfare (favored by the administration), employment supplementation through wage subsidies, and job training and services through the existing work incentive program.[42] Since that time, various states have experimented with all three, usually on a small scale, in order to evaluate their costs and effectiveness.

Dissatisfied with the limited progress being made, the administration has tried to force faster state action. In an attempt to make the community service approach mandatory, it sought to require that states involve seventy-five percent of eligible AFDC and Food Stamp recipients in such programs or face fiscal sanctions for inadequate compliance. To date, however, the states have successfully resisted such mandates. Concerned that workfare programs may significantly raise administrative and social service costs and provide few long-term benefits for recipients, they have sought to retain the flexibility necessary to experiment with and refine alternative approaches.

Another case of social policy prescription involves administration attempts to force changes in affirmative action hiring plans at the local level. Ironically, many of the plans in question were initially imposed on local governments by lawsuits undertaken by earlier administrations. Today, however, these plans are accepted by most of the cities involved and by their employees, who resent yet another wave of federal intervention.

The immediate source of the controversy stems from the U.S. Supreme Court's ruling in Firefighters Local Union 1784 v. Stotts. In this 1984 decision, the Court ruled that contractually established seniority rights assumed precedence, in making layoffs, over the rights of black employees hired later through a court-ordered affirmative action plan. Since that time, lower courts have interpreted the Stotts ruling narrowly, in part because it was a statutory interpretation of the Civil Rights Act of 1964 and not a constitutional interpretation.

Rather than wait for further clarification and a stronger constitutional footing before challenging locally supported plans, the Reagan Justice Department took Stotts to be a mandate against "quotas" and "reverse discrimination."[43]  It has sought reversal of consent decrees in fifty-six localities and, meeting strong resistance from many of these, it has taken Indianapolis to court.  Such actions strike the mayor of that city, and many less involved observers, as inconsistent with the president's New Federalism.  In the words of Neal Peirce:  "By initiating expensive legal action to force cities to back down on affirmative action, Justice makes something of a joke of the 'New Federalist' ideal of returning power to the grassroots."[44]

## POLICY DILEMMAS AND THE FUTURE OF FEDERALISM

The Reagan administration has been confronted with many difficult policy decisions.  Forced to choose between policies supportive of its federalist objectives--devolution, enhanced state autonomy, and balanced intergovernmental relationships--and those supportive of other presidential priorities--reduced federal domestic spending, lighter regulatory burdens on the private sector, and conservative social policy objectives -- the Administration chose, in each case examined here, a course that was openly or implicitly contrary to its stated intergovernmental goals.

Some of these decisions were reached reluctantly.  Some may have been products of bureaucratic momentum or political compromise rather than the products of a calculated strategy.  Others can be defended on their merits.  Moreover, there have been certain cases that have gone the other way.  In 1983, the Department of Transportation declined to preempt local airport noise restrictions despite calls for uniformity from the airline industry.[45]  Within the courts, the Administration sided with states against a Citicorp challenge to regional banking agreements.  It also long resisted legislative efforts to preempt state pesticide regulations before ultimately relenting.  Finally, in his federalism package, the president agreed to nationalize funding of the costly Medicaid program in his effort to achieve a comprehensive sorting out of intergovernmental roles.  Nonetheless, when truly difficult decisions were on the line, the overall thrust of policy by this administration seemed to bear little resemblance to the president's rhetoric on intergovernmental reform.

This pattern of policymaking has important impli-

cations for the current political status and future
prospects of federalism in the United States. The point
is not that Reagan is less supportive of strengthening
federalism than other recent presidents have been. On
balance, he has seemed more committed to this end.
Nevertheless, President Reagan resembles his more liberal
predecessors in his willingness to sacrifice federalism
whenever it conflicts with his other deeply held policy
objectives. Summarizing four years of federal grants
policy, George Peterson concluded that: "The Administration performed in the traditional manner as senior
partner in the federalist grants partnership. The change
... was that the new financial inducements ... were meant
to achieve expenditure reduction."[46] Similarly, in
regulatory policy, when opportunities arose to use
preemptive national action to advance policy goals, the
temptation to do so often proved too great to resist. As
former Nixon economic aide Herbert Stein has written,
"Even conservative governments when in office do not want
to limit their own powers."[47]

This tendency appears to be consistent with popular
attitudes. Most Americans continue to pay lip service to
the ideals of federalism and decentralization, but they,
like the politicians who represent them, appear to be
generally unwilling to sacrifice specific policy goals to
pursue these ideals. The situation is not unlike the
contradiction in public attitudes discovered by Lloyd Free
and Hadley Cantril in 1964. They found that in terms of
abstract political values, a majority of Americans could
be classified as political conservatives, voicing support
for the Jeffersonian ideals of small, decentralized
government and reduced public interference in the private
sector and in the lives of individuals. Yet, when asked
about specific public policy issues, a substantial
majority of respondents favored increased federal
government involvement in nearly every aspect of the
welfare state.[48]

It appears that hardly anyone today believes that
maintaining the integrity of the federal system is
sufficiently important to justify sacrificing other
important values. This does not mean that federalism is
irrelevant. Politicians and interest groups continue to
use federalist arguments for tactical purposes, as
vehicles to pursue other policy ends, but fewer and fewer
people appear committed to federalism as a worthwhile end
in itself. Although this may be understandable, it is
very different from the commitments commonly invested in

other aspects of the U.S. Constitution. There are many passionate defenders of absolute adherence to the guarantees of free speech or to restrictions on search and seizure, for example, who are willing to endure the dissemination of offensive or unpopular publications or to accept less effective law enforcement to pursue these larger goals. Once common, such tradeoffs on behalf of federalism are increasingly rare.

Ultimately, this tendency may represent the most fundamental challenge to the federal system. It gives rise, not to a wholesale onslaught on the system or to a wellspring of support for a unitary system, but to a subtle process of erosion that eventually leaves an archaic, sterile structure bound together only by a web of mundane administrative relationships. As Laurence H. Tribe expressed it:

No one expects Congress to obliterate the states, at least in one fell swoop. If there is any danger, it lies in the tyranny of small decisions--in the prospect that Congress will nibble away at state sovereignty, bit by bit, until someday essentially nothing remains but a gutted shell.[49]

Perhaps the United States can survive without a strong federal system, just as many other countries do. But considering the prominent role that federalism was intended to play in the U.S. system of government, we ought to evaluate federalism's real and potential contributions to U.S. political life and weigh the gains and losses resulting from its quiet diminution.

For example, the federal system can still perform a variety of traditionally valued functions such as: providing multiple arenas of collective decisionmaking and public participation, permitting the expression and preservation of local diversity within a framework of nationally shared values, and promoting democratic government through a system of shared and separated powers. In addition to such traditional functions, the federal system in recent years has proven to be of increasing value in the formation of viable public policy. Though long appreciated, the value of state and local governments as "laboratories of experimentation" has never been more evident than it is today--from demonstrating how to cope with fiscal stringency and new modes of service delivery to promoting educational reforms and economic development.

Moreover, the past twenty years of experience with

domestic policy initiatives has underscored the potentially complementary roles played by governments in designing and implementing new federal programs. Freed from the burdens of actually delivering most public services, national policymakers have often been able to focus on the abstract objectives of public policy (equity, fairness, health and safety, freedom of choice) and to set ambitious goals for their achievement. Because they are insulated from the day-to-day responsibilities for actually accomplishing these and other competing goals, however, federal policymakers have also risked under-estimating the constraints on governmental performance, placing excessive strains on state and local governments and society at large, and overlooking the merits of existing institutional arrangments and patterns of behavior.

As the principal implementors of governmental programs, state and local governments have been firmly rooted in the realities of service delivery, aware of the constraints on government's abilities, and reflective of legitimate variations in community preferences and values. Yet these governments have sometimes appeared to loose sight of the ends to which policies are directed, becoming co-opted by established institutions and modes of operation or excessively constrained by the fear of resource competition with other jurisdictions.

Both policy perspectives are vital to effective public policy. But to gain the advantages of both perspectives requires a degree of political equilibrium between the different levels of government. In the contemporary intergovernmental context, this especially means reserving sufficient autonomy for state and local governments to enable them to be viable centers of power and decisionmaking, with adequate resources for experimentation and the ability to gain on a regular basis policy concessions from the federal government. Some observers fear that the United States has already passed the point where state and local governments retain enough autonomy to resist federal policy encroachments and to ensure federal consideration of their policy perspectives. They fear, in short, that the United States has slipped into a quasi-unitary form of government.[50] Although such fears seem premature, the maintenance of federalism will require deliberate choices in cases of conflicting goals. Recognition of this by federal policymakers would be a useful first step.

NOTES

Author's Note:    I wish to thank David Beam, Cynthia Colella, Robert Dilger, Donald Kettl, Lester Levine, Ann Martino, David Walker, and Margaret Wrightson for their helpful advice on earlier drafts of this article.

1.    "First Phase in Revitalizing Federalism," Alabama Municipal Journal (September 1981): 4.
2.    Richard S. Williamson, "The Self-Government Balancing Act:   A View from the White House," National Civic Review 71 (January 1982):   19.
3.    Advisory Commission on Intergovernmental Relations (ACIR), Significant Features of Fiscal Federalism (Washington, D.C.:  Government Printing Office, 1984), pp. 11, 120.
4.    See ACIR, Regulatory Federalism:   Policy, Process, Impact, and Reform (Washington, D.C.:  Government Printing Office, 1984).
5.    See Timothy J. Conlan, "Back in Vogue:  The Politics of Block Grant Legislation," Intergovernmental Perspective 7 (Spring 1981):   11,12
6.    Eugene Eidenberg, "Federalism:   A Democratic View," in American Federalism:   A New Partnership for the Republic, ed. Robert B. Hawkins, Jr. (San Francisco: Institute for Contemporary Studies, 1982), p. 112.
7.    For more details on these proposals, see David R. Beam, "New Federalism, Old Realities:   The Reagan Administration and Intergovernmental Reform," in The Reagan Presidency and the Governing of America, eds. Lester M. Salamon and Michael S. Lund (Washington:  The Urban Institute, 1985).
8.    U.S. Office of Management and Budget, Budget of the United States Government, Fiscal Year 1986 (Washington, D.C.:  Government Printing Office, 1985), p. 5-151.
9.    Timothy J. Conlan and David B. Walker, "Reagan's New Federalism:   Design, Debate and Discord," Intergovernmental Perspective 8 (Winter 1983):   9.
10.  For more on this, see Laurence I. Barrett, Gambling With History (Garden City, N.Y.:   Doubleday, 1983), pp. 342-343.
11.  Richard S. Williamson, "The 1982 New Federalism Negotiations," Publius 13 (Spring 1983):   31.
12.  "New Federalism:   A Special Story," Governors' Priorties:   1983 (Washington:   National Governors' Association, 1983), p. 39.

13. Williamson, "The 1982 New Federalism Negotiations," p. 26.

14. Quoted in Milton Coleman, "U.S. Mayors Asked to Back Tax Plan," Washington Post, 18 June 1985, p. A4.

15. U.S. Congress, Senate, Committee on Government Affairs, Limiting State-Local Tax Deductibility, Committee Print 98-77, 98th Cong., 1983-84 1st sess., p. 17.

16. Rep. Robert Matsui, quoted in Timothy Clark, "The Tax Reform Spotlight is Falling on State and Local Tax Deduction," National Journal, 29 June 1985, p. 1511.

17. "States Contribute More Than Fair Share," Capitol to Capitol, 8 July 1985, p. 3.

18. Government Finance Officers' Assoication, "GFOA Opposes the Administration's Tax-Exempt Bond Provisions," Unpublished Position Statement, 21 June 1985, Washington, D.C., p. 1.

19. Edwin M. Yoder, Jr., "Demogoguery Over a Deduction," Washington Post, 18 June 1985, p. A15.

20. For more details about such "partial preemption" programs, see ACIR, Regulatory Federalism: Policy, Process, Impact, and Reform.

21. Quoted in Daniel Gottlieb, "Business Mobilizes as States Begin to Move into the Regulatory Vacuum," National Journal, 31 July 1982, p. 1342.

22. Felicity Barringer, "U.S. Preemption: Muscling in on the states," Washington Post, 25 October 1982, p. A11.

23. Alan B. Morrison, "N*w Fed*ral*sm Holes," New York Times, 20 September 1982, p. A15.

24. Alfred R. Light, "Federalism, FERC v. Mississippi, and Product Liability Reform," Publius 13 (Spring 1983): 85.

25. Ibid., p. 96.

26. C. Boyden Gray, "Regulation and Federalism," Yale Journal of Regulation 1 (1983): 96, 97.

27. Caroline Mayer, "Product Liability Dispute is Settled," Washington Post, 16 July 1982, p. D3.

28. Tom Wicker, "Welcome, Killer Trucks," New York Times, 1 November 1982, p. E14.

29. Ernest Holsendolph, "Lewis Offers Plan on Trucks as Exchange for a Tax Rise," New York Times, 5 May 1982, p. A20.

30. 1982 Congressional Quarterly Almanac, (Washington, D.C.: Congressional Quarterly, 1983), p. 317.

31. Barbara Harsha, "DOT Sets Final Routes for Large Trucks," Nation's Cities Weekly, 18 June 1984, p. 2.

32. Steven Weisman, "Reagan Signs Bill Tying Aid to Drinking Age," New York Times, 18 July 1984, p. A15.

33.  Douglas Feaver, "Reagan Now Wants 21 as Drinking Age," Washington Post, 14 June 1984, p. A1.
34.  Weisman, "Reagan Signs Bill," p. A1.
35.  Michael Lerner, "Coastal Mismanagement," The New Republic, 14 October 1981, p. 14.
36.  Ibid., p. 12.
37.  1982 Congressional Quarterly Almanac, p. 448.
38.  See Joseph A. Davis, "Senate Commerce Moves Bill on Offshore Leasing Actions," Congressional Quarterly, 12 May 1984, p. 1138; and "House Passes Coastal Zone Bill," Congressional Quarterly, 3 August 1985, p. 1552.
39.  Morrison, "N*w Fed*ral*sm Holes," p. A15.
40.  Pacific Gas and Electric Co. v. State Energy Resources Conservation and Development Commission, 51 LW 4449.
41.  Ronald Reagan, "Conservative Blueprint for the 1970s," reprinted in Congressional Record, 94th Cong., 1st sess., 1975, p. 31186.
42.  Linda Demkovich, "The Workfare Ethic," National Journal, 26 February 1983, p. 453.
43.  Eric Wiesenthal, "Municipal Affirmative Action Plans Attacked," Public Administration Times, 1 June 1985, p. 1.
44.  Neal R. Peirce, "Republican Mayor Blasts Reagan on Civil Rights," County News, 3 June 1985, p. 19.
45.  Randy Arndt, "DOT Sees Airport Noise as State, Local Problem," Nation's Cities Weekly, 4 April 1983, p. 4.
46.  George Peterson, "Federalism and the States:  An Experiment in Decentralization," in The Reagan Record, eds. John L. Palmer and Isabel V. Sawhill (Cambridge, MA:  Ballinger, 1984), pp. 234-35.
47.  Herbert Stein, "The Reagan Revolt that Wasn't," Harpers, February 1984, p. 48.
48.  Lloyd Free and Hadley Cantril, The Political Beliefs of Americans (New York:  Simon and Schuster, 1968).
49.  Laurence H. Tribe, American Constitutional Law (Mineola, N.Y.:  The Foundation Press, 1978), p. 302.

50.  See, for example, Theodore J. Lowi, "Europeanization of America?  From United States to United State," in Nationalizing Government:  Public Policies in America, eds. Theodore J. Lowi and Alan Stone (Beverly Hills, CA: Sage, 1978); Daniel J. Elazar, "Is the Federal System Still There?" in Hearings on the Federal Role, Advisory Commission on Intergovernmental Relations (Washington, D.C.:  Government Printing Office, 1980); and Stephen L. Schechter, "The State of American Federalism in the 1980s," in American Federalism:  A New Partnership for the Republic, ed. Robert B. Hawkins, Jr. (San Francisco: Institute for Contemporary Studies, 1982).

# 3

# Reagan Federalism:
# Goals and Achievements

*Richard S. Williamson*

The deep roots of Reagan federalism can be traced to his years as governor of California (1967-1974). There he gained first-hand experience with the competence of state government. Through his own successful welfare-reform program in California, he demonstrated the potential in state experimentation--the benefits of diversity. Also, while governor of the largest state, he experienced the frustrations that result from federal intervention in state business. Reagan saw the inefficiencies of the long arm of Washington.

Therefore, there was no surprise when the 1980 rhetoric of presidential candidate Ronald Reagan was a call for bold federalist reform. He recognized that the centralized federal government had become overloaded, assuming more than it could handle. Accountability between voters and government had waned. And, too often, state and local officials were judged more by their grantsmanship[1] in Washington than by their responsiveness and effectiveness in governing.[2]

President Reagan clearly set before the American people his plans in his inaugural address when he said,"It is my intention to curb the size and influence of the Federal establishment and to demand recognition of the distinction between the powers granted to the Federal government and those reserved to the states or to the people. All of us need to be reminded that the Federal government did not create the states: the states created the Federal government."[3]

As President Reagan's assistant for intergovernmental affairs, I was involved in the early White House meetings in 1981 as President Reagan's goals were translated into

41

specific proposals. From the outset President Reagan made clear that he wanted to focus his political capital on his economic reform package of budget cuts, regulatory reform, tax cuts, and a stable monetary policy. Further, in the early Cabinet and Budget Review Board meetings, he made it clear to all of us that he wanted to graft federal proposals onto the economic reform package.

Consequently, his budget proposals and the congressional budget reconciliation process were used to advance block grants; a concept for decentralizing decision making about which President Reagan was enthusiastic. The Regulatory Reform Task Force that Reagan established under Vice President Bush was requested, among other things, to ease the federal regulatory burdens on state and local governments. And the tax cut proposal was seen by President Reagan to be one means of getting the federal government off the backs of citizens and freeing up revenue sources for state and local governments. This was the strategy in 1981, and in large measure it remained intact throughout President Ronald Reagan's first term in office.

After substantial success in his first year, the President attempted in 1982 a tactical gambit of a bold federalism proposal. This over $40 billion proposal to sort out responsibilities amongst the various levels of government and return revenue sources to the states ultimately failed. It faced opposition on many fronts: the strong skepticism and rivalries between the intergovernmental players (local vs. state vs. federal); the strong resistance in established Washington to changes of the status quo (interest groups, Congress, and the bureaucracy); conflicting power centers within the administration (White House, Office of Management and Budget (OMB), cabinet departments); and, most important, the budget crisis that crowded out all other issues on the domestic agenda.

Nonetheless, Reagan federalism has made noteworthy progress with block grants, regulatory relief, and budget trends. The following discussion seeks to set forth what was done in the first term -- more specifically, block grants, regulatory relief, the federal budget, and federalism initiative.

BLOCK GRANTS

Over the years a system of allocating federal funds to state and local areas developed that was organized into a myriad of specific categorical grants that serve narrowly defined groups. It is the view within the Reagan administration that this system of categorical grants had become a confusing tangle of small programs that overlap, conflict, and overregulate. These categorical grants systematically took discretionary authority away from state and local officials and transformed them into administrators of federal programs.[4] As President Reagan said in 1981,

A major aspect of our federalism plan is the eventual consolidation of categorical grants into blocks. Today there are too many programs within too many strings offering too small in return ... Block grants are designed to eliminate burdensome reporting requirements and regulations,unnecessary administrative cost and program duplication. Block grants are not a mere strategy in our budget plan, as some have suggested; they stand on their own as a federalist tool for transforming power back to the state and local level.[5]

The growth trend and proliferation of categorical grants had been dramatic. On June 16, 1959, during hearings that resulted in the creation of the Advisory Commission on Intergovernmental Relations, former Governor and then Senator Edmund Muskie made the following observation: "There is a feeling on the part of some people that states are always reaching out for federal dollars. There are upward of 40 grant-in-aid programs depending on how they are classified. I don't know how you keep track of them all."[6]
In 1959, the total spending for these grant-in-aid programs was $6.5 billion, accounting for 1.4 percent of the gross national product (GNP).[7] By 1970, there were 130 categorical grant programs, and by 1980 the number of categorical programs stood at 492; total federal spending had skyrocketed to over $91.5 billion, accounting for 3.6 percent of GNP.[8]
Furthermore, the categorical grant programs described by Senator Muskie in 1959 dealt principally with transportation and income security programs. The 492 programs of 1980 covered virtually every facet of state and local government.

## 1981 BLOCK GRANT PROPOSALS

In 1981 President Reagan proposed the most far-reaching effort ever attempted to consolidate federal grant-in-aid programs to state and local governments. He asked Congress to consolidate nearly ninety categorical grants into seven block grants: Health Services, State Education Services, Community Development, Preventive Health Services, Social Services, Energy, and Emergency Assistance and Local Education Services.

When the president's 1981 block grant proposals were unveiled, few thought they could be successful. As governors Richard Snelling of Vermont and James Hunt of North Carolina wrote in August 1981: "Last year, knowledgeable observers predicted that legislation proposing new block grants would never be scheduled for a hearing in the Senate or the House of Representatives; enactment was viewed as an impossibility."[9]

Such skepticism was understandable given the prior record of block grant proposals. Only five had been enacted out of approximately twenty that had been proposed during the previous two decades. In contrast to the prior record of disappointment, President Reagan's 1981 block grant proposals achieved substantial success. Admittedly, Congress made significant changes in the Reagan proposals, but the basic framework was retained. The Omnibus Budget Reconciliation Act of 1981[10] consolidated fifty-seven categorical grants into nine new or modified block grants with budget authority of over $7.5 million. The reconciliation bill, as signed by the president, included the following block grants: Alcohol, Drug Abuse and Mental Health; Preventive Health and Health Services; Primary Care; Social Services, Community Services; Low Income Home Energy Assistance; Elementary and Secondary Education; and Community Development. (See Appendix A for detailed description of these 1981 block grants.)

The states accepted most block grants quickly. For example, thirty-seven states participated in HUD's Community Development Block Grant in Fiscal Year (FY) 1982 even though it was optional; forty-eight states participated in FY 1983. The primary reason for nonparticipation was a problem of timing, which was resolved during 1982.[11] All fifty states chose to accept five of the HHS block grants; forty-one states accepted a sixth HHS block grant, community services, during its first year of availability. Finally, when the Department of Education block grant became available in July 1982, forty-eight states applied in the first week. Applications from the remaining two states were received shortly thereafter.

The administration followed through on the new block
grants by dramatically cutting costs to states for these
programs. For example, in implementing the consolidation
of more than thirty categorical programs into a single
block grant, the Department of Education eliminated 118
printed pages of regulations in the Federal Register,
200,000 pages of grant applications, 7,000 pages of
financial reports, and 20,000 pages of programmatic
reports. This reduction of paperwork represented per year
a $1.5 million savings to grant application preparants,
$70,000 in financial reports that the Department of
Education otherwise would have requested, and nearly
$145,000 in the preparation of reports for the various
programs.[12]

The Office of Management and Budget estimated that
the new block grant regulations resulted in a reduction in
the paperwork burden on state and local officials from 6.5
million worker hours in FY 1981 to 1.1 million worker
hours in FY 1982, an 83 percent reduction.[13]

Notwithstanding his 1981 block grant achievements,
President Reagan was not satisfied. The very next day
after passage of the Omnibus Budget Reconciliation Act of
1981, he said he would seek more in the future. He said
in an address to the National Conference of State
Legislators on July 30, 1981,

In normal times what we've managed to get through the
Congress concerning block grants would be a victory. Yet
we did not provide the states with the degree of freedom
in dealing with the budget cuts we had ardently hoped
for. We got some categorical grants incorporated into
block grants but many of our block grant proposals are
still on the Hill. That doesn't mean the end of the
dream. Together you and I will be going back and back and
back until we obtain the flexibility you need and
deserve.[14]

Unfortunately, with one exception, the Reagan administration's block grant proposals of 1982 and 1983 did not
realize success on Capitol Hill.

## 1982 BLOCK GRANT PROPOSALS

As the president promised, he proposed seven new
block grant or program consolidations in 1982. In
addition, three existing block grants were proposed to be
expanded to include new categorical programs. These ten

new proposals would replace forty-six more of the existing categorical programs.[15] In 1983, amendments would also be proposed to replace four child nutrition programs with a simple $448 million program of more flexible grants to the states.[16]

The new 1982 block grant proposals were Child Welfare,[17] Combined Welfare,[18] Rehabilitation Services,[19] Vocational and Adult Education,[20] Education for the Handicapped,[21] Rental Rehabilitation,[22] and the Job Training. Expansions of the following three block grants established by the Omnibus Budget Reconciliation Act of 1981 were proposed for FY 1983: Primary Care,[23] Maternal and Child Health,[24] and the Energy and Emergency Assistance.[25]

The Job Training Block Grant proposal was signed into law on October 13, 1982,[26] creating a new single block grant to states for training and employment programs. This grant replaced the Comprehensive Employment and Training Act, which had expired. An appropriation level of $1.8 billion was proposed for the first year.[27]

In 1981, officials of the Department of Labor worked out a proposal with the Cabinet council working group. The proposal included a block grant program to the states and placed the emphasis for training and jobs on the private sector.[28]

On February 11, 1982, Labor Secretary Raymond Donovan met with President Reagan and others to discuss job training legislation. Following that meeting, agreement was reached for senators Dan Quayle (R-Ind.) and Orrin Hatch (R-Utah) to introduce the administration's bill. The bill, S.2184, was introduced on March 9, 1982.[29] The administration bill differed from an earlier Quayle bill, S.2036, as well as another House bill, H.R.5320, which continued the old CETA program with little change. As a result of subsequent meetings of administration officials with senators Hatch and Quayle, the Senate bill was modified to conform more closely with administration goals. At the mark-up of the Senate bill (S.2036) Senator Quayle said, "This bill is based on a proper recognition of the role of the states. It transfers to the state many functions previously vested in the federal government, such as approval of local plans, designation of service delivery areas, and management and fiscal controls."[30]

On September 30, 1982, and October 1, 1982, the Senate and House, respectively, approved the conference report on S.2036, the Job Training Partnership Act of 1982.[31] The bill incorporated the key features of the

president's original proposal.    President Reagan signed
the bill into law on October 13, 1982,[32] which represented, as Governor Scott Matheson said, "the most
significant federalism step in 1982."[33]    This was the
first block grant to be enacted in 1982.

## REGULATORY RELIEF

Over the years, Ronald Reagan made well known his
concerns about Washington's over-regulation.    The
administration's view of how federal over-regulation had
distorted U.S. federalism was perhaps best expressed by
President Reagan's first Chairman of the Council of
Economic Advisors, Murray Weidenbaum:

(I)n the past decade we have seen a boom in federal social
regulation with devastating consequences for the federal
system ... the federal government, through many of its
regulatory actions, has reduced the autonomy of state
governments and centralized the responsibilities for many
important social, economic, and regulatory programs.  This
loss of autonomy has weakened the states and reduced their
independence, while the centralization of responsibilities
better handled at state and local levels has limited the
effectiveness of the federal government.[34]

Indeed, there had been a dramatic proliferation of
federal regulations affecting state and local governments
during the 1960s and 1970s.   A large portion of this
growth resulted from the increase in numbers of federal
grants and, particularly, direct grants to local
governments during these twenty years.   Over 1,200 new
federal regulations affecting state and local governments
were promulgated during this period.[35]    Of the new
regulations, 80 percent accompanied the new grants-in-aid,
and were thus conditional.[36]    They could be imposed only
on the condition that a jurisdiction accepted the grant.
This was Washington's "carrot" approach to regulation.
Perhaps the most troubling aspect of growing federal
regulations on state and local governments has been the
growth of crosscutting regulations.  One of the first and
most important was the 1964 Civil Rights Act, barring
social discrimination under any federal assistance
programs.[37]    By 1980 there were fifty-nine of these
regulations that cut across all grants-in-aid.[38]    They
were expanded in the civil rights area to include the
handicapped, women, and the elderly.[39]  In environmental

protection they included air and water pollution,[40] historic preservation,[41] endangered species,[42] and land management.[43] The Davis-Bacon Act, Anti-kickback (Copeland) Act,[44] and Contract Work Hours and Safety Standards Act[45] engendered crosscutting rules in labor standards. Health, welfare, and worker safety had crosscutting protections,[46] as did the Freedom of Information Act.[47]

Crosscutting requirements are particularly menacing to state and local officials because they are imposed without regard to how they affect specific programs or how they collectively alter the efficiency of government. As concluded in a 1980 study by the OMB,

Individually, each crosscutting requirement may be sound. But cumulatively the conditions may be extraordinarily burdensome ... They can distort the allocation of resources, as the conditions are frequently imposed with minimal judgment as to relative costs and benefits in any given transition. Frequently, the recipients must absorb substantial portions of the costs.[48]

President Reagan moved swiftly to make necessary institutional arrangements to help implement his regulatory relief goals. The day after the inaugural, he established a cabinet-level Task Force on Regulatory Relief chaired by Vice President Bush. The next week he sent a memorandum to the heads of eleven cabinet departments and the Environmental Protection Agency, asking them to delay for sixty days the effective date of all final rules that had not yet taken affect. And on February 17, 1981, he issued an executive order to establish a strong centralized mechanism for presidential managment of agency rulemaking activity that would use cost-benefit analysis in reviewing proposed regulations.[49] Ten regulatory policy guidelines were developed by the Office of Management and Budget to apply the economic principles of Executive Order 12291 to the most frequently encountered issues of regulatory policy in order to "guide agencies in the administration of regulatory programs, to the extent permitted by law." One of the guidelines reads as follows: "Federal regulations should not preempt state laws or regulations, except to guarantee rights of national citizenship or to avoid significant burdens on interstate commerce."[50]

In other words, the Reagan administration sought fewer overall regulations and respect for (and in many cases deference to) alternative governmental sources of rules.[51] The Vice President released on August 1982 a progress report on the Regulatory Relief Task Force that listed twenty-four actions that have greatly reduced the regulatory burdens on state and local governments.[52] The OMB estimated that these initial actions deregulating state and local governments saved between $4 and $6 billion in total investment costs, and $2 billion in annual recurring costs. The OMB estimated these actions reduced paperwork reporting requirements by almost 11.8 million worker hours per year for state and local government employees.

As discussed previously, a great deal of this regulatory relief was achieved through quick implementation of the Reagan administration's block grant legislation which dramatically reduced federal interference in grant-in-aid programs administered by state and local governments.[53] However, the Reagan administration's regulatory relief for state and local governments went far beyond just block grants, covering a broad range of federal programs directed at diverse operating functions of government.

In education, for example, the proposed bilingual education rules were rescinded.[54] This reform is estimated to save school systems $900-2,950 million in investment costs. A Department of Education regulation prohibiting discrimination in dress codes on the basis of sex was rescinded.[55] School systems were given flexibility in accounting requirements under the National School Lunch Program, reducing by an estimated 11.7 million hours the time spent filling out forms each year.[56]

In health care, states received greater flexibility in revising reimbursement levels, making eligibility determinations, and deciding which services to offer in what settings.[57]

In the area of transportation, the Federal Highway Administration determined that it was asking for more statistical data than it was using, and reduced reporting requirements by 50 percent.[58] New rules were issued to permit states to design their own procedures and criteria for highway maintenance.[59] And handicapped accommodation requirements for public transit implementing section 504 of the Rehabilitation Act were revised, with an estimated savings of over $2.2 billion.[60]

The Department of Housing and Urban Development revised rules to speed up environmental impact evaluations and allow greater local autonomy under the new Community Development Block Grant (CDBG) program.[61] States also were permitted to determine their own CDBG administrative requirements, and were relieved of burdensome reporting.[62] Another HUD rule revision streamlined the application process and liberalized the governing rules under the Modernization of Public Housing Program.[63]

At the Environmental Protection Agency, air quality rule-review procedures were relaxed to eliminate a backlog.[64] This allowed clean air goals to be achieved faster, more efficiently, and at a lower cost. Similarly, regulations governing sewage treatment plants were changed to permit jurisdictions receiving grants to choose the most cost-effective process.[65]

The most sweeping change made in federal government philosophy and procedures in regulating the intergovernmental system came on July 14, 1983, when President Reagan signed Executive Order 12372, "Intergovernmental Review of Federal Programs." This allowed elected state and local officials to decide which federal grant and development programs to review and how. The order required federal agencies to accommodate the recommendations of state and local officials where possible. Federal agencies were ordered to allow states to simplify and consolidate federally required state plans and to discourage continuation of special purpose, federally dominated state planning agencies. This action sought to insure federal consideration of state and local priorities in the regulation of federal programs. Concurrently, OMB Circular A-95 was rescinded.[66] On June 24, 1983, final regulations and notices implementing the order were published simultaneously in the _Federal Register_ by twenty-eight federal agencies.[67]

## THE BOLD STROKE

Encouraged by the success of his first block grant initiatives and budget progress in 1981, President Reagan took a high risk, bold stroke for decentralizing government. In January 1982, President Reagan delivered his first State of the Union message and the cornerstone of that address was his federalism initiative.[68] "Let us solve this problem with a single bold stroke, the return of some $47 billion in federal programs to state and local governments, together with the means to finance them, and

a transition period of nearly ten years to avoid unnecessary disruption."[69]

The President's initiative called for an approximately $47 billion turnback of federal programs and tax
bases to be phased in over an eight-year period beginning
in FY 1984 (October 1983). It sought to achieve a
"sorting out" of responsibilities among the various units
of government.[70] The program was divided into two
distinct components: the swap and the turnback.[71]

Under the swap, the federal government was to take
full responsibility for Medicaid (saving the states $19.1
billion in FY 1984). In exchange, the states were to
assume full responsibility for Aid to Families with
Dependent Children and Food Stamps (at a cost of $16.5
billion for FY 1984).

The turnback component involved phasing out
approximately forty education, transportation, community
development, and social service programs. Financing was
to be provided for the states to pick up these programs or
to use the money in other ways. This was to be
accomplished in two stages.

The programs would be financed by a trust fund with
money from two principal sources: (1) $11 billion out of
the $13 billion collected by the federal government in
excise taxes on alcohol, telephone, tobacco, and gasoline;
and (2) approximately $15 billion from the Windfall
Profits Tax on oil. In FY 1987, when stage two was to
begin, the trust fund would have been reduced by 25
percent per year over four years with the federal
government concurrently reducing excise taxes by 25
percent each year for the states to pick up.

President Reagan's Federalism Initiative, as set
forth in the 1982 State of the Union Address, was not a
detailed plan, but rather a conceptual framework.[72] In
the spring and summer of 1982 the President commenced
unprecedented thorough and complete consultations with the
state and local officials designed to reach a consensus on
a package of Federalism Legislation. Unfortunately,
notwithstanding major efforts by all parties, consensus
was never achieved.

In 1983, President Reagan introduced the Federalism
Initiative Legislation that was the culmination of the
year-long effort to develop, in consultation with state
and local elected officials, a major initiative for
decentralizing government. The proposal consisted of four
mega-block grants, which sought to consolidate thirty-four
programs, with a proposed total FY 1984 funding level of

approximately $21 billion. It provided for level funding for each of five fiscal years from 1984 through 1988.

Unfortunately, the continuing hemorrhage of the federal budget throughout 1983 and the consuming battles over budget cuts crowded out serious congressional consideration of nonbudgetary domestic initiatives. The President's mega-block grants were among the victims of this phenomenon. They remain, however, on the table and present a vehicle for sigificantly increased flexibility for state and local officials.

## THE FEDERAL BUDGET AND THE NEW FEDERALISM

A major step in the Reagan administration's campaign to return authority and revenue to state and local governments was to cut the size of the federal government itself; and cut the growth of Washington's role in the federal system, President Reagan intended to halt and then reverse the dominance of federal aid and interference in state and local governments.

The great expansion of federal aid funds to other political jurisdictions began during Franklin D. Roosevelt's presidency. Between 1932 and 1934 federal intergovernmental aid quadrupled.[73] In the 1930s, "the states lost their confidence, and the people lost faith in the states."[74] The attitude of the Roosevelt administration was perhaps best described by one of its members, Professor Samuel Beer, "I vividly recall our preoccupation with persuading people to look to Washington for the solution to problems and one sense of what a great change in public attitude this involves."[75]

During the 1930s, federal domestic spending[76] increased more than sixfold--from 1.2 percent of gross national product to 7.1 percent.[77] Federal aid to state and local governments grew by 1,000 percent in ten years.[78] Expansion continued after World War II. The Employment Act of 1946 gave permanence to the federal role in public welfare, and, with the 1949 urban renewal program, even broader support for enlarging the federal role in urban affairs.

In 1953 federal aid represented 10 percent of the annual budgets of state and local governments. In 1973, it represented just over 20 percent; by 1978 federal aid financed 26 percent of state and local spending.[79] Viewed from a different perspective, although the federal share of all government spending has remained fairly constant since 1950 (between 65 and 70 percent), intergovernmental grants have assumed a dramatically increasing proportion of federal spending. In 1950 federal intergovernmental grants were approximately 6 percent of all federal spending; by 1978, they had risen to 17 percent.[80] Government employment figures show that state and local government employment grew by 42 percent.[81] This would suggest that growing federal intergovernmental grants allowed Washington to use state and local governments as their administrative agents.

President Reagan's first budget proposals demonstrated his commitment to hold this growth of Washington's role in the intergovernmental system. As President Reagan's first chairman of the Council of Economic Advisors, Murray Weidenbaum, said that year, "The Administration's budget also reflects a shift in federal priorities to truly national needs. Both national defense and an adequate social safety net for the truly needy are national priorities and federal responsibilities." (italics added)[82] Other existing programs, however, were not seen as paramount federal responsibilities. As the president said in addressing the nation's mayors at the time he sent his first budget to Congress, "I know that accepting responsibility, especially for cutbacks is not easy. But this package should be looked at by state and local governments as a great step toward not only getting America moving again, but toward reconstructing the power system which led to the economic stagnation and urban deterioration.(italics added)[83]

In FY 1981 the federal government spent $657.2 billion. Within this budget, federal aid to state and local governments was $94.8 billion in outlays, or 14.4 percent of all budget expenditures. This total combines payments that were federally funded but administered by state and local governments (welfare)[84] and federal grants that do not go to individuals but to state and local governments for their operations or capital projects (categorical grants, block grants, and General Revenue Sharing).[85] Since FY 1971, federal aid to (and consequent interference in) state and local governments had increased $66 billion in current dollars, increased $18.2 billion in 1972 constant dollars, and increased 0.5 percent of the GNP[86] President Reagan sought to and, in fact, did reverse this trend.

The Omnibus Budget Reconciliation Act of 1981[87] and consequent congressional budget actions resulted in a FY 1982 budget authority reduction of $45.1 billion, causing a total outlay reduction of $44.1 billion from the level they would have reached if Congress had not adopted President Reagan's new policies. This reduced budget authority by 5.7 percent and outlays by 6 percent. Excluding defense expenditure increases and interest on the public debt, the cuts were 12.3 percent in budget authority and 9.4 percent in outlays.[88] Of these budget reductions, a substantial amount came in cuts of federal aid to state and local governments.

Federal grants payments funded federally but administered by state and local governments were reduced $16.350 billion, a 23.5 percent reduction, in 1981, while federal grants to state and local governments for their operations and capital projects were reduced $19.075 billion, a 37.7 percent reduction. All federal aid to state and local governments bore 54.6 percent of reductions in fiscal year 1982 budget authority, when measured from current policy. On the average, each budget account had its budget authority reduced by 29.5 percent compared with current 1981 policy levels.

"In fiscal year 1982, federal aid to states registered its first decline since the Advisory Commission on Intergovernmental Relations had been tracking intergovernmental aid flows."[89] From FY 1981 to FY 1982, Present Reagan achieved a federal aid drop from $94.8 billion to $88.8 billion. Major components of this reduction included a $2.6 billion decline in the Department of Labor employment and training assistance program, a $814.4 million decline in temporary employment assistance, a $1 billion decline in payments to states from the Highway Trust Fund, a $130 million decrease in Airport and Airway Trust Fund payments, a $490 million decrease in the child nutrition programs administered by the Department of Agriculture, a $341 million drop in the Department of Health Service maintenance assistance (Aid to Families with Dependent Children) payments. The net $6 billion reduction in federal aid to state and local governments was realized despite increases in certain other intergovernmental programs such as the $600 million increase in Medicaid and modest increases in refugee assistance and preventive health services.[90]

Although the FY 1982 budget provided a 12 percent reduction in constant dollars in federal intergovernmental aid, it was projected that FY 1983 would show a 0.7 percent increase. Generally, intergovernmental aid was held constant for FY 1983, but increased funding for transportation programs under the new Surface Transportation Assistance Act (Pub. L. 97-424)[91] would push up all federal aid to state and local governments to $93.5 billion.[92]   However, in contrast to historic funds for fifty years, President Reagan had made substantial cuts in domestic spending and trimming in the government role in domestic program areas.[93]

President Reagan said a week after he sent his first 1981 budget requests to Congress, "We are not cutting the budget simply for the sake of sounder financial management.  This is only a first step toward returning power to states and communities, only a first step toward reordering the relationship between citizen and government."[94]   His budget has reflected that reordering of relationships.  As political commentator David Broder wrote near the end of Reagan's third year in office: There is no doubt that Reagan has won the first stage in his battle to halt almost fifty years of unbroken growth of Washington's role in the federal system.[95]

LOOKING AHEAD

In 1984 federal aid to state and local governments continued to grow more slowly than did state and local own-source revenue.  It dropped for the sixth straight year as a percentage of state-local expenditures.  It fell to state and local governments to raise taxes, to cut services or to do both in order that revenues would match expenditures.[96]   Fiscal stringency in the federal budget propelled fiscal decentralization.

Reagan continues to face a serious federal budget hemorrhage in his second term.  The pressure to hold the line or cut federal domestic programs is enormous.  This fiscal pressure to curb federal aid to state and local governments coupled with the strong public support for Reagan's conservative and decentralist philosophy suggests further gradual decentralization in the years ahead.

Devolution is happening in the form of federal retrenchment and state-local ascendency.  As political commentator David Broder wrote in the summer of 1985: "(T)he initiative on education, social and most economic environmental issues now rests in state capitols rather than in the U.S. Capitol and the White House.  That shift is what Reagan set out to accomplish four years ago, and the extent of his success ... truly is revolutionary."[97]

While the federal government has cut back spending for education, most states increased outlays for elementary and secondary schools and public colleges.  At the same time that the Reagan administration proposed cuts in Medicaid, Arkansas and West Virginia set up special funds to finance care for the indigent.[98]

Most states have developed some economic cooperative ventures, using their universities and small amounts of public money to leverage private funds for new technology-based companies or stepped-up application of new technology and worker-training in old firms.[99] Massachusetts has transformed itself from a dying textile-based economy to a modern high-tech economy with low unemployment due to local-state government cooperation with business, labor, and education. Similarly, Pennsylvania is replacing its declining steel jobs with service and manufacturing employment.[100] As Delaware Governor Michael Castle said during the summer of 1985, "We're looking to Washington less and less. We're taking our futures into our own hands."[101]

The federal government austerity, guided by a president with a deep decentralist philosophy, will continue gradual fiscal federalism in the years ahead.

## APPENDIX A

### THE NINE BLOCK GRANTS
### SIGNED INTO LAW IN 1982

#### Alcohol, Drug Abuse and Mental Health

| | |
|---|---|
| Consolidates: | *Drug Abuse Community Services<br>*Alcohol Treatment and Rehabilitation<br>*Alcohol Formula Grants<br>*Drug Abuse Prevention Formula Grants<br>*Community Mental Health Centers |
| Date of Eligibility: | October 1, 1981, or subsequent fiscal quarters up to October 1, 1982 |
| Status on 10/8/81:<br>(State applications received) | Yes:  50 (46 states & Columbia, Puerto Rico, Virgin Islands, Northern Mariana Islands, and 210 Indian tribes) No:  6 states (California, New Hampshire, Montana, Hawaii, Guam, Trust Territories) |
| Funding Authorization: | FY 1982:  $491 million<br>FY 1983:  $511 million<br>FY 1984:  $532 million |

Preventive Health and Health Services

Consolidates:                          *Health Incentive
                                       Grants
                                       *Rape Crisis Center
                                       *Urban Rat Control
                                       *Fluoridation Grants
                                       *Health Education and
                                       Risk Reduction
                                       *Emergency Medical
                                       Services
                                       *Home Health Services
                                       *Hypertension Program
Date of Eligibility:                   October 1, 1981, or
                                       subsequent fiscal
                                       quarters up to October
                                       1, 1982.
Status on 10/8/81:                     Yes: 50 (46 states &
(State applications received)          (District of Columbia,
                                       Puerto Rico, Virgin
                                       Islands, Northern
                                       Mariana Islands, and
                                       185 Indian tribes)
                                       No: 5 (New Hampshire,
                                       New York, Hawaii,
                                       California, Trust
                                       Territories)
Funding Authorization:                 FY 1982:  $95 million
                                       FY 1983:  $96.5
                                       million
                                       FY 1984:  $98.5
                                       million

## Maternal and Child Health Services

| | |
|---|---|
| Consolidates: | *Crippled Children Services<br>*Maternal and Child Health Services<br>*Disabled Children (SSI)<br>*Sudden Infant Death Syndrome<br>*Hemophilia Centers<br>*Lead-Based Paint<br>*Genetic Diseases<br>*Adolescent Pregnancy Prevention |
| Date of Eligibility: | October 1, 1981, or subsequent fiscal quarters up to October 1, 1982. |
| Status on 10/8/81:<br>(State applications received) | Yes: 51 (47 states & District of Columbia, Puerto Rico, Virgin Islands, Northern Mariana Islands)<br>No: 5 (New Hampshire, New York, California, Guam, Trust Territories) |
| Funding Authorization: | FY 1982: $373 million, and each year thereafter. |

## Primary Care

| | |
|---|---|
| Consolidates: | *Community Health Center |
| Date of Eligibility: | October 1, 1982 |
| Status on 10/8/81: | This block grant will |
| (State applications received) | not be available until October 1, 1982. |
| Funding Authorization: | FY 1982:  $286.5 million (284 million under categorical authorities and $2.5 million for block grant planning grants) FY 1983:  $302.5 million FY 1984:  $327 million |

## Social Services

| | |
|---|---|
| Consolidates: | *Title XX Social Services *Title XX Child Day Care *Title XX Training |
| Date of Elibility: | States must assume this block grant on October 1, 1981. |
| Funding Authorization: | "Such sums as necessary"  Bill sets minimum state entitlement levels. |

## Low Income Home Energy Assistance

| | |
|---|---|
| Consolidates: Assistance Program | *Low Income Energy |
| Date of Eligibility: | States must assume this block grant on October 1, 1981. |
| Funding Authorization: | FY 1982-1984:  $1.875 billion annually. |

## Elementary and Secondary Education

| | |
|---|---|
| Consolidates: | *30 education categorical grant programs |
| Date of Eligibility: | July 1, 1982 |
| Status on 10/8/81: (State applications received) | This block grant will not be available until July 1, 1982. |
| Funding Authorization: | Chapter I: Financial Assistance to Meet Special Educational Needs of Disadvantaged Children FY 1982-1984: $3.48 billion Chapter II: Consolidation of Federal Programs for Elementary and Secondary Education FY 1982-1984: $589 million |

## Community Services

| | |
|---|---|
| Consolidates: | *Community Services Administration |
| Date of Eligibility: | October 1, 1981, or subsequent fiscal quarters up to October 1, 1982 |
| Status on 10/8/81: (State applications received) | Yes: 42 (36 states plus C.C., Puerto Rico, Virgin Islands, Northern Mariana Islands, Samoa, Trust Territories and 180 tribes) No: 14 (Connecticut, New Hampshire, New York, Virginia, West Virginia, Texas, Florida, Georgia, New Mexico, California, Maryland, Colorado, Montana, Alaska) |

## Community Development

Consolidates:

*Replaces community
development block
grant for small cities
and rural areas.

Date of Eligibility:

60 days after
regulations are
published in Federal
Register.

Status on 10/8/81:

Not applicable.

Funding Authorization:

FY 1982-1983: $1.1
billion annually.

NOTES

1. For a good discussion of intergovernmental "grantmanship" see D. Haider, When Governments Come to Washington: Governors, Mayors and Intergovernmental Lobbying (New York, The Free Press 1974); G. Hale and M. L. Palley, The Politics of Federal Grants (Washington, D.C: Congressional Quarterly Press, 1981).

2. See generally Ronald Reagan, remarks made in Seattle, Wash. June 8, 1980; Ronald Reagan, acceptance speech delivered to the Republican National Convention, Detroit, Mich. July 17, 1980. Also note Ronald Reagan, speech delivered to the Chicago Executive Club, Chicago, Ill. September 1975; and Ronald Reagan, White Paper on Federalism, February 8, 1976, wherein he outlined "a systematic transfer of authority and resources to the state--a program of creative federalism for America's third century".

3. President Ronald Reagan, Inaugural Address, Washington, D.C., Jan. 20, 1981.

4. See generally President Ronald Reagan, State of the Union Address: address delivered before a joint session of the Congress, Washington, D.C., January 26, 1982.

5. President Ronald Reagan, Address to the National Conference of State Legislators, Altanta, Ga., July 30, 1981.

6. Senator Edmund Muskie (D-Maine), Senate Committee on Governmental Operations, "To Establish an Advisory Commission on Intergovernmental Relations," June 16, 1959.

7. Office of Management and Budget, Federal Grants-in-Aid to State and Local Governments Vol. 5 (March 1981).

8. Office of Management and Budget, Number of Funded Federal Grant Programs in the Catalogue of Federal Domestic Assistance Included in the Budget Concept of Grants to State and Local Governments Vol. 5 (October 28, 1982).

9. Governors Richard Snelling (R-Vt.) and James Hunt (D-N.C.), Governors' Guide to Block Grant Implementation, Council on State Planning Agencies and National Governors' Association, August 1, 1981.

10. Omnibus Budget Reconciliation Act of 1981, Pub. L. No. 97-35, 95 Stat. 357 (1981).

11. Department of Hous. and Urb. Dev., Block Grants--One Year Later 1 (August 1982).

12. Block Grant Report, Memorandum from the Secretary of Education to the Director, Office of Cabinet Affairs, at 2 (August 1982).

13. Office of Management and Budget, Information Collection Budget of the United States Government Fiscal Year 1982, at 16-17 (February 4, 1982).

14. President Ronald Reagan, Address to the National Conference of State Legislators, Atlanta, Ga., July 30, 1981.

15. Office of Management and Budget, Information Block Grants and Program Consolidations in the Fiscal Year 1983 Budget 156 (Feb. 18, 1982).

16. Office of Management and Budget, New Block Grants and Consolidations Proposed for Fiscal Year 1983 (Aug. 1982).

17. The Child Welfare Block Grant proposed to consolidate into a single block grant to each state four categorical programs for foster care and child services. The program would support state services designed to strengthen and unite families or place children in adoptive homes when they cannot be reunited with their families. This program was sent to Congress on June 8, 1982.

18. The Combined Welfare Administration proposed to consolidate payments for state expenses to administer three welfare programs:  Food Stamps, Medicaid, and Aid to Families with Dependent Children.  No state match would be required and states would be given added flexibility to design efficient public assistance programs.  In lieu of open-ended funding, states would be given added flexibility to design efficient public assistance programs.  In lieu of openended funding, states would receive fixed grants even if caseloads declined due to tighter eligibility requirements.  This program was sent to Congress on July 17, 1982.

19. The Rehabilitation Services Block Grant proposed to consolidate and simplify five separate authorities designed to help disabled individuals become self-sufficient.  Authority for administering the new programs would be transferred from the Department of Education to the Department of Health and Human Services.  This bill will not be submitted until the next Congress.

20. The Vocational and Adult Education Block Grant would consolidate into a single grant program nine separate education authorities--eight vocational and one adult education.  A bill was sent to Congress on March 28, 1982.  An amended version was introduced by Senator Orrin Hatch on March 31.

21. The Education for the Handicapped Block Grant would consolidate into a single grant program thirteen programs currently authorized by two sources, the Education of the Handicapped Act and the education of the handicapped activities authorized by Chapter 12 of the Education Consolidation and Improvement Act of 1981 (Title I, Elementary Secondary Education Act Handicapped State grants).

22. The Rental Rehabilitation Block Grant would replace two existing housing rehabilitation programs--the Rehabilitation Loan fund and Section 8 Moderate Rehabilitation Program. The new program will provide grants to states and units of local government for up to half the cost of rehabilitating multifamily rental properties, principally for low-income families. A bill was introduced on March 30, 1982.

23. The existing block grant proposes to provide primary health care services to populations in need, beginning in FY 1983. Legislation will propose adding three programs to this block grant--Black Lung Clinics, Migrant Health, and Family Planning. This proposal was submitted to Congress on May 12 and has not been introduced yet.

24. The existing Maternal and Child Health (MCH) block covers seven programs to assist and improve the health of mothers and children. This proposal will add one program --currently administered by the U.S. Department of Agriculture--Women, Infants, Children (WIC). It will thus authorize provision of nutrition services, as well as other services to improve the health of mothers and children. This program was sent to Congress on April 12, 1982.

25. The existing Low Income Home Energy Assistance block grant would redesign the federal program for low-income home energy assistance to increase state program discretion. This proposal will add one program (Emergency Assistance) to the existing block grant and will thus permit states to respond to emergencies for low income families as part of the block grant. This program was sent to Congress on May 24, 1982, and introduced as S.2775 on July 2, 1982.

26. The Job Training Block Grant proposal was signed into law on October 13, 1982. Training Partnership Act, Pub. L. No. 97-300, 96 Stat. 1322 (1982).

27. White House Office of Policy Information, The Job Training Partnership Act of 1982, Issue Alert No. 6 (Oct. 19, 1982).

28. See Office of Management and Budget, supra note 15.

29. Memorandum from Don Shasteen, Department of Labor, to Jocelyn White, my staff assistant, New Federalism Aspects of the Job Training Partnership Act 1 (Oct. 20, 1982).

30. Ibid.

31. 128 Cong. Rec. S.12731 (daily ed. Sept. 30, 1982); 128 Cong. Rec. H 8447 (daily ed. Oct. 1, 1982).

32. New Federalism, supra note 29.

33. Governor Scott Matheson, American Enterprise Institute Seminar on The Deeper Dimensions of the New Federalism, in Washington, D.C. (Dec. 7, 1982).

34. Murray Weidenbaum, "Strengthening Our Federal System," Journal of Contemporary Studies 4,4 (Fall 1981), pp. 71-72.

35. Catherine Lovell, "Federal Deregulation and State and Local Governments", Reductions in U.S. Domestic Spending, Ed. John Williams Ellwood (New Brunswick: Transaction Books, 1982), pp. 99-129, 101-102.

36. For a general discussion of the overloading and congestion of the federal system, see "A Crisis of Confidence and Competence," The Federal Role in the Federal System: The Dynamics of Growth (Advisory Commission on Intergovernmental Relations, A-77, 1980).

37. Applicable provision of the 1964 Civil Rights Act (Pub. L. 88-352, July 2, 1964) is Title VI.

38. For a general discussion, see U.S. Office of Management and Budget, Managing Federal Assistance in the 1980s; A Report to the Congress of the United States Pursuant to the Federal Grant and Cooperative Agreement Act of 1977 (Pub. L. 94-244), Washington, D.C., March 1980.

39. Examples include the Age Discrimination Act of 1975 (42 U.S.C. 6101); Title IX of the Education Act Amendments of 1972, as amended by Pub. L. 93-568, 88 Stat. 1855 (20 U.S.C. 1681 et seq.); and the Architectural Barriers Act of 1968, as amended, Pub. L. 90-480 (42 U.S.C. 4151 et seq.).

40. Examples include the National Environmental Policy Act of 1969, as amended, Pub. L. 91-190 (42 U.S.C. 4321 et seq.); Sec. 508 of the Federal Water Pollution Control Act Amendments of 1972, Pub. L. 92-500 (33 U.S.C. 1251 et seq.); and Conformity of Federal Activities with State Implementation Plans Under the Clean Air Act Amendments of 1977, Title I, Sec. 129(b).

41. Examples include Sec. 106 of the National Historical Preservation Act of 1966, Pub. L. 89-665 as amended (16 U.S.C. 470), 84 Stat. 204 (1970), 87 Stat. 139 (1973), 90 Stat. 1320 (1976), 92 Stat. 3467 (1978); Procedures for the Protection of Historic and Cultural Properties (36 CFR 800); and Executive Order 11593, May 31, 1971, Protection and Enhancement of the Cultural Environment (36 CFR 8921, 16 U.S.C. 470).

42. For example, The Endangered Species Act of 1973, Pub. L. 93-205 (16 U.S.C. 1531 et seq.), as amended by Pub. L. 95-632.

43. Examples include Executive Orders 11988 and 11990, May 24, 1977, Floodplain Management and Protection of Wetlands, respectively, the Wild and Scenic Rivers Act of 1968, Pub. L. 90-542, as amended (16 U.S.C. 1271 et seq.); and Secs. 307(c) and (d) of the Coastal Zone Management Act of 1972, as amended (16 U.S.C. 1451 et seq.).

44. 40 U.S.C. 276a-276b-7 and 27 CFR Pt. 1, 46 Stat. 1494, Appendix A.

45. 40 U.S.C. 874; 40 U.S.C. 276C.

46. 40 U.S.C. 327-332.

47. Examples include the Comprehensive Alcohol Abuse and Alcoholism Prevention, Treatment, and Rehabilitation Act of 1970, Pub. L. 91-616 (42 U.S.C. 4581); Lead-Based Paint Poisoning Prohibition (42 U.S.C. 4831(b)); and the Animal Welfare Act of 1966 (7 U.S.C. 2131-2147).

48. 5 U.S.C. 552. Office of Management and Budget.

49. Executive Order 12291, 46 Fed. Reg. 13193, Feb. 19, 1981.

50. President's Task Force on Regulatory Relief, Reagan Administration Regulatory Achievements, August 11, 1983, pp. 17, 19. Also see statement of Christopher Demuth, Administrator for Information and Regulatory Affairs, Office of Management and Budget, before the Subcommittee on Administrative Law and Governmental Relations, Committee on the Judiciary, U.S. House of Representatives, on H.R. 2327, The Regulatory Reform Act of 1983, July 28, 1983.

51. See George C. Eads and Michael Fix, "Regulatory Policy," The Reagan Experiment, Eds. John Palmer and Isabel Sawhill (The Urban Institute Press, Washington, D.C., 1982) pp. 129, 150.

52. Presidential Task Force on Regulatory Relief, _Reagan Administration Achievements in Regulatory Relief; A Progress Report_, August 1982. The total number of regulatory reviews undertaken by August 1982 numbered 119. For a more conceptual review of the first year's accomplishments in regulation relief, see Donald F. Kettl, "The Uncertain Bridges: Regulations Reform in Reagan's New Federalism," Ed. Stephen L. Schectator, _Publius: Annual Review of American Federalism 1981_, p. 19.

53. See section discussion Block Grants, infra. Also, see discussion of the deregulation of block grants in Catherine Lovell, "Effects of Regulatory Changes on State and Localities," in _The Consequences of Cuts_, Ed. Richard P. Nathan, Fred C. Doolittle and Associates (Princeton Urban and Regional Research Center, Princeton, N.J., 1983) pp. 169, 172.

54. ED/Bilingual Education (Law Rules), 45 Fed. Reg. 52052. Proposed regulations withdrawn February 3, 1981.

55. ED/Personal Appearance Codes, 34 CFR 106. Rule rescinded July 8, 1982. A good example of federal overreach, this rule had resulted in schools unable to require boys to wear ties or girls to wear skirts unless the same requirements were imposed on the opposite sex.

56. USDA/National School Lunch Program--Cost Accounting, 7 CFR 210. Final rule published July 20, 1982.

57. HHS/Health Care Financing Administration Rules, 42 CFR 431, 435, 440, 441, 447, 456. Final rules published Sept. 30, Oct. 1, and Dec. 3, 1981. HHS/Health Care Facility Capital Expenditures, 42 CFR 122. Final rule published January 26, 1982.

58. DOT/Guide to Reporting Highway Statistics. Reduced paperwork requirements cleared by OMB May 5, 1982.

59. DOT/Highway Geometric Design Standards for 3R Projects, 23 CFR 625. Final rule published June 10, 1982.

60. DOT/Section 504 of the Rehabilitation Act, 49 CFR 27. Interim final rule published April 12, 1982.

61. HUD/Environmental Policies, 24 CFR 58. Interim final rule published April 12, 1982.

62. HUD/Community Development, 24 CFR 570, subpaort F. Final rules published Feb. 23 and April 8, 1982.

63. HUD/Modernization of Public Housing Projects, 24 CFR 868. Final rule published May 21, 1982.

64. EPA/Emissions Trading Policy. Statement released April 7, 1982. EPA/State Implementation Plans, 40 CFR 51. Policy announced June 23, 1982.

65. EPA/Construction Grant Regulations, 40 CFR 35. Interim final rule published May 12, 1982.

66. OMB/Local Clearinghouses (Circular A-95). Executive Order 12372 signed July 14, 1982.

67. Federal Register, Vol. 48, No. 123, June 24, 1983, pages 29096 ff (Washington, D.C. U.S. Government Printing Office.

68. President Ronald Reagan, "State of the Union Address," Washington, D.C., 26 January 1982.

69. Ibid.

70. The National Governors' Association, "Agenda for Restoring Balance to the Federalism System," adopted at 1980 Annual Meeting, Denver, Col. The Executive Committee of the National Conference of State Legislatures and the National Governors' Association jointly adopted a "Statement on Federalism Reform," in December 1980. See Appendix II of statement on ...

71. See generally Fact Sheet: Federalism Initiative, Office of the Press Secretary, The White House, Jan. 27, 1982; and the President's Federalism Initiative: Basic Framework, Office of the Press Secretary, The White House, January 26, 1982.

72. The President had promised consultations on the federalism framework in his State of the Union Message, January 26, 1982, saying: "I will shortly send this Congress a message describing (the initiative), I want to emphasize, however, that its full details will have been worked out only after close consultations with congressional, state and local officials."

73. Federal aid funds to other political jurisdictions grew from $232 million in the last year of the Hoover administration to more than $1 billion in the second year of the Roosevelt administration.

74. Terry Sanford Storm Over the States, (McGraw Hill Book Company, New York), 1967 p. 21.

75. Deil S. Wright "'New Federalism' Recent Varieties of an Older Species," paper drafted for symposium on federalism in the American Review of Public Administration, July 1982, p. 4.

76. These figures excludes major national security, international affairs and finance, veterans' services and benefits, and interest on the national debt.

77. U.S. Bureau of the Census, Historical Statistics of the United States, Colonial Times to 1970 (Washington, D.C. 1975), pp. 225, 1115.

78. Ibid., p. 1125.

79. Advisory Commission on Intergovernmental Relations, Recent Trends in Federal and State Aid to Local Governments (July 1980) p. 8, Table 5 (Note: This declined to 21 percent in 1982.)

80. Congressional Budget Office, The Federal Government in a Federal System: Current Intergovernmental Programs and Options for Change (August 1983, p. 14. (Note: This declined to 11 percent in 1982.)

81. Economic Report of the President, 1983, p. 205, Table B-37.

82. Murray L. Weidenbaum "Strengthening Our Federal System," in American Federalism: A New Partnership for the Republic, Ed. Robert Hawkins (Institute for Contemporary Studies, San Francisco, 1982), pp. 89, 93.

83. President Ronald Reagan, remarks to the National League of Cities, Washington, D.C., March 2, 1981.

84. John W. Ellwood "Controlling the Growth of Federal Domestic Spending," in Reductions in U.S. Domestic Spending, Ed. John W. Ellwood (New Brunswick: Transaction Books, 1982), pp. 7, 8. This category would include "Medicaid, Aid to Families with Dependent Children (AFDC), housing assistance, and child nutrition programs. These grant programs spent $39.9 billion in Fiscal Year 1981, or 6.1 percent of all budget outlays."

85. Ibid. "In Fiscal Year 1981, the federal government spent $54.8 billion, or 8.3 percent of all budget outlays, for such grants."

86. Ibid., p. 9, taken from Office of Management and Budget, Federal Government Finances: 1983 Budget Data (Washington, D.C.: Office of Management and Budget, February 1982), pp. 59-78, Tables 10, 11, and 12.

87. John W. Ellwood "The Size and Distribution of Budget Reductions," Ibid., pp. 33, 39.

88. Ibid.

89. Advisory Commission on Intergovernmental Relations (ACIR), "Federal Aid to States Registers First Decline," news release, Washington, D.C., April 28, 1983.

90. Ibid. See Department of Treasury, Federal Aid to States Fiscal Year 1982, Washington, D.C.

91. Surface Transportation Assistance Act (Pub. L. 97-424).

92. ACIR, Op. Cit.

93. For an excellent detailed analysis of these budget trends, see Richard P. Nathan, Fred C. Doolittle and Associates, The Consequences of Cuts: The Effects of the Reagan Domestic Program on State and Local Governments (Princeton Urban and Regional Research Center, Princeton, N.J., 1983).

94. President Ronald Reagan, remarks to the Conservative Political Action Committee Conference, Washington, D.C., March 20, 1981.

95. David Broder "States Learn to Live with End of New Deal," The Des Moines Register, Nov. 30, 1983, 9A.

96. Kenneth S. Howard "DeFacto New Federalism," Intergovernmental Perspective, Winter 1984, p. 4; and John Shannon, "1984 - Not A Good Fiscal Year for Big Brother," Intergovernmental Perspective, Winter 1985, p. 4.

97. David Broder "Reagan's Ironic Revolution," The Washington Post, Aug. 11, 1985, A1.

98. Robert Pear "States Are Found More Responsive On Social Issues," The New York Times, May 19, 1985, A1.

99. David S. Broder "Midwesterners Cite Signs of Turnaround," The Washington Post, Aug. 21, 1985, A4. See also, Terry Nicholas Clark "A New Breed of Cost-Conscious Mayors," The Wall Street Journal, June 10, 1985, 15; Editorial, "Leadership to the States," Chicago Tribune, May 11, 1985, 24.

100. David S. Broder "State of Economic Leadership," Chicago Tribune, Aug. 5, 1985, 12.

101. David Shribman "Governors Feel Limited by U.S. Deficit But Enjoy Freedom From Washington," The Wall Street Journal, August 6, 1985, 62.

# PART TWO

# Administrative Impacts on Subnational Governments

One of the primary sources of concern related to the changes under the New Federalism has been the impacts on state and local governments. As a result of the shifting emphasis away from nation-centered federalism and cuts in the levels of federal funding support, state and local governments have undergone fiscal, programmatic, and administrative changes. The impacts of these changes provide the focus of inquiry for the following five chapters.

In Chapter 4, George J. Gordon and Irene Rothenberg examine the intent and the impact of the centerpiece of the New Federalism, Executive Order (EO) 12372, on state-federal relations. Gordon and Rothenberg outline the essentials of EO 12372 and present the problems that have complicated effective implementation of the order.

The impacts of the Reagan administration's numerous block grant consolidations on the planning processes, service delivery capabilties, and administrative functions of state governments are detailed by Paul Posner. Posner also outlines the overall impacts of Reagan's block grants on the abilities of states to provide assistance to local governments.

The remaining three chapters in Part Two examine the impacts of New Federalism on specific state and local governments. Stein, McManus, and Savage review the positive and negative effects of New Federalism funding cuts on the operating, entitlement, and capital improvement programs of the State of Texas and the City of Houston. The impact of funding cuts also provides the focus for Beverly Cigler's examination of survival strategies which have been employed by smaller local governments (under 50,000) in North Carolina. The approaches and strategies discussed by Professor Cigler include increasing program efficiency, volunteerism, borrowing, user fees, and program elimination.

When local governments are faced with significant budget cuts, frequently it is the capital improvement budget that is the first to be reduced or even eliminated. In exploring the impacts of federal budget cuts on the capital improvement budget of Tulsa, Oklahoma, Rosenfeld and Frankle outline the alternatives facing municipalities throughout the country. Their examination reveals that creative alternatives can be developed to save threatened capital improvement budgets.

# 4

# "Out with the Old, in with the New": The New Federalism, Intergovernmental Coordination, and Executive Order 12372

*Irene Fraser Rothenberg
and George J. Gordon*

Ronald Reagan's New Federalism policy initiatives--so boldly trumpeted during his first year in the White House as heralding dramatic changes in contemporary federalism-- now appear to have lost their early momentum. Although Congress approved the consolidation of dozens of cate- gorical grants into fifteen new block grants and also authorized significant reductions in spending for inter- governmental assistance, other proposals encountered stiff political resistance. Some were enacted in modified form; some were defeated outright. On still others, no definitive action was taken--for example, the contro- versial proposal for state and federal governments to "swap" programs, involving state assumption of Food Stamps and Aid to Families with Dependent Children (AFDC) in exchange for federal assumption of Medicaid. As other priorities came to the fore, federalism concerns seemed to wane in relative importance.

With the president's highly touted changes "on hold," the focus of attention has shifted to the adjustments state governments have had to make in coping with federal budget cuts and grant reforms instituted in 1981 and 1982. However, the Reagan administration has undertaken important initiatives in at least one other area, affecting local as well as state governments. These initiatives have centered on easing what the adminis- tration regarded as the excessive burdens of inter- governmental regulation.[1] A specific change was a replacement of one complex of existing intergovernmental coordination procedures with another. The course of action taken in revising these mechanisms is indicative of several underlying themes in the New Federalism.

A LOOK AT THE "OLD":  THE LOCUS OF CHANGE

In intergovernmental relations, "coordination"--adapting an individual decision within a set of inter-dependent decisions to the others in that set[2]--has long merited attention by both practitioners and scholars.[3] But coordination issues took on greater urgency after the rapid proliferation of federal categorial grants in the middle and late 1960s, within a vastly more complicated fabric of intergovernmental relations.[4] As the number of "categoricals" mushroomed, the political opportunities for effective grantsmanship increased but so too did the problems of grant administration. These problems included unnecessary duplications, inconsistencies, and outright conflicts between grant programs and individual awards; the failure of those designing federal aid programs to consider program impacts on state, regional, and local plans; and the fact that state and local planners and elected officials often were not consulted--or even informed--about federally funded projects in their areas.[5] These aspects of intergovernmental coordination generated more attention (and some controversy) in the late 1960s and 1970s, leading to systematic efforts to address these problems meaningfully.

Among the most significant federal efforts were two statutes enacted by Congress. Section 204 of the Demonstration Cities and Metropolitan Development Act (Model Cities) of 1966 stipulated that applications from local governments in metropolitan areas must first have been screened by an areawide comprehensive planning agency. Then, in 1968, came passage of the Inter-governmental Cooperation Act (ICA), containing three important provisions. Title IV directed that more regularized evaluation and review procedures be set up for grant requests. Section 401(b) directed that the planning process take into consideration as fully as possible all national, state, regional, and local viewpoints that might be pertinent to the policy under consideration. And Section 401(c) made it national policy to seek maximum congruence between national program objectives and the objectives of state, regional, and local planning. These lofty (if somewhat ambiguous) goals were adopted in the face of widespread local and state unwillingness to consider effects of their own programs and planning on those of neighboring jurisdictions and sister agencies.

Implementation of these provisions came under the growing managerial responsibility of the Office of Management and Budget (OMB). The tactics OMB employed were aimed at increasing consultation with states and localities, and at providing "governors and mayors with the information and management tools necessary to achieve some degree of control over their functional bureaucracies"[6] (an increasingly important aspect of "improving intergovernmental coordination"--then and now). A number of specific implementation devices were adopted, chief among them OMB Circular A-95. This circular established a Project Notification and Review System under which state, regional, and metropolitan area "clearinghouses" were to receive, from agencies and governments in the respective jurisdictions, notification of their <u>intent</u> to apply for federal aid.

The clearinghouses, under Part I of Circular A-95, were then to exercise two functions: 1) transmitting this information to other government entities in the affected area and soliciting their comments; and 2) assessing the applications for conformity with established state, regional, and local planning. (Other parts of A-95 required federal agencies engaging in direct development projects to consult in advance with state and local officials, and provided that governors would have an opportunity to review state plans required by some federal aid programs before those plans were submitted to the funding agency.) These procedures were predicated on the assumption that improved intergovernmental communication--<u>before</u> grant applications were formally submitted--would contribute to improved coordination and cooperation among federal, state, and local governments.[7] This, it was hoped, would lead in turn to "dollar savings, better projects, and more value for the public investment."[8]

The A-95 review process is credited with having made it possible for state and local officials to obtain more complete information about grant applications. As a result, it also made possible less duplication of effort in seeking grants, as well as providing government officials a more effective way of expressing their opinions to others in the grant application process. However, many problems were associated with A-95 implementation as well. Chief among these were insufficient funding of the process; reviews that were often subjective, ineffective, or both; serious gaps in compliance with the circular, especially by federal agencies; and a growing perception that the A-95 process was becoming heavily laden with paperwork and increasingly "bureaucratized."[9]

In 1982 the Reagan administration came forward with a major reform in coordination machinery. On 14 July 1982 President Reagan rescinded A-95 and replaced it with Executive Order (EO) 12372. The year 1983 witnessed myriad and fast-paced developments, as participants in intergovernmental consultation familiarized themselves with the new "rules of the game." What those rules are, the rationales for their promulgation, the reactions of affected parties, the developments in the rules themselves, and the "agenda" of unfinished business in the immediate future are the subjects of this article.

## EXECUTIVE ORDER 12372: THE ESSENTIALS

The principal components of EO 12372, as originally issued, were as follows. Section 1 required federal agencies to "provide opportunities for consultation by elected officials" of state and local governments providing matching funds for, or directly affected by, proposed aid or direct development programs. Section 2 permitted--but did not direct--states to develop new processes, or refine existing ones, for state and local elected officials to "review and coordinate" federal programs--all this in close consultation with local general-purpose governments and "appropriate" (in the state's view) special-purpose organizations. Section 2 provided that where such processes are made operative, federal agencies shall, to the extent permitted by law:

1. utilize the state process to determine official views of state and local elected officials;
2. communicate with state and local elected officials "as early in the program planning cycle as is reasonably feasible" to explain specific plans and actions;
3. "make efforts to accommodate" state and local elected officials' concerns communicated through the designated state process, and, "where the concerns cannot be accommodated," explain "in a timely manner" why that is so;
4. allow states to simplify and consolidate existing federally required state plan submissions;
5. seek to coordinate views of elected state and local officials in affected states when proposed aid or direct development has interstate impact; and

6.   discourage the creation or reauthorization of any
     planning organization that is federally funded, has a
     federally prescribed membership, is established for a
     limited purpose, and is not "adequately repre-
     sentative of, or accountable to," state or local
     elected officials.

Section 3 provided that states were to be permitted
to delegate to local elected officials responsibility for
reviewing, coordinating, and communicating with federal
agencies. At the discretion of elected state and local
officials, the state process could exclude particular
federal programs from review and comment. Section 4
called for "official State entities designated by the
States" to direct the new process. The order also
required federal agencies to propose new rules and
regulations governing inter-governmental reviews, to take
effect 30 April 1983 (Section 5); authorized OMB to
prescribe any appropriate rules and regulations (Section
6); ordered rescision of A-95 itself (Section 7); and
called for a report by the director of OMB within two
years on federal agency compliance with 12372, within two
years (Section 8).

Moreover, the review process under 12372 was to be a
<u>neutral</u> one, meaning that the federal government would
neither define the nature of the state process nor
predetermine who would be involved in that process, as it
was designed and put into operation.[10]

RATIONALES FOR 12372: LINKS TO THE NEW FEDERALISM

An explicitly articulated objective of Ronald
Reagan's presidency has been to enhance the relative
position of the states in the U.S. federal system.
Beginning with his inaugural address, the president made
it clear that he viewed as a matter of great urgency the
task of "returning power to the states" and "restoring the
historical balance" between national and state government
power. In each year since then, including 1983, there
have been major efforts to "roll back" a host of federal
government activities, and to enlarge the areas of responsibility in U.S. governance formally entrusted to state
governments and public officials. A companion objective
has been to strengthen the influence of <u>elected</u> officials,
on all planes, in deciding on policy priorities and
program activities, but with emphasis, again, on elected
<u>state</u> officials. These concepts and objectives of the New

Federalism have been central to much of this administration's domestic policy.

Proposal of EO 12372 as a replacement for A-95 was represented from the start as consistent with the philosophical underpinnings of the New Federalism. In early congressional testimony, OMB justified the change in terms of simplifying review and comment processes by reducing federal regulation; promoting agency respon-siveness to state concerns and, through the state, to local concerns; and increasing state and local flexibility by permitting substantial discretion in choosing which programs to review and how to review them.[11] The order was characterized as "one of the fundamental components" of the New Federalism for "providing an opportunity for state and local officials to have more influence on federal financial assistance ... and [on] direct-development activities that affect the states."[12]

Perhaps the clearest statement of the linkages between 12372 and the New Federalism came at a national meeting of state and federal officials in Washington D.C. in late October of 1983:

The Executive Order is an important part of the new federalism policy. We consider it a significant opportunity for state and local government. President Reagan is committed to restoring the Constitutional balance between state and federal government. That has three aspects: structural changes, shifting responsibilities to state and local government; regulatory relief and reducing federal intrusiveness; and federal responsiveness to state and local concerns.
...
The Executive Order is related to federalism in two ways: (1) federal responsiveness, and (2) restoration of state/local authority, state/local flexibility, and regulatory relief.[13]

These statements and others like them clearly reflect a preference for state decisional authority and an intention to lighten regulatory burdens on both states and localities. (The A-95 process was one of the regulations targeted by the Vice President's Task Force on Regulatory Relief prior to 1983.) Whatever else might be said about EO 12372, it is clear that its issuance was a conscious, deliberate step within the larger framework of the Reagan administration's philosophical and political objectives.

IMPLEMENTING CHANGE: WHAT HAPPENED IN 1983

The early transition from A-95 to 12372 was characterized by unexpectedly intense opposition to the new order. The criticisms were broad-gauged and directed toward various dimensions of the new process-- some a part of the formal provisions, others stemming from OMB or federal agency interpretations of them. The events of 1983 began unfolding when federal agencies, per instructions from OMB, published proposed rules for implementing 12372 in the Federal Register on 24 January 1983. These proposed rules sparked a wave of protest from diverse sources. Local government officials made known their fears that, among other things, their ability to influence grant allocation decisions could be severely diminished under the new state-established processes. State officials sought more time to organize those processes and clearer direction about the operation of the key elements involved. Some members of Congress (including Republican Senator David Durenberger of Minnesota, chairman of the Senate Subcommittee on Intergovernmental Relations) saw a major omission in the order's failure to mention, as statutory bases for 12372, either Section 204 of the Model Cities Act or Sections 401(b) and 401(c) of the ICA.

Protests were also heard regarding the role that state governors were to play and regarding proposed agency regulations that contained extensive lists of programs excluded from the scope of 12372. This last point rankled state and local officials alike, who believed that agencies had contravened a provision in Section 3 of the order that permitted program exclusions "at the discretion of the State and local elected officials," with no mention of federal agency discretion.

Many of these reactions were made known in public hearings sponsored by OMB in Washington, D.C. in early March of 1983 and focusing on the notices of proposed agency rulemaking. Other significant developments in late 1982 and early 1983 included threats of litigation from the National Association of Regional Councils (NARC), which was fearful that regional Councils of Governments (COGs) would find their access to the consultation process severely limited[14]; and (after the March hearings) a well-publicized letter to President Reagan from Senator Durenberger and several of his colleagues that temporarily halted implementation of 12372.

Because the order's effective date (30 April 1983) was fast approaching and because of the intense and diverse criticisms of the order, the White House moved quickly to defuse the situation. On 8 April, President Reagan issued EO 12416, which amended 12372 in several ways. First, the effective date was moved back to 30 September 1983 to permit states more time in devising their consultation processes. Second, a citation of Section 204 of the Model Cities Act was explicitly included in 12416.[15] Shortly thereafter, OMB scheduled another public meeting for early May in Washington and extended the period for public comment until 19 May. It also directed federal agencies to publish final rules no later than 30 June, so that state and local officials would have three months to finalize the new state processes with full knowledge of federal implementing regulations and program scope.[16] A national meeting of federal and state officials was scheduled for late October in Washington, D. C., to be followed by a series of regional meetings in November, at which implementation issues and problems could be discussed jointly by the parties most directly involved.

When final agency rules were published on 24 June in the wake of these developments, major changes were evident; these seemed to respond to the harshest public comments and the most effective political pressure. The most important changes are as follows:

1. The review and comment period is sixty, not thirty, days.
2. Federal agencies must provide a written explanation of "nonaccommodation" in all instances, not only at the request of a state's governor.
3. The waiting period between notice of nonaccommodation and final agency action on a grant application is fifteen days, rather than ten, to cover mailing time.
4. Comments differing from those sent through the state level "Single Point of Contact" (SPOC) must also be forwarded and must be "considered" by an agency.
5. Federal agencies must directly notify affected entities about program decisions if a program or activity is not within the scope of 12372 or if there is no state process established.
6. States will consult with local officials before changing program coverage.

7.  Recommendations prepared by local governments or designated interstate agencies will be "accommodated or explained" if submitted through the SPOC, in the absence of a state-process recommendation (or of a state process, which was the case in two states as 1983 ended).

8.  An agency is required to keep records of emergency waivers as well as of nonaccommodations.

9.  Agencies are required to undertake interagency coordination within the framework of the review process.[17]

The political impact of these changes was indicated by the reaction of NARC--one of the most vocal critics of the regulations proposed in January--when it called the new regulations a "significant step forward for local governments and regional councils," noting that the changes included "significant clarifications" of points that had been intensively negotiated between January and June.[18] (NARC's threat of litigation was not carried out, in light of the revisions in the new regulations.)

Also significant, however, were changes requested in public comments, but not made in the final rules. Among these were the viewpoint, noted previously, that federal agencies should not determine which programs and activities should be included or excluded from the order's scope; that OMB should expand its oversight role; that a specific right of legal appeal and review should be established; and that more definitions should be provided concerning the 12372 process itself.[19] Clearly, despite a considerable amount of movement on OMB's part (and on that of the president) during 1983, a number of concerns remain about both substance and procedure in implementing EO 12372.

IMPLEMENTING CHANGE: WHAT DID NOT HAPPEN IN 1983

Even after a year of fast-paced regulation writing, political maneuvering, negotiation, and regulation rewriting, 1983 ended with many fundamental inter-governmental review issues unresolved. As is often the case, these nondecisions were at least as interesting as the decisions. Thus, any analysis of developments in intergovernmental consultation in 1983 would be incomplete without discussion of what did not happen in that year.

At the 26-27 October national meeting in Washington, D. C., a spokesperson characterized state officials' feelings on EO 12372 as "ambivalence, consternation, confusion, and lamenting some missing links," but with a "continued belief in the EO and its potential for flexibility and responsiveness." Most of the states' reservations stemmed from the failure to resolve four interrelated issues: (1) rules for notifying applicants and SPOCs, (2) definitions of the 60-day review period, (3) federal responsiveness, and (4) determination of future program exclusions and review thresholds. Ironically, the year's experience also left some deeper doubts about the intergovernmental structure of decision making, on the intergovernmental review issue.

## Notification Rules

Even though the new review process officially is "state-established," active federal involvement is as necessary now as it was under A-95. Most of the unresolved issues concern the extent and depth of that federal commitment. For example, the first step in the process must be informing potential applicants of their responsibility to comply with 12372. Under the old system, federal agencies had the obligation to inform applicants, and most agencies eventually fulfilled this requirement in a fairly satisfactory way by including A-95 instructions in their program announcements and application packages. But rescision of the circular reopened the question of whether, and how, funding agencies would notify applicants. Decentralization under the order also complicates the issue because each state could have a slightly different process, with varying rules and filing dates. Although states drafted their 12372 procedures under the assumption that federal agencies would inform applicants, at the end of 1983 states still were not entirely sure that this battle had been won.

The October meeting achieved a general consensus that federal agencies would tell applicants to contact the appropriate state SPOC, which then would instruct them regarding the particular requirements in that state. But because there was no real agreement on exactly how this could be done, states still considered this to be high-priority unfinished business.

A related issue concerns how agencies would inform SPOCs of grant application opportunities. Most states want to know about such opportunies well in advance, so that they can urge appropriate agencies to apply, establish state priorities, seek out matching funds, and "head off at the pass" any "renegade applications."[20] At the October meeting, most federal agencies said that SPOCs could become familiar with the grants available by reading the Federal Register, but most states claimed they had neither time nor staff to do this. There was lengthy discussion of alternative notification mechanisms but no agreement. One state, taking OMB's declarations of state flexibility at face value, simply wrote into the state process a provision that the state "will receive a weekly letter notification from the Secretary of each federal department that has EO 12372 responsibilities."[21]

## 60-Day Review Period

Like the notification issue, 60-day review is a technical question with great political and practical signficance. According to the final agency regulations, SPOCs must be given sixty days to review most funding applications.[22] What is not entirely clear, however, is where in the grant cycle these sixty days will occur. This presents two problems. First, federal agencies, applicants, and state and local reviewers have to know exactly what they must do by precisely what date, or compliance and enforcement will be impossible. To complicate matters, states had to define the 60-day period for themelves in writing their procedures, so there already are many varying interpretations.

More importantly, it seems likely that this issue will be resolved in such a way that state and local agencies will find it difficult to perform what has traditionally been the most significant function of intergovernmental review: the negotiation of conflict and advising of applicants before applications are submitted to funding agencies. As one state official pointed out at the November regional meeting in Chicago, final application reviews in the past functioned like the goalie in a hockey game: coordination and review ideally worked early in the process, and the "goalie" had to be called upon only when the rest of the system failed. But to perform the early negotiation function, reviewers need considerable time at the preapplication state.

Assuming that all the participants can agree on a 60-day period, the consensus definition probably will be one proposed by the federal Department of Health and Human Services (HHS). Under this plan, federal agencies will set a closing date for submission of comments which is sixty days later than the application deadline. Applicants will be told that they should contact the SPOC for their state and probably will also be told that the SPOC should have at least sixty days to review the application. This way, according to HHS, each state can set whatever rules it wishes regarding preapplications, because "it is really not our concern how many steps states require the applicant to go through, how soon you ask the applicant to get in touch with you, whether you require notification of intent, etc."[23]

While this plan does fulfill the need for a straightforward, easily understood deadline for review (except for grant programs which have no specified application due dates), its implementation could make it very difficult to enforce state regulations concerning application reviews. An individual applicant, when told that SPOCs must have sixty days for review and that the review period ends sixty days after the application due date, is likely to assume that simultaneous submission to the SPOC and the funding agency is the accepted practice, no matter what else the instructions might say. If contacted in advance, SPOCs could try to persuade applicants to provide materials at an earlier time, but they would have no way to enforce this request. This may be one reason why the General Accounting Office (GAO), which is conducting a comprehensive evaluation of the order, already has expressed concern that applications under 12372 will be sent to funding agencies and SPOCs simultaneously, thereby precluding early negotiation and encouraging a reviewer-applicant adversary relationship.[24]

## Federal Responsiveness and Quality Control

In a 1975 study of A-95, GAO found that the intergovernmental review system was severely weakened by lack of federal support for the process, demonstrated by federal agency tolerance of "renegade" applications (that is, applications which bypassed the process entirely) and by lack of agency feedback to clearinghouses.[25] These problems supposedly will be corrected under the new system, but doing so will require resolving many questions of detail still outstanding. For example, OMB announced in October that "in 100% of cases where federal agencies receive an application without evidence that the state has seen it, they will notify the SPOC."[26] As yet, however, states and federal agencies have not achieved consensus on what "evidence" will be required (such as, an applicant check-off or a state identifier number). Nor have they decided whether federal agencies will be required--or even encouraged--to withhold funds from "renegade" applicants or, again, how any of this will be enforced.

Similarly, OMB asserts that the order will ensure responsiveness by requiring federal agencies to accommodate a state process recommendation or to explain in writing why they cannot. But states and federal agencies still have not reached common definitions of "accommodation" or "state process recommendation." More fundamentally, according to many state officials the critical issue is not "accommodation" at all, but the funding agencies' broader receptivity and responsiveness to state and local concerns. Noting that the states never even asked for "accommodation," one spokesperson explained:

We want due consideration of the comments that are generated by the states, and some consideration in responding to them, some feedback that the federal agency has thought through the comments and given them some kind of weight. We are looking for responsiveness, not necessarily accommodation on every issue. It should be kept in mind that we are looking for intergovernmental communication, due process that has a responsive element, and not just one that highlights accommodation and nonaccommodation.[27]

Because the various parties still differ on federal obligations to "be responsive," there is also considerable disagreement on how federal performance is to be evaluated. Agencies are required to keep records of all waivers and nonaccommodations, and OMB will review these records for its one-year evaluation of 12372. But, as one observer noted at the national meeting (in a statement that seemed to reflect the feelings of many state and local officials), "just looking at nonaccommodation is a narrow conception, looking at it from a narrow point of view. Nonaccommodation might not necessarily be bad."[28] As one might expect, state concerns about the scope and depth of the evaluation also led to questions about OMB as the most appropriate evaluator:

In the private session of state representatives following the plenary session, states expressed a concern that a year from now, when implementation is being evaluated and changes are being considered, we will have forgotten the

big issues we fought and lost during the OMB interpretation of the Order--like scope issues. The states
agreed that it is incumbent on states to take on some of
the responsibility for evaluating aspects of the Executive
Order process which will not be covered by OMB's assessment. It was agreed that consideration would be given to
outside groups doing an evaluation, because another group
than OMB should be involved.[29]

## Program Exclusions and Thresholds

As noted earlier, one of the bitterest areas of
controversy during 1983 was the funding agencies'
determination of which programs would be excluded from
12372 coverage. The year ended with no resolution of this
matter. States continued to claim that the order gave
them--and them alone--the right to exclude programs, while
federal agencies maintained that the order gave states
only the right to choose from a prescreened list. States
continued to object to many specific exclusions and to the
high dollar thresholds which precluded review of applications for many of the remaining programs. For example,
officials in one state pointed out that the state
government would not be able to review a single Housing
and Urban Development (HUD) application if the current
thresholds were retained. Other SPOCs, such as those in
Connecticut, Delaware, Maryland, Puerto Rico, and Texas,
decided to test the system by including in their state
regulations many programs the federal agencies had
excluded. OMB was not amused, however, and offered the
following advice:

Some states want to include programs in their systems
which were not included by federal agencies, and we
encourage the states to tell their applicants to follow
state requirements on those programs. As to the federal
government, however, we can't guarantee extension of the
Executive Order to these additional programs. The
agencies will be available to talk with you on a case-by-
case basis if there are specific programs that you would
like to have included. If you can work out a deal with
them, you are home free. If you can't, and it's something
you feel you should include, talk with us.[30]

The more pragmatic states accepted the existing list of
covered programs as a given but expressed concern about
how states might have greater input into <u>future</u>

determinations of program coverage.

## THE INTERGOVERNMENTAL STRUCTURE OF 12372 POLICY MAKING

Running through the continuing negotiations over notification, the 60-day period, federal responsiveness, and program exclusions is a broader, more fundamentally political controversy: What should the intergovernmental structure of decisionmaking be, regarding 12372-related issues? While this question inevitably emerges in some form in any endeavor in which many federal agencies and several layers of government are involved, the rhetoric of New Federalism which surrounds 12372 highlights the issue.

The controversy takes two forms. First, what plane of government will have the authority to make, or significantly influence, basic rules and procedures? As noted earlier, the order implies that states will have a great deal of flexibility and discretion. OMB's "marketing campaign" did nothing to dispel this image. The agency regulations were a rude awakening for the states, but at least they clarified some of the uncertainty regarding the locus of power. On the other hand, the year ended with no answer to a second question: How will communications and negotiations between states and federal agencies be structured, and where will OMB fit into this picture?

Almost all analyses of the A-95 process criticized OMB's passive role regarding the circular's implementation. Critics claimed, in particular, that OMB's deliberately low profile was a major reason for federal agency noncompliance with A-95.[31] OMB made it quite clear during 1983 that it intends to assume an even smaller role regarding compliance under EO 12372. On the other hand, OMB took a very visible part in the design, negotiation, and early implementation of 12372. Ironically, this increase in its level of activity has only escalated the criticism.

OMB served as the intermediary between federal agencies and the states. In part because of this role OMB drew intense criticism, from federal and state participants alike, while coordinating federal agency regulation writing, serving as the liaison between agencies and the states, and organizing hearings, briefings, and meetings involving agencies and the states. To some extent, this resulted from differences of both style and perception. Intergovernmental review personnel from both federal and state agencies tend to be pragmatic, career civil servants. On the other hand, the most visible OMB participants evidenced all the characteristics of what Chester Newland has termed President Reagan's "ideological political administration,"[32] and therefore carried a considerable amount of ideological "baggage." It appears that OMB used its central position under pattern A as a way of presenting a unified administration position. In the words of one OMB official, "We will do it as one government, we will not have 23 federal governments."[33] Many federal agency and state officials have found this arrangement very unsatisfactory, however. In private conversations, some indicated they were deliberately defying OMB, by exchanging information with other officials behind OMB's back.

During the October meeting, OMB began suggesting that for certain kinds of issues, each state should try to negotiate an agreement with each federal agency, as illustrated in pattern B. Many of the states, however, viewed this as an OMB effort to "divide and conquer" and therefore preferred to treat important policy matters with a unified state front (pattern C). They were supported in this position by the Council of State Planning Agencies (CSPA), which had a contract to organize the October and November meetings, and which began to assume more and more of OMB's "facilitator" role. This third pattern also seemed to be the one most advantageous to federal agencies, since they do not have the time or the resources to negotiate and then implement separate agreements with each state. By the time of the regional meetings in November, some communications at the policy level were beginning to follow pattern C, but there were widespread expectations that OMB would continue to assert an important role. In the words of a CSPA official, "Although states understand that they are to deal directly with each federal agency in implementing the Executive Order, they see that OMB will play a role in that 'direct' relationship--and do not know what to expect of OMB."[34] Not all states would welcome a resurgence of OMB visibility, for, as one state spokesperson put it, "The irony of the intergovernmental consultation process is that there has been no intergovernmental consultation by OMB."[35]

## FINAL OBSERVATIONS, CONCLUSIONS, AND SMALL IRONIES

This was not the only irony of 1983. For example, states were vehement in their demand that they--not federal agencies--decide which programs to exclude from intergovernmental review. When the time came to select programs from the federal agency list, however, most states decided to review everything, at least initially. While federal prescreening undoubtedly was one reason for this, one suspects that many states would have decided to review all eligible programs in any case simply because the process of sifting through programs for inclusion or exclusion would have been both time consuming and politically sensitive.

On another front, the Reagan administration billed 12372 as an important vehicle for states--and, specifically, for governors--to use in increasing their clout with the Washington bureaucracy. The SPOC was seen as an important part of this new system, since it provided a way for states to consolidate, underline, and edit the views of local officials. But the states showed little interest in these new powers. Indeed, a number of states sent a letter to OMB suggesting that the SPOC system was not needed![36] When it came time to decide whether or not to participate in the new system, however, most states decided to have an official state process as a service to local government. As one state official said, there would have been a severe backlash from local government officials had state officials decided not to go ahead with a formal state-level review process. (On the other hand, local governments and regional planning commissions were not invited to any of the meetings where the 12372 procedures were worked out.)

In yet another irony, New Federalism (at least in its intergovernmental review manifestation) is not likely to be viewed as "deregulation" or "decentralization" from the perspective of local and regional governments. The reason is that, thus far, the major effect of 12372 has been to interject another government between themselves and the funding agencies.

Finally, given the poor record of federal agency compliance with A-95 and OMB's reluctance to move forcefully in persuading federal agencies to take A-95 seriously, many observers are still very anxious to discover how compliance will be achieved under 12372. According to OMB's 16 September memo, OMB and the federal agencies have found a novel solution to this dilemma. The states are to be in charge of assuring compliance:

The state responsibility is shared, but the state has principal responsibility ... Under the Executive Order, states, in consultation with local officials, have flexibility to design their own review and comment process. Thus, the consultation procedures and review requirements which an applicant follows are principally those of the state, not the Federal Government.[37]

Those familiar with the "layer cake" and "marble cake" models of federalism may ask whether 12372 may be adding an "upside down cake" model to the array of confectionary selections.

Although 1983 was a very active year for change and issue resolution in the intergovernmental review system, it clearly ended with many questions still unanswered. To those experienced in A-95 matters, however, this comes as no surprise. As one twelve-year veteran of A-95 review put it, "It takes a long time to get this in place. Some of these broad issues are going to be broad issues next year and the year after. It is going to come through evolution.[38] What that portends for an effective system of intergovernmental review, and for the distribution of poltical influence within such a system, is thus very much an open question.

NOTES

1. Inceasing attention has been paid in recent years to the various aspects of regulation in intergovernmental relations. Among the most useful studies of this phenomenon are Catherine H. Lovell, et al., Federal and State Mandating on Local Governments--Issues and Impacts, Report to the National Science Foundation, June 1979; U. S. Advisory Commission on Intergovernmental Relations (ACIR), State Mandating of Local Expenditures (Washington, D.C.: ACIR, 1978); Catherine H. Lovell and Charles Tobin, "The Mandate Issue," in Public Administration Review 41 (May/June 1981): 318-331; and Donald F. Kettl, The Regulation of American Federalism (Baton Rouge: Louisiana State University Press, 1983).

2. This definition of coordination is derived from the discussion of the concept in Charles E. Lindblom, The Intelligence of Democracy (New York: The Free Press, 1965), at p. 24.

3. See, for example, Herbert Kaufman, "Organization Theory and Poltical Theory," in American Political Science Review 58 (March 1964): 7; and James L. Sundquist with the collaboration of David W. Davis, Making Federalism Work (Washington, D.C.: The Brookings Institution, 1969), especially Chapter 1.

4. See, among others, Catherine H. Lovell, "Where We Are in IGR and Some of the Implications," in Southern Review of Public Administration 3 (June 1979): 6-20.

5. See, for example, U. S. General Accounting Office (GAO), Improved Cooperation and Coordination Needed Among All Levels of Government--Office of Management and Budget Circular A-95, Report to the Congress by the Comptroller General of the United States (Washington, D.C.: GAO, processed, 11 February 1975), p.2.

6. Gary Bombardier, "The Managerial Function of OMB: Intergovernmental Relations as a Test Case," in Public Policy 23 (1975): 328.

7. GAO, Improved Cooperation and Coordination, pp. 5-6.

8. Ibid., p. 6.

9. See, among others, George J. Gordon, "Office of Management and Budget Circular A-95: Perspectives and Implications," in Publius: The Journal of Federalism 4 (Winter 1974): 45-68; and "OMB Circular A-95: An Overview," paper delivered at the annual meeting of the American Society for Public Administration, Phoenix, Arizona, 1978; Philip A. Russo, Jr., "In Search of Intergovernmental Coordination: The A-95 Project Notification and Review System," in Publius: The Journal of Federalism 12 (Spring 1982): 49-62; Bruce D. McDowell, "Intergovernmental Consultation Changes Provide Opportunities," in U. S. Advisory Commission on Intergovernmental Relations Bulletin No. 82-3, (December 1982): especially pp. 23-26; and Irene Fraser Rothenberg, "Regional Coordination of Federal Program: Has the Difficult Grown Impossible?" in Journal of Policy Analysis and Management (forthcoming).

10. Statement of Joseph R. Wright, Jr., Deputy Director, OMB, before the U.S. Senate Subcommittee on Intergovernmental Relations, Committee on Governmental Affairs, on EO 12372, Intergovernmental Review of Federal Programs, 3 March 1983, pp. 6-7; Memorandum from Harold I. Steinberg, Associate Director for Management, OMB, to Interested Federal, State, and Local Officials, regarding EO 12372--Federal Implementation Activities, 14 October 1982.

11. Statement of Joseph R. Wright, Jr., pp. 6-7.

12. Ibid., p. 3.

13. Statement of Barbara Young, OMB, at National Transition Meeting on EO 12372, 26-27 October 1983, Washington, D.C., as reported in a synopsis of that October meeting, prepared by the Council of State Planning Agencies (CSPA), dated 2 November 1983 (cited hereafter as CSPA, "Synopsis").

14. McDowell, "Intergovernmental Consultation Changes Provide Opportunities," p. 6, note 5.

15. One additional amendment to the order, of lesser significance, changed the due date of the OMB Director's first evaluation of 12372 to 30 September 1984, rather than "within two years" of its taking effect.

16. Memorandum to State EO Contacts and OMB State Network, from James F. Kelly, Deputy Associate Director, Management Reform Division, OMB, 28 April 1983.

17. Memo to federal agencies concerning public comments on the proposed agency rules, dated 4 August 1983.

18. Public Administration Times (Washington, D.C.: American Society for Public Administration, 15 July 1983), p. 8.

19. Memo to federal agencies, 4 August 1983.

20. CSPA, "Synopsis," p. 4.

21. Ibid., p. 5.

22. Only thirty days are allocated for certain programs and activities such as noncompetitive continuation grants, and the Department of Housing and Urban Development's mortgage insurance and Urban Development Action Grant programs. Most federal agencies authorize emergency waivers of the regulation "only in the rare instances in which an unanticipated situation necessitates prompt action, and does not allow for full compliance with the rules." Office of Management and Budget, "Federal Rules for EO 12372," Intergovernmental Review of Federal Programs, 25 August 1983.

23. CSPA, "Synopsis," p. 6.

24. Ibid., pp. 24-25.

25. GAO, Improved Cooperation and Coordination. See, also, Irene Fraser Rothenberg, "National Support for Regional Review: Federal Compliance and the Future of Intergovernmental Coordination," in Publius: The Journal of Federalism 13 (Fall 1983): 43-58.

26. CSPA, "Synopsis," p. 7.

27. Ibid., p. 10.

28. Ibid., p. 23.

29. Ibid., p. 24.

30. Ibid., p. 14.

31. GAO, Improved Cooperation and Coordination.

32. See Chester A. Newland, "A Mid-Term Appraisal--The Reagan Presidency: Limited Government and Political Administration," in Public Administration Review 43 (January/February 1983): 1-21. This conflict between "political" and "career" policymakers in the executive branch is suggestive of the broad thesis of Hugh Heclo, in A Government of Strangers: Executive Politics in Washington (Washington, D.C.: The Brookings Institution, 1977).

33. CSPA, "Synopsis," p. 17.

34. Ibid., p. 22.

35. Notes of the authors from 26-27 October 1983 transition meeting, held in Washington, D.C., and from the regional meeting for Federal Region V held in Chicago, Illinois, on 9 November 1983.

36. Notes from 9 November 1983 regional meeting, Chicago.

37. Office of Management and Budget, "Questions and Answers to Implementation of EO 12372," 16 September 1983.
38. CSPA, "Synopsis," p. 18.

# 5

## State Managerial Responses to the New Federalism

*Paul Posner*

Passage of the 1981 Omnibus Budget Reconciliation Act signaled a major shift in the direction of our federal system. Not only were substantial cuts instituted in many domestic programs, but greater authority was delegated to the states in allocating reduced federal funds in nine new block grant programs. Although in subsequent years Congress mitigated these cuts by at least partially restoring funds, the block grants have proven to be more lasting in status and effect. Implementation of these block grants, along with a federal deficit that chilled new expensive national domestic initiatives and substantive deregulation of categorical programs, shifted the focus of authority, political pressure, and analytic attention to the states. Richard Nathan, in fact, argues that the lasting impact of Reagan's domestic program changes will be the shift of authority to the states, not the much heralded or feared budget cuts.[1]

Since 1981, block grants have been established in a number of program areas. Although their "broad-based" aid still comprises only 20 percent of total fiscal year (FY) 1985 federal grant outlays, Congress did create 12 new block grant programs so far in the 1980's, for a total of 13 including the Community Development Block Grant created in 1974.[2]

THE MANAGERIAL IMPETUS FOR BLOCK GRANTS

One of the primary rationales for the conversion of categorical programs to block grants was to improve public management of intergovernment programs. Block grants were promoted as a mechanism to overcome perceived problems

96

with the categorical approach to delivering services. In 1981, the federal government funded over 500 categorical programs that comprised 80 percent of the $94 billion in federal grants provided to state and local government. These grants were typically narrow in scope and generally accompanied by numerous federal programmatic and administrative requirements.

At their outset, categorical programs served to stimulate state and local involvement in a host of national priority services that may not otherwise have received attention. Yet, over time, the accumulation of numerous narrow-purpose federal grant programs was alleged to have fostered an overcentralized, inefficient service delivery system.

According to several major studies by the Advisory Commission on Intergovernmental Relations (ACIR) and the U.S. General Accounting Office (GAO),[3] the categorical approach promoted a fragmented, overly restricted approach to service delivery, inhibiting effective coordination with related state programs to meet actual service needs at the state and local level. Further, satisfying numerous federal administrative requirements for the host of overlapping categorical grants was alleged to impose excessive costs and burdens on states and localities. Finally, the inextricable linkages among the multiple layers of government involved in setting policy and running these programs confused or diluted accountability, according to ACIR. Oversight by elected officials at state and local levels was discouraged because their discretion was so constrained.[5]

Considerable interest was aroused, then, over whether the federal government and the states would implement the new block grants to overcome some of these categorical management problems. Several major questions were posed: Would states use their newly won authority to integrate related services and make other changes to better reflect state or local needs as determined by publicly accountable officials? Did states have the capacity to manage their new responsibilities without strong federal guidance? Would the management changes result in cost savings and administrative improvements sufficient to offset some or all of the budget cuts accompanying these programs?

Reflecting the strong interest in this area, several field studies were initiated to assess this effort. The GAO--the evaluation and audit arm of the Congress--began a thirteen-state study of the implementation of seven of the nine 1981 block grants in response to numerous congressional inquiries. The information from this GAO effort serves as the basis for the following discussion of the six key managerial impacts of block grants. However, the inferences drawn are those of the author alone.[6]

STATE ADMINISTRATIVE IMPACTS

Varieties of Block Grants

The study revealed that a variety of variables condition the potential managerial impacts of block grants. While the political debate in 1981 considered block grants as a unidimensional phenomenon, important differences existed among the block grants that were enacted--differences that have a direct bearing on the field impacts of these federal changes on state management and service delivery.

Specifically, the programs differed in the degree of additional discretion provided to the states. For instance, states were given new authority to set service standards and income eligibility criteria under the Social Services block grant (SSBG)--a considerable change from the prior Title XX program where the federal government was moving to impose national standards on day care providers. Under the Maternal and Child Health (MCH) block grant, states could decide how to allocate federal funds among ten programs that used to be separately funded as categorical programs.

State authority was more limited under other programs. For example, while the Community Services block grant (CSBG) gave states a new role in managing community services providers, states were required to spend 90 percent of their block grant allocation on organizations receiving federal money under the prior categorical structure. Under the Education block grant, state authority to determine how local school districts used the pass-through funds was limited, since the federal intent was to promote local discretion in the use of funds.

Other key differences include the extent of consolidation of prior categorical programs and the degree of prior state involvement with the programs. States had considerable state funds invested in many of the areas supported by block grants. For instance, over 50 percent of total expenditures for maternal and child health was provided by state sources in most states GAO visited. Under the Alcohol, Drug Abuse and Mental Health Services

(ADAMH) block grant, the federal allocation of $10 million
to California for alcohol services pales by comparison to
the state investment of $90 million. On the other hand,
states generally did not invest their own funds in
Community Services or Low-income Energy Assistance. Table
5.1 capsulizes these differences for the seven programs
studied by GAO.

Of course, other factors could be hypothesized to
play a role in determining the state managerial impact of
change. For instance, the size of the grant, either
absolutely or in relation to state spending, might be
expected to affect the degree of change that could be
expected from changes in grant structures and responsibilities. Federal funds for these block grants range
from $2.7 billion for the SSBG social services to less
than $100 million for the Preventive Health and Health
Services (PHHS) block grant. One recent study suggests a
linear relationship between the influence of federal
priorities on state behavior and the size of federal
funds. The following section discusses how the funding
changes and administrative changes brought about by block
grants affected state fiscal and managerial responses.

State Funding Changes and Priorities:  Findings

GAO concluded that states often maintained program
funding and service priorities, in spite of the federal
funding cuts accompanying most of the block grants,
through the fiscal year 1983. For the three health block
grants (PHHS, MCH, and ADAMH), and the SSBG total expenditures for these programs increased between 1981 and 1983
in about 75 percent of the cases in the thirteen states.
However, when adjusted for inflation, "real" expenditure
growth was registered in only 30 percent of the cases.

States used three principal strategies to help offset
the initial federal funding cuts. The applicability and
use of these strategies varied greatly by block grant.

1.  Prior categorical funds. Overlapping federal funding
    from prior categorical programs awarded to service
    providers prior to the onset of the block grant were
    available well into the first and second years of
    block grant implementa-tion. As a result, service
    providers used these funds to continue program
    implementation, en-abling states to carry forward
    block grant funds into future years.

2. <u>Fund transfers among block grants</u>. In a number of cases, states took advantage of statutory provisions allowing a portion of the funds from one block grant program to be transfered to another. Most states transferred funds from the Low-Income Home Energy Assistance block grant (LIHEA), which actually received increased federal appropriations, to the SSBG, which received the largest federal dollar reduction.

3. <u>Increased state funds</u>. Most states increased their own contributions to health and social services programs to compensate for the federal cuts. This increased state support reflects the states' long-standing financial and administrative investment in these programs areas. Most states, however, did not allocate additional funds to two block grant programs--community services and low-income energy--where they had little or no prior involvement or commitment.

Overall, states chose to maintain continuity in services provided in the first several years of the block grant experience, especially for those block grants where states have been traditionally involved in the service delivery process. Nevertheless, their expanded flexibility enabled the states to reassess service priorities in some cases to better address state needs and to cope more effectively with funding limitations. States provided more support for broader health programs they had previously funded and relatively less support for more narrowly targeted activities previously mandated or directly funded by the federal government. The following is a brief summary of findings for each of the seven block grants examined in the GAO study.

- Under the MCH and the PHHS block grants, the thirteen states tended to provide more support for program areas over which they formerly had greater control, such as crippled children's services and fluoridation, and relatively less support for areas that used to be primarily federally controlled or mandated, such as lead-based paint poisoning prevention and emergency medical services.

- Although changes varied considerably by state under the SSBG, the thirteen states usually gave a higher priority to adult and child protective services, adoption and foster care, home-based services, family

Table 5.1
State Authority in Financial and
Administrative Involvement

| | Substantial State Authority | | Limited State Authority | |
|---|---|---|---|---|
| | Consolidation | No Consolidation | Consolidation | No Consolidation |
| Prior State Financial and Administrative Involvement | Maternal and Child Health (MCH)<br><br>Preventive Health and Health Services (PHHS) | Social Services (SSBG) | Education Block Grant (EDBG)<br><br>Alcohol, Drug Abuse, and Mental Health (ADAMH) | |
| Prior State Administrative Involvement Only | | Low-Income Home Energy Assistance (LIHEA) | | |
| No Prior State Involvement | | | | Community Services (CSBG) |

planning, and employment, education, and training. Many states also tightened eligibility standards for day care services and decreased expenditures for a wide range of other services.

- Under the CSBG, nine of the thirteen states introduced new methods for distributing funds that included poverty-based factors. Such changes and the substantial decrease in federal assistance led to funding changes for many service providers in the thirteen states; over 90 percent that received funds in 1981 had their funding reduced in 1983.
- While heating assistance remained the major program activity under the LIHEA block grant, heating expenditures tended to decline as most of the thirteen states increased funding for weatherization and crisis assistance, transferred funds to other block grants, and carried over energy funds into the next year.
- Program changes were less evident in the ADAMH block grant, in part due to legislative provisions controlling the allocation of funds among the three program areas.
- Under the education block grant, states were required to pass on at least 80 percent of their allocation to local education agencies, which have virtually complete control over the use of these funds. Thus, state authority was limited to deciding how to use the remaining 20 percent, and state program officials reported that funds retained by the states were generally used to support activities similar to those funded under the prior categorical programs. GAO estimated that over 50 percent of the funds used by local educa-tion agencies funded in the thirteen states were spent on instructional materials and equipment.

## STATE PLANNING PROCESSES USED FOR BLOCK GRANT DECISIONS

These state decisions were most often made through broader state planning and budgeting processes used for state-funded programs. The extent to which planning for the block grant programs was integrated into broader state processes, however, varied among the block grant programs based on the degree of discretion delegated to the states and the level of state involvement in the program areas addressed. Where states share a financial and adminis-trative commitment, additional flexibility afforded under the block grant enabled states to consider these funds as additional resources available to support state service priorities. Thus, state decisions on the use of social services, health, and the state portion of the education block grant funds were often developed concurrently with, or reflected, goals established for broader state programs. Plans prepared for these block grants generally were either derived from, or are consistent with, basic allocational decisions made during the state budgetary or other broad decision-making process.

For example, programs listed in Washington's MCH, PHHS, and SSBG applications were identified primarily through the process used to develop the state health and social services agency budget for the 1981-1983 biennium. The agency instituted a detailed budget planning process to review services and existing priorities in response to actual state and anticipated federal funding reductions. State officials noted that block grant funds were considered as revenue sources available to support state efforts. In Vermont, the comprehensive services plan prepared by the Agency for Human Services was used for both state legislative and public consideration during the state's budgetary process as well as submitted as the fiscal year 1983 application for six block grants and five major categorical programs.

For some of the larger predecessor programs, states were also most likely making decisions through these broader planning and budgeting processes. For instance, only four of GAO's thirteen states noted that the Social Services block grant provided additional flexibility over the prior Title XX program. Nevertheless, the lifting of federal categorical restrictions promoted the states' integration of planning for related federal and state programs for a greater number of program areas.

This was especially true for programs like ADAMH, where states had only limited control over predecessor categorical funds that were allocated directly to service providers before the block grant. Nearly all the funding under the prior categorical community mental health center program and a large share of the project grant money for alcohol abuse treatment went directly to local level providers that also receive funds from the state government or were otherwise considered as part of the states' service delivery network. Under these prior categorical programs, state health agencies reviewed local provider grant applications and incorporated their activities in state plans but had little real control over provider use of the federal funds. A number of state officials noted that the increase in state control over federally funded alcohol and drug abuse and community mental health programs under the ADAMH block grant encouraged improvements in state planning and budgeting.

States' new authority over federal funds dedicated to these program areas allowed them to consider the ADAMH block grant as a revenue source to support state priorities and served to strengthen the planning process in place for state programs. For example, Florida officials reported that the block grant is now included in the state appropriation process, thereby providing greater control over total resource expenditure for substance abuse and mental health.

In contrast to the health and social services block grants, states set priorities separately for the Community Services and Low Income Home Energy Assistance block grants, reflecting the lower level of state financial involvement in these programs. CSBG presented states with new responsibilities for a program area for which few had any prior financial or administrative commitment. Generally, states approached planning their CSBG programs cautiously; few took advantage of the flexibility available to mandate what community services would be offered at the local level and to design programs to meet state needs. Instead, most delegated significant discretion to the local service providers to determine the services to be delivered within the broad parameters set in the federal legislation.

## PUBLIC INVOLVEMENT IN STATE PLANNING

In making these decisions, states provided greater opportunities for public participation than were available for the prior categorical programs.[8] Typically, multiple channels for public input were made available for each program, including hearings, advisory groups, and comments on plans.

In over half of the cases, governors and legislatures responding to GAO's questionnaire noted increased involvement for block grants over levels reported for prior categorical programs. Although many legislatures had been moving to increase their oversight of federal funds before 1981, the advent of block grants directly spurred legislatures in three of the thirteen states--Kentucky, Iowa, and Colorado--to develop new formal procedures to either appropriate federal funds or to approve state applications for federal grants. The new discretion provided to state officials as well as the specific federal provision requiring state legislatures to hold public hearings on several block grants helped stimulate state legislative interest in these programs. Legislatures in ten of the thirteen states assert a relatively specific level of control by appropriating block grant funds along with related state funds to specific subprogram activities within each block grant.

Nevertheless, legislative staff and Governors report that the level of oversight devoted to federal block grant funds is still lower than the attention they devoted to state funded programs--block grants receive the same or greater level of state legislative attention as state programs in 65 percent of the cases, compared to 82 percent of the governors. State legislative staffs report devoting greater attention to those health and social services block grant programs where states have had significant funding and administrative involvement, than to the Community Services and LIHEA programs. Governors, on the other hand, report relatively equal levels of involvement for most of the block grants, including Community Services. Although lacking state funding, Community Services required a high level of administrative attention since most states lacked prior administrative experience with this program and its providers. Among the seven block grants, the Education Block Grant received the lowest levels of involvement from both legislatures and governors, probably due to the traditional autonomy accorded to education programs in state government.

Interest groups active at the state level also reported a higher level of interaction with state officials for block grant programs than under prior categorical programs. The 534 interst groups in 13 states responding to GAO's survey were split, however, in their assessment of states' efforts. The groups had mixed views about various aspects of state public participation procedures: while most were satisfied with their informal access to state officials and state advisory groups, most were dissatisfied with the timing of hearings in relation to when state decisions were made. They were equally divided regarding their satisfaction or dissatisfaction with states' program decisions on services.

The characteristics of the groups themselves explain much of the variance. Those groups presumably more familiar with state policymaking--that is, those who were active at the state level and those who actually participated in state hearings--were more satisfied with state processes and state program decisions. Those interest groups primarily active at the substate or regional level and, perhaps concurrently, those who did not participate in state processes were more dissatisfied.

## EFFECT ON STATE ORGANIZATION AND SERVICE DELIVERY SYSTEMS

Although the block grants generally expanded the scope of their involvement in federal assistance programs, states were not required to make major organizational changes to assume their new responsibilities for most block grants. Proceeding from their involvement in administering the prior categorical grant programs, and more importantly, their prominant role in the funding of most block grant-supported activities, states had an administrative structure in place to deliver these services. States' decisions to basically maintain the funding patterns established prior to the block grant served to maintain the existing service delivery network.

GAO did find some examples of states consolidating, eliminating, or transferring program responsibilities among state offices, reflecting their new role and authority under the block grants. For example, seven states consolidated or were in the process of folding the prior categorical Supplemental Security Income (SSI) program for disabled children into their crippled children's services under the MCH Block Grant.

In response to the change in federal administrative requirements attached to the social services program, Pennsylvania and Vermont eliminated offices responsible for the specific data collection and reporting requirements attached to the prior Title XX program. Five of the thirteen states GAO studied made organizational changes in response to the program consolidation and reduced administrative requirements under the education block grant.

While the network of institutions delivering services at the local level has remained fairly stable in the early years of block grant implementation, some changes have been made as states changed emphases placed on the scope and location of services provided or in the role of various organizations in the delivery system. Frequently, states sought to broaden funding to a greater number of providers throughout the state. Of the twelve states that continued to support emergency medical services through 1983 under the PHHS block grant, six broadened the program's geographic coverage or the types of services offered. Michigan now funds thirteen local providers instead of the three regional systems funded by the federal government prior to the block grant. Pennsylvania distributes block grant moneys to all emergency medical services regional systems, including those that did not receive categorical funds. These changes in the substate service delivery network more often affected those providers that had received direct federal categorical funds for more narrowly defined activities prior to the block grants.

As with their planning and budgeting processes, states were able to integrate ADAMH block grant funds into the service delivery systems used for related state programs. In some states, the service delivery networks used for state-funded activities paralleled those supported by certain federal categorical grants--most notably for community mental health centers and alcohol abuse treatment projects--where funds were directly awarded to local service providers. Although none of the states GAO visited revised policies governing the types of organizations eligible to receive ADAMH funds, integration of all funds into state system strengthened the role of the counties or regional entities in planning and allocating funds for these services. In some cases, the inclusion of these federal monies into the state system broadened geographic coverage. For example, in Pennsylvania all forty-three county authorities for substance abuse received federal block grant money, fourteen of which had not previously received federal alcohol or drug abuse funds.

States' ability to alter the existing service delivery network was curtailed by legislative provisions for certain of the block grant programs. The CSBG legislation restricted state options for determining which organizations could receive 90 percent of their block grant allocation; Colorado was the only state GAO studied that received a waiver allowing the state to distribute funds to counties beginning in 1983. Also, under ADAMH, states were required to continue support for certain community mental health centers that received direct federal funding prior to the block grant.

While states generally had some involvement with the protected community mental health centers prior to FY 1982, they were required to forge new relations with CSBG service providers, primarily community action agencies, with which they had very little previous involvement.

States continued funding for these providers, but used their new authority to institute new methods of distributing funds, which included funding of new entities or otherwise expanding the program's geographic coverage. Texas, for instance, extended service to ninety-one previously unserved counties by providing additional funds to existing service providers to expand their operations.

By utilizing their existing service delivery arrangements, states did not delegate additional flexibility or discretion to local providers receiving block grant funding. Rather, states continued to apply controls and restrictions traditionally imposed for state-funded programs. In most cases, GAO's thirteen states applied additional state restrictions to service providers, over and above the federal block grant requirements. These restrictions included obtaining prior state approvals for hiring or procurement and the requirement to provide local matching funds. For instance, seven of the thirteen states required local service providers to match CSBG funds, even though the federal matching requirement was eliminated.

In several states, however, the advent of the federal block grant did spur rethinking and change in state-local relationships. Several states visited by GAO began mini-block grants with their local providers that consolidated several programs, enabling greater local discretion in determining the use of both federal and state funds. Further, under the Education block grant, the federal legislation provides nearly complete discretion to local education agencies in the use of block grant funds passed through by the state.

EFFECTS ON ADMINISTRATIVE PROCEDURES AND COSTS

Although structural changes in state service delivery systems were generally not forthcoming during the early years of block grants, considerable change occurred in state administrative procedures. GAO's study found that block grants prompted the thirteen states to change or standardize their administrative requirements in 67 percent of the cases across the seven programs studied. In areas such as substate applications and reporting, states standardized procedures across block grants and extended state procedures to block grant programs. In some cases, these state actions reduced or simplified administrative requirements, while in others states increased accountability requirements to improve their ability to oversee service providers.

States realized considerable reduction in the administrative burden imposed by the federal government. Specifically, in 64 percent of the cases, GAO's thirteen states reported devoting less time and effort to preparing their federal applications, while 73 percent of the cases states were able to reduce their reporting effort to the federal government. In many cases, improvements in the use of state staff were also noted, as personnel were able to spend more time on state program activities and less on federal administrative requirements. The lifting of prior categorical constraints, further, enabled several states to use the same staff to administer several related program activities.

Although states were able to institute many management improvements, they also experienced increased grants management responsibilities. For instance, one Mississippi official claimed that state administrative costs for the health block grants were greater due to the increased state managerial responsibilities assumed for such areas as regulatory development, oversight, and auditing.

GAO found it could not measure the net effects of these two competing forces on the levels of states' administrative costs. Neither comprehensive baseline data on the costs of prior categorical programs nor uniform cost data at the state level based on consistent state definitions of such costs were available to permit the measurement of change. The presence of significant amounts of state funds in several of these programs also complicates efforts to measure trends in state administrative costs promoted by one of several funding sources.

While it is clear that administrative burdens on states were reduced, data on state staffing levels indicate that this did not necessarily lead to a reduction in state staff, but more typically in improved utilization of existing staff. In some cases, however, particularly under the social services and education block grant, federal and state administrative simplifications did permit staff reductions. Florida, for instance, was able to reduce its staff due to consolidation of education offices prompted by the block grant. In other cases, states recorded increases in staffing, particularly for CSBG where states assumed a central management role they never had before.

## MANAGEMENT OVERSIGHT

States have traditionally been given an important role as the administrative arbiter of federal categorical grants. Functioning as overseers and pass-through agents, states had considerable latitude to determine substate fund allocations and administrative rules for substate entities to follow, often adding their own state requirements to federal rules.[9] States performed this function within a web of prescriptive federal rules, as well as federal management oversight of the states' administration, including application approval, monitoring, reporting, and auditing.

Thus, when block grants arrived, states had built a considerable record of experience in managing federal funds for many of the program areas funded by block grants. Of the seven block grants studied by GAO, states were involved in administering most of the prior categorical programs, with the exception of community services, the mental health portion of ADAMH, and several programs encompassed by MCH, PHHS, and the education block grant.

Accordingly, most states in GAO's study did not increase their levels of monitoring or data collection to accommodate block grants. For the health block grants, SSBG, and LIHEA, states already had ongoing relationships with service providers as well as established rules, regulations, and monitoring systems to assess performance.

In contrast to the past, states' management oversight efforts under block grants were driven more by state rather than federal needs and requirements. In 69 percent of the cases GAO studied, state officials reported that state planning and management requirements had a great influence on their data collection efforts, while only 34 percent cited federal block grant requirement as having a great impact. For instance, while the prior categorical energy assistance program required states to report quarterly on household characteristics prescribed by HHS, states indicated that the 1981 LIHEA block grant permitted them to direct data collection to address specific state needs.

Significantly, states' block grant oversight has been subsumed under broader state frameworks used to oversee the expenditure of state funds, reflecting the view of block grants as funding sources supporting broader state efforts. Although it is probable that federal and state funds were monitored jointly under the prior categorical programs, the reduction in federal requirements and in the

federal oversight presence enabled states to further integrate the oversight of funds into broader state systems.
For instance, the ADAMH block grant has spurred some
states to eliminate prior federal categorical data
collection in favor of a single state data and monitoring
system. In some states, like Vermont, the legislature's
demands for greater oversight of state funds resulted in
the collection of more detailed information for block
grants supporting these state efforts than before.

The integration of block grant funds into broader
state management frameworks may assure that the federal
funds receive the same level of attention as state
funds. Although the quality of the states' own oversight
systems has yet to be systematically examined, this
attention may be a distinct improvement over the
relatively low levels of attention reportedly devoted by
state and local central management officials for federally
funded programs with little or no state or local financial
involvement.[10] Yet, the federal funds easily lose their
identity in this broader state context, creating potential
federal accountability issues to be discussed later. For
the health and social services block grants, state program
officials in 63 percent of the cases GAO studied indicated
they do not maintain data systems that separately indicate
those clients or program services supported specifically
with the federal, as opposed to state, funds.

There is one distinct exception to this pattern among
the seven programs studied by GAO--the Community Services
block grant. Most states had to establish new monitoring
and oversight processes for CSBG because they had little
prior involvement with either community services programs
or providers. Not only were most prior federal community
services grants sent directly to local providers, but also
ten of the thirteen states had no comparable state-funded
program for community services. To handle their expanded
grant management role, states established new oversight
mechanisms for monitoring and data collection, including
development of administrative requirements and hiring of
additional staff. While six of thirteen states initially
adopted procedures used by the federal government for
prior programs, they later established, or had plans to
establish, their own requirements.

IMPLICATIONS OF CHANGING INTERGOVERNMENTAL ROLES

In comparison with the general absence of major
changes in state roles in block grant-supported programs,

the advent of block grants prompted a dramatic change in the federal government's oversight role. The change in managerial accountability under block grants was, in fact, more a function of the reduction in the federal role and in federal requirements than any major increase in responsibility thrust on the states.

Traditional federal management and regulatory activities were curtailed as part of the Reagan administration's effort to reduce federal intrusion in state block grant management. For example, in reviewing block grant applications, the Department of Health and Human Services (HHS) limits its role to assuring that applications are complete and contain the information and assurances required by statute. The department contends it has no explicit authority to approve a state's intended use of block grant funds beyond verifying that states make certain statutory assurances, such as maintaining adequate fiscal controls and complying with civil rights laws, in their application.

Also, unlike the regulations accompanying the prior categorical programs, the block grant regulations do not interpret many legislative provisions. Rather, HHS has chosen to rely on state interpretations partly because several federal statutes specifically preclude the Secretary from prescribing the manner of compliance with legislative requirements. HHS has not, for instance, defined state administrative costs, which are limited to certain dollar percentages in several programs, or explained the meaning of prohibited activities, such as construction. HHS further indicates that it will not challenge state actions or interpretations unless they are clearly erroneous.

In the data collection area, federal agencies have not prescribed the form or content of states' annual reports. Rather, states were given the flexibility to determine the amount, nature, and format of information provided in applications or intended use reports and in annual reports submitted to federal agencies.

This reduced federal oversight presence has, however, prompted considerable debate about the requisites of block grant survival in what remains a necessarily intergovernmental process. Block grants were initially justified as a "decongestion" strategy that would promote a renewal of dual federalism, where state and federal governments retreat to their respective spheres of authority. However, the record of these block grants illustrates that a continuing and vital federal-state partnership is needed if the block grant is to become a stable, continuing mechanism used to fund intergovernmental programs.

The inherent instability of block grants stems from the delicate balance that is sought between the benefits of recipient discretion and the need to assure the Congress that federal funds are promoting national purposes. As ACIR observed 8 years ago, although the block grant changes the nature of federal agency involvement, it doesn't abrograte federal responsibility.[11]

One area of intergovernmental stress caused by the reduced federal oversight presence was in the area of federal technical assistance and guidance on interpreting statutory requirements. In most cases, GAO's thirteen states requested technical assistance from the federal government to assist them in assuming their new responsibilities, especially for those programs where states had little previous involvement. Although the states reportedly received the assistance they requested, in some cases the federal agencies refused to provide clarification or interpretations of federal reporting requirements or statutory restrictions due to the administration's desire to maximize state discretion in program implementation.

States responded differently to this new federal hands-off policy. Some welcomed the absence of federal interference and grew to rely more on nonfederal sources of guidance such as advice from other states; however, some states registered discomfort with the absence of federal guidance. The uncertainty over interpreting federal statutory provisions created confusion and, at times, a reluctance by states to use their new flexibility to depart from prior categorical policies or procedures. These states were concerned that they would be subsequently second-guessed by state auditors, federal officials, or the courts applying different interpretations of these provisions.

The absence of federal regulatory interpretations or oversight does not confer autonomous status to the states. Auditors and courts remain as an independent oversight force and check on state actions. In this context, federal regulatory guidance can help states in their exercise of discretion by providing them with "iron-clad" support in audit or court challenges. Further, federal guidance can provide "political assistance" in shielding state officials from interest group pressures when making difficult choices. One state official observed that discretion is an empty word unless states get federal help in exercising it. This state played it safe by declining to fund local portable school buildings with Education block grant funds after the federal agency refused to indicate whether this was an eligible expense.

In retrospect, the much-denounced picket fence helped resolve or buffer intergovernmental conflict through close, harmonious working relationships among like-minded professionals. In its absence, federal-state conflicts may come to be fought among strangers in more unfamiliar and less predictable surroundings, including the courts. Ironically, the prospect of this kind of intergovernmental conflict can chill the exercise of state discretion that minimal federal guidance was expected to universally promote.

Another stress point in the continuing debate over the federal role in the current block grants involved the data collection area. When federal money is appropriated, Congress has a continuing need to ascertain what is being accomplished. Especially in an era of federal budget constraints, programs exhibiting little national benefit or payoff are likely to lose congressional support and wither away.

Due to the administration's efforts to reduce federal involvement for these block grants, however, states were given the discretion to determine the form and content of data collected and reported to the federal government. Accordingly, consistent national data across states on the uses of funds and program activities were not available. Federal officials could not respond to key congressional oversight questions on the number of people served by these programs or on the characteristics of program clientele.

Reflecting their need for national information on these programs, the Congress acted in 1984 to require the collection of more systematic and uniform data for five of the seven block grant programs studied by GAO. Although national reporting standards may entail some loss of state flexibility, states may find this to be desirable tradeoff if the availability of national data promotes congressional support for these programs.

Yet, the design of federal provisions to promote national goals and evaluate state actions through block grants is complicated by another intergovernmental dilemma--the "fungibility" problem. Block grants are inherently difficult to evaluate because when federal funds are allocated for such broad functional areas, it becomes difficult to distinguish the federal money from the state and local money for financial accounting purposes--that is, what was the money spent for? Second, because federal funds comprise such a small part of total state and local spending for certain broad functional areas funded by block grants, the always-uncertain task of evaluating the effects or impacts of these funds--that is, what did the money accomplish--becomes magnified.

The fungibility problem also makes it difficult, if not impossible, to enforce restrictions on the use of funds. If state funds significantly outweigh the federal funds, they can simply shift their own money to fund the prohibited activity and switch the federal money to an eligible activity previously funded with state money. This shell game enables states to conform to the letter of the requirement without fulfilling its spirit. For example, most of the 1981 block grants place limits on state administrative costs. Yet, any state that was investing its own money could maintain or increase its actual administrative costs for the entire program area funded by the block grant by simply shifting federal and state funds in the manner shown in Table 5.2.

While tracking block grants is difficult when states outspend the federal government, it could become an impossible task under block grants that do not include a maintenance of effort provision requiring that federal funds be used to supplement existing state and local spending levels. Without maintenance of effort, federal funds ostensibly provided for broad functions would, in effect, be transformed into general fiscal relief because states could, and probably would, use some or all of their federal block grants to substitute for their own money invested in the functional program area. To the extent that this occurs, the ultimate effect of these federal dollars would be to either increase state spending in other functional areas or reduce taxes.[12]

Ironically, the very same properties of blocks that promote managerial improvements--integrating related federal and state programs into broader state policy and management frameworks--also contribute to the fungibility dilemma. The federal government's options to promote accountability for national objectives are limited. The imposition of federal categorical data requirements forcing states to separately track expenditures and accomplishments achieved with only the federal portion of funds could not only be inefficient, but, like the revenue sharing experience, fail to capture more than a book-keeping perspective on the actual use and impact of the

Table 5.2

Shifting Administrative Costs

| | Pre-Block | | | Post-Block (Assume no admin. costs allowed with Federal block grant funds) | | |
|---|---|---|---|---|---|---|
| | State | Federal | Total | State | Federal | Total |
| Direct Costs | 10 | 10 | 20 | 5 | 15 | 20 |
| Admin. Costs | 0 | 5 | 5 | 5 | 0 | 5 |
| Total | 10 | 15 | 25 | 10 | 15 | 25 |

federal funds.[13]

Another federal approach to the fungibility problem could be to redefine federal accountability expectations. Instead of tracking accomplishments of the federal funds alone, monitor the extent to which the entire federal-state effort promotes national goals. Federal goals could be expressed in terms of minimum service levels to be achieved through combined intergovernmental spending, regardless of funding source. Yet, this option extends federal influence to the domain of state funds--a familiar federal response but perhaps inappropriate in a block grant context. Restrictions or limitations on the use of federal funds (for example, administrative cost ceilings) should also be re-examined in this context, since they are so easily evaded when states have significant funds invested in the program area.

Finally, if evaluating the specific accomplishments of federal funds proves to be difficult, federal oversight could focus on the procedural adequacy of state frameworks used to manage the funds. Under revenue sharing, for instance, GAO recommended eliminating recipient reports on the use of revenue sharing funds alone, and substituting instead a financial audit of the recipient's entire budget regardless of funding source.

Congress has moved in this direction for other federal aid programs in passing the Single Audit Act of 1984 (P.L. 98-502). This act establishes a uniform audit process covering all federal grants to state and local governments. Most aid recipients are required to obtain an annual audit of the financial statements and internal controls of the entire state or local agency or governments receiving federal funds. Although including provisions for testing compliance with key federal grant requirements, this single audit will focus primary attention on assessing whether the state or local financial management systems encompassing federal funds meet certain minimum standards.

CONCLUSIONS: THE EVOLUTION OF INTERGOVERNMENTAL PROGRAMS

The record of block grant implementation says as much about the impact of the prior categorical programs as it does about the block grant itself. The categorical programs initially served to stimulate new initiatives and spending at the state level for national purpose program areas. Their prescriptive fiscal and organizational requirements succeeded in promoting and institutionalizing state fiscal commitment and an in-place service delivery network to support these new services. Clientele became politically entrenched and self-aware, often coalescing as an organized interest group at the state level.

Having incubated the requisite state commitment under the categorical era, the move to block grants begins to appear less risky from the national level and, in fact, necessary in an evolutionary sense. Indeed, states' financial and service decisions for block grants reflected strong state support for many previous national initiatives that involved the states. In an evolutionary process, categorical grants can be viewed as seed-money programs that took root at the state level. Once this occurred, the federal regulatory trappings become unnecessary and expendable. In a broad sense the categorical programs made the world safe for block grants.

The analytic framework for assessing the impacts of federal policies on states needs to be re-examined also in light of these trends. Much intergovernmental analysis has focused on the adverse impacts of the growing federal role on states and localities. This body of work decried the effects of prescriptive categorical provisions on the intergovernmental system, arguing that the growing federal role was making intergovernmental programs more unmanageable and unaccountable at the state and local levels.

While this perspective may aptly characterize federal impacts during the early stages of categorical programs, it may no longer be the most appropriate way to understand the evolution of that system. If the federal categorical programs were presenting as much burden as hypothesized, it would be reasonable to expect states to have instituted far more fundamental changes under block grants than they did. A more reasonable explanation is that states internalized these national goals as their own at some point in time. The same evolutionary process has occurred with other federal regulatory requirements: most states now have their own "mini" Davis-Bacon laws, environmental review procedures, and uniform relocation requirements that began as prescriptive federal mandates.

Students of the intergovernmental process need to be more aware of how federal aid actually is used by states today before making judgments about program impact. Even in areas where states don't share federal values, the growing state investment in these programs itself implies that federal policies have a far more modest impact on service delivery than has heretofore been acknowledged.

Some studies have shown how states can frustrate the

implementation of the most onerous federal policies through the application of their political resources at the national level.[14] The analysis of fungibility indicates that on a less profound level states can escape the full impact of certain federal restrictions through artful bookkeeping when they have significant state money invested in programs.

Thus, for program areas dominated by state funds, it can be argued that state policies are the driving force in determining who gets what, when, where, how, and why. This perhaps accounts for the considerable variability observed by Kirlin and others in state and local implementation of national programs. Kirlin further argues that changes in state policies are caused more by fiscal and political factors internal to the state than by changes in federal grant policies.[15]

When viewed from this perspective, traditional distinctions drawn between block versus categorical programs become eclipsed by a new distinction that has considerable explanatory power: state-dominated versus federal-dominated grant programs, defined principally by the extent of state fiscal and managerial involvement in programs. Federal policies and changes in those policies are likely to have a far more profound effect on federal-dominated programs like community services than on state dominated programs in the areas of health or social services. In impact terms, block grants and larger categorical grants with heavy state investment and involvement (for example, the categorical Vocational Education program) have more in common than block grants with great differences in state involvement (for example, Social Services vs. Community Services block grants).

This distinction was perhaps the most crucial variable explaining differential state management responses to block grants. In fact, different issues are salient for each of these two types of grants. For state-dominated programs, states were able to subsume block grants within ongoing state frameworks with little change. A principal block grant management issue for these programs was whether states would improve the integration of federal programs with related state efforts in a manner that promoted more effective and less costly service delivery.

For federal-dominated block grant programs, states faced a different management challenge in assuming new responsibilities for a program that had generally not been managed by the states before. Unlike state-dominated programs, administrative cost savings and improved coordination were largely irrelevant issues. Rather, here the concerns were how well and how quickly states could articulate new systems to manage federal funds.

This emerging distinction should also be useful in the design and oversight of federal assistance. Federal officials need to be more aware of the existing inter-governmental relationships when designing federal programs and oversight systems. Some recognition of this is evident in the 1981 block grants from the inclusion of transition provisions providing states with a year to assume the new block grants. However, little awareness of the fungibility problem is evident, as Congress included several restrictions on administrative costs and prohibitions that can be easily circumvented by many states.

Differing federal oversight standards might also be appropriate for federal-versus state-dominated programs. If it is found that state-dominated programs benefit from greater oversight attention by state elected and management officials due to the presence of state funds, it might be reasonable to reduce federal accountability requirements and reviews for these programs in comparison with federal-dominated programs that may not benefit from extensive state attention. Further study of the behavioral implications of this distinction for public management is needed to promote more informed federal policymaking on intergovernmental programs.

NOTES

1. Richard Nathan and Fred C. Doolittle, "The Untold Story of Reagan's New Federalism", The Public Interest, No. 77 (Fall, 1984), p. 97.

2. The nine block grant programs established in 1981 were Maternal and Child Health Services (MCH); Preventive Health and Health Services (PHHS); Alcohol, Drug Abuse and Mental Health (ADAMH); Social Services (SSBG); Community Services (CSBG); Low-Income Home Energy Assistance (LIHEA); Education (ED); Small Cities Community Development Block Grant (CDBG); and Primary Care. In 1982, Congress created the Job Training Partnership Act block grant (JTPA) from the old CETA program, and a mass transit block grant (Section 9, Surface Transportation Act). Finally, in 1984, an additional block grant for crime control was established.

3. ACIR's critique can be found in a number of their reports, including the 14-volume study, The Intergovernmental Grant System: An Assessment and Proposed Policies (Washington, D.C.: U.S. Government Printing Office, 1976-1978). The General Accounting Office evaluated the categorical approach in their 1975 report, Fundamental Changes Are Needed in Federal Assistance to State and Local Governments, (GGD-75-75) (Washington, D.C.: U.S. General Accounting Office, August 19, 1975).

4. One study estimated nearly $2 billion a year was spent at state and local levels on federal grant paperwork requirements. See Commission on Federal Paperwork, Impact of Federal Paperwork on State and Local Governments: An Assessment by the Academy for Contemporary Problems (Washington, D.C.: U.S. Government Printing Office, 1977).

5. One state legislator aptly stated: "Why should I spend my time on federal programs which I can't control, when I can spend my time on state programs which I can control." Quoted in Comptroller General, Federal Assistance System Should Be Changed to Permit Greater Oversight By State Legislatures (GGD-81-3) (Washington, D.C.: U.S. General Accounting Office, 1980).

6. The GAO studied these seven programs: Maternal and Child Health Services (MCH); Preventive Health and Health Services (PHHS); Alcohol, Drug Abuse and Mental Health (ADAMH); Education Block Grant (ED); Social Services (SSBG); Community Services (CSBG); and Low-Income Home Energy Assistance (LIHEA). GAO issued 12 reports: 7 on each program; 4 assessing trends in state financial decisions, management, public participation, and civil rights; and an overall summary report. For a complete listing of reports and overview of the study, see Comptroller General, Block Grants: Overview of Experiences To Date and Emerging Issues, (HRD-85-46) (Washington, D.C.: U.S. General Accounting Office, April 3, 1985).

7. Richard C. Elling, "Federal Dollars and Federal Clout in State Administration: A Test of 'Regulatory' and 'Picket Fence' Models of Intergovernmental Relations", paper presented at 1985 Midwest Political Science Association Meeting, Chicago, April 17-20, 1985.

8. Information on state public accountability processes is drawn from Comptroller General, Public Involvement in Block Grant Decisions: Multiple Opportunities Provided But Interest Groups Have Mixed Reactions to States' Efforts, (HRD-85-20) (Washington, D.C.: U.S. General Accounting Office, December 28, 1984).

9. Advisory Commission on Intergovernmental Relations, Management of Federal Pass-Through Grants: The Need for More Uniform Requirements and Procedures, (A-102) (Washington, D.C.: ACIR, 1981).

10. Paul Posner, "Separating Money From Authority in Intergovernmental Programs: Whither Accountability," paper delivered at the 1981 annual conference of the National Assistance Management Association, Washington, D.C., 1981.

11. Advisory Commission on Intergovernmental Relations, Block Grants: A Comparative Analysis (Washington, D.C., Government Printing Office, 1977) p. 39.

12. Most of the 1981 block grants do not contain a maintenance of effort requirement. For further discussion of fiscal substitution in federal aid programs, see Comptroller General, Proposed Changes in Federal Matching and Maintenance of Effort Requirements, (GGD-81-7) (Washington, D.C.: U.S. General Accounting Office, 1981).

13. GAO concluded that the reports filed by revenue sharing recipients did not reflect the actual impacts of these funds, due to the fungible nature of these funds. Comptroller General, Revenue Sharing: An Opportunity for Improved Public Awareness of State and Local Government Operations, (GGD-76-2) (Washington, D.C.: U.S. General Accounting Office, 1975).

14. Helen Ingram, "Policy Implementation Through Bargaining: The Case of Federal Grants-in-Aid," Public Policy 25 (Fall 1977) pp. 499-526.

15. John J. Kirlin, et. al., "California," paper prepared for a research conference on the Reagan Domestic Program, Princeton University, June 7-8, 1984.

# 6

## The Texas Response
## to Reagan's New Federalism
## Program: The Early Years

*Susan A. MacManus,*
*Robert M. Stein,*
*and V. Howard Savage*

President Reagan's New Federalism resembled federalism programs of his predecessors in that it was designed to strengthen the power of state and local governments by reducing the national government's role in a number of domestic policy arenas. Reagan's programs proposed to restore balance to the federal system by means of budget cuts, block grants channelled through state governments (rather than directly to local governments), functional and fiscal reassignments, heavier reliance on the private sector, and the revision and reduction of costly federal rules and regulations.[1]

There was no expectation that these changes would have the same impact on all state and local governments. Rather, it was anticipated that reactions to these decentralization strategies would vary because of inter- and intra-state differences in demographic, socioeconomic, and political conditions. This was regarded as a highly desirable outcome reflecting the basic premise of decentralization, namely that grass-roots decision making on most domestic issues is the optimal way to target resources to a very diverse U.S. population.[2] The expectation was that each state and local government would restore funding cuts and/or alter the programmatic thrust in only those programs it regarded as essential.

At the same time fiscal and programmatic variations in state and local government responses were anticipated, so were differences in the timing of the responses. For example, students of the budgetary process know that changes in the funding level of capital-intensive programs take longer to show up than changes in programs with a more current operational thrust.[3] This is largely due to differences in the appropriation cycle (multi-year for capital improvement programs; annual for current operations activities).

The purpose of this article is to examine the impact of the first enactments of Reagan's New Federalism: budget cuts and state block grants. We focus on the State of Texas and its largest city, Houston. The time frame of the analysis is 1981-1983. We begin by examining the socioeconomic and political context in which the Reagan program was implemented. We then examine specific changes in funding levels for major federal programs routed through the state, focusing first on current operational programs, then on capital improvement programs. This is followed by a description of the state's fiscal and programmatic responses to these changes. We then shift to an analysis of the impact of federal funding cuts and greater state control at the local level, looking at the reactions of governments in the Houston metropolitan area. We conclude that contrary to the preliminary negative expectations of both state and local officials in Texas there was relatively little change in funding levels or programmatic thrusts directly attributable to Reagan's New Federalism policies during the first three years of their implementation. Most of the changes were more a consequence of the state's changing economic, demographic, and political makeup. The Texas response was undoubtedly different from that of other states and localities primarily because of the Texas governments' initially lower levels of dependency on federal funds.[4]

## A CHANGING TEXAS

At the time Reagan's New Federalism programs were being implemented, Texas was undergoing some dramatic economic, demographic, and political changes. In order to better understand the magnitude and significance of these changes a closer look at each is warranted.

### Economic Changes

The state that had been characterized as "recession proof" on the basis of its phenomenal growth in jobs, people, industries, and investments during the late 1970s and early 1980s was ultimately struck by the national recession in late 1982.[5] This, along with a worldwide drop in oil prices, devaluations of the Mexican peso, and severe weather conditions, sharply reversed the state's economic growth.

The Impact of the National Recession. Historically, Texas has depended on tax receipts that are closely related to economic conditions, namely elastic taxes such as retail sales, oil and natural gas, and motor vehicle sales. (The state does not have a personal or corporate income tax). Consequently, because of the recession the state's sales tax collections dropped from $3.5 to $3.3 billion between FY 1982 and 1983 (a 4.5 percent decline). Similar declines characterized oil production tax revenues (-9.6 percent) and motor fuels taxes (-1.2 percent). Local governments also felt these declines. For example, sales tax receipts for the city of Houston dropped from $152 to $142 million (a 6.6 percent decline) during this same period. In both instances the slump in the petroleum industry exacerbated the effect of the recession.

The Impact of the Engergy Glut. Declining worldwide energy prices spelled trouble for the state's finances. For every dollar drop in the price of Texas crude oil, an estimated $70 million in sales and oil production tax revenue was lost.[6] At that time the state generated about 27 percent of its revenue from energy-based taxes; 30 percent of the state's sales tax was tied directly or indirectly to the energy sector. The effect was a serious strain on the state's revenue growth.

The Impact of the Mexican Peso Devaluation. Declining oil prices also affected Texas' neighbor to the south which compounded the impact of the energy glut. There was an 80 percent drop in sales tax revenue along the Texas-Mexico border, which had economic ramifications as far north as San Antonio and Houston following two devaluations of the Mexican peso in FY 1982.[7]

The Impact of Severe Weather Conditions. Texas suffered through a series of weather-related crises that drastically reduced revenue intake in 1983. Estimates from the Texas Department of Agriculture showed the drought cost Texas farmers a half-billion dollars in lost crops and livestock. In addition to the short-term effects of these losses on the state treasury, the long-term costs of farm failures and diminished production capacity caused greater state expenditures in other programs. The Gulf Coast region (Galveston and Houston) experienced bad weather of a different sort. Hurricane Alicia caused an estimated

$1.2 billion in damages. Damages to publicly owned property approached 26.5 million, one-fourth of which local governments had to pay. In addition, the state lost $27.5 million in taxes from insurance company write-offs alone.[8] A severe freeze in December 1983 followed Hurricane Alicia. By the end of 1983 over one-third of the state had been declared a disaster area.

In summary, the sharp reversal in the economy of this heretofore "boomtown" state for the reasons cited above precluded any rampant replacement of lost federal funds by the state legislature when it met in January-June 1983. (The Texas Legislature meets biennially, which meant the first session to address the full scope of the Reagan budget cuts and state block grant mandates was this 1983 session during the depths of the recession). However, there was evidence that state lawmakers and departmental officials increased their targeting efforts within established federally-funded program areas primarily in response to changes in the Texas demographic and political environments.[9]

## Demographic Changes

During the 1970s, Texas was one of the fastest-growing states in the nation. Its population increased 27 percent more than twice the national average for the same period. Over half of the population increase resulted from people moving to Texas from other states and Mexico.[10] This immigration continued through the first part of 1982. Texas boomed as the Northeast and Midwest went bust. However, once the recession hit Texas in late 1982 net migration slowed down significantly, although it remained positive.

The Texas of the 1980s is not, however, the Texas of 1970. It is a more socially diverse state than it was ten years ago. Lieberson's measure of social diversity provides a means of assessing the degree of homogeneity of a state's population.[11] The diversity score for Texas, based on the number of traits shared among state residents (for example, income, race, education, occupation and homeownership) shows that the state's population has become more heterogenous over time, a condition normally associated with urbanized northeastern states. Hispanics now make up 21 percent of the state's population, blacks 12 percent, and orientals 1 percent. The state's dependent populations (youth and aged) have also increased. Those under fifteen years of age were up six percent and

those over sixty-five are up 38 percent. The increase in
needy and dependent populations obviously affected the
state's social service program targeting decisions. These
groups were very adept at exercising their growing political clout, especially with the new state-level policymakers whom they helped elect, along with more liberal
newcomers.

As is often the case, recent arrivals to a state act
as agents of change for the newcomers seem less committed
to the status quo than older residents and tend to bring
new perspectives. The president of the Texas League of
United Latin-American Citizens (LULAC) has remarked
that: "Today (the typical Texan) is more urbane and
technologically-oriented, more sophisticated and le native
more compassionate, more sensitive to minority
interests."[12] Of course, this statement is truer in some
regions of the state than others.

## Political Changes

In November, 1982, Democratic challenger Mark White
defeated Republican incumbent Governor William P.
Clements, Jr., in a high-turnout election. White received
53 percent of the vote, including heavy support from
women, blacks, Mexican-Americans, and the poor. According
to one political analyst, "The race turned primarily on
economic issues (the economic downturn). Those on the
bottom of the economic ladder--one third of whom voted for
Reagan in 1980--decided in the final ten days to punch the
straight Democratic ticket."[13] Democrats were also
elected to the offices of attorney general, agriculture
commissioner, treasurer, and state land commissioner.
Each of these new agency heads was regarded as more
progressive than his or her predecessor.

In the same election the character of the Texas
Legislature changed significantly. Forty-four new members
were elected to the House of Representatives (almost a
one-third turnover) and ten new members (one-third) went
to the Senate. Many of these new members were elected
from the heavily populated urban areas of the state where
district lines had been redrawn due to population gains
reflected in the 1980 Census. Like the newly elected
agency heads, these first-term legislators were described
as "a bit less conservative and a little bit more moderate
in political philosophy," regardless of party affilia-
tion.[14] This "liberalization" mirrored the changing
demographic and political composition of the state and

helps explain the state's responses to Reagan's New Federalism programs.

## CHANGES IN FEDERAL FUNDING LEVELS

Like many other states, Texas experienced a rollercoaster ride with the federal aid system between 1981 and 1983. In 1982 the state experienced a 14.7 percent decrease in total federal assistance. In 1983, total federal aid allocations increased 17 percent. (See Figure 6.1.) Thus, for the three-year period the state experienced an almost negligible decreased in federal assistance (.002 percent), which along with the state's biennial budget cycle and its relative low level of federal aid dependency, helps explain the minimal impact of Reagan's New Federalism during this period.

What's interesting to note is that the rate of change in federal aid as a percent of total general revenue in Texas ran ahead of the national average. The decline in federal aid as a percent of total state revenues in Texas (5.2 percent) was nearly twice the national average of 2.9 percent. Increases in state revenues did not explain this drop, since the effect of a national recession reduced tax collections by 4.1 percent between 1982 and 1983.[15] As noted earlier, the changes were felt earliest in programs with more annualized funding cycles (current operating and entitlement programs). (See Table 6.1.)

### Changes in Current Operations Program Funding Levels

The bulk of the funding cuts occurred in the current operating budgets and entitlement programs. At the same time the shift from a categorical to a block grant mechanism provided state policymakers much wider discretion in the targeting and spending of federal aid monies that they exercised in response to politically influential clientele groups.

Block Grant Programs. As Table 6.1 shows, under the first year of the Social Service Block Grant (SSBG), Texas lost 13.4 percent of its 1981 categorical aid allocation. This cut was replaced only modestly by a 1.5 percent increase in the state's 1983 SSBG allocation. One of the most significant effects of this cut was the change in priority assigned to various program components. The big winners were protective services, family violence, employment, and community care activities; the losers were family plan-

Table 6.1
Changes in federal aid for the state of Texas:  FY 1981-1983
(millions of dollars)*

| Area/Program | Federal Aid | | | % Change in Aid | | |
|---|---|---|---|---|---|---|
| | 1981 | 1982 | 1983 | 81-82 | 82-83 | 81-83 |
| | ($) | ($) | ($) | (%) | (%) | (%) |
| **Current Operating Program** | | | | | | |
| Social Service Block Grant (Title XX)(A) | 173.1 | 149.8 | 152.0 | -13.4 | 1.5 | -12.2 |
| Protective Services | 61.2 | 70.3 | 81.9 | 14.1 | 16.5 | 20.7 |
| Family Planning | 11.9 | 14.2 | 14.8 | -15.9 | 4.2 | -12.4 |
| Child Day Care | 36.0 | 29.4 | 31.5 | -19.6 | 71.4 | -13.9 |
| Family Violence | 0.330 | 0.790 | 0.910 | 139.0 | 15.0 | 175.0 |
| Community Service | 2.1 | 1.3 | 1.6 | -38.0 | 23.0 | -23.8 |
| Employment | 0.600 | 2.6 | 4.3 | 333.0 | 653.0 | 616.0 |
| Community Care | 86.5 | 92.1 | 101.6 | 6.4 | 10.3 | 17.6 |
| Preventive Health and Health Services | 3.8 | 3.3 | 3.5 | -13.1 | 6.0 | -7.8 |
| Hypertension | - | 0.600 | 0.400 | - | -33.0 | - |
| Fluoridation | - | 0.300 | 0.300 | - | 0 | - |
| Home Health | - | 0.030 | 0.030 | - | 0 | - |
| Health Ed. | - | 0.300 | 0.300 | - | 0 | - |
| Emergency | - | 1.0 | 1.1 | - | 10.0 | - |
| Rodent Control | - | 0.900 | 0 | - | -100.0 | - |
| Health Incentives | - | 0.500 | 1.1 | - | 110.0 | - |
| Emergency Jobs Act | - | - | 62.7 | - | - | - |
| Community Services | - | - | 1.0 | - | - | - |
| Social Services | - | - | 10.8 | - | - | - |
| Alcohol, Drug Abuse | - | - | 1.2 | - | - | - |
| Maternal and Child Care | - | - | 6.4 | - | - | - |
| Community Dev. (entitle.) | - | - | 34.5 | - | - | - |
| Community Dev. (non-entitle.) | - | - | 9.8 | - | - | - |
| Maternity and Child Care Block Grant | 17.6 | 16.1 | 24.3 | -8.5 | 50.9 | 38.1 |

(Table 6.1 con't.)

| Area/Program | Federal Aid | | | % Change in Aid | | |
|---|---|---|---|---|---|---|
| | 1981 | 1982 | 1983 | 81-82 | 82-83 | 81-83 |
| | ($) | ($) | ($) | (%) | (%) | (%) |
| Maternal and Child | - | 10.9 | 24.3 | - | 57.8 | - |
| Crippled Children | - | 5.2 | 7.1 | - | 36.5 | - |
| Alcohol, Drug Abuse and Mental Health Block Grant | 24.0[b] | 16.8 | 18.3 | -30.0 | 8.9 | -23.7 |
| Alcohol | - | 4.0 | 4.2 | - | 5.0 | - |
| Drug | - | 6.1 | 6.4 | - | 5.0 | - |
| Mental Health | - | 6.7 | 7.6 | - | 13.4 | - |
| Community Services Block Grant | 23.0[b] | 17.0[b] | | 15.8 | 26.1 | -7.1 |
| -31.3 | | | | | | |
| Education Block Grant | - | - | 27.6 | - | - | - |
| Low Income Energy Assistance Block Grant | - | 42.3 | 44.6 | - | 5.4 | - |
| Job Training Partnership Act | - | - | 119.3 | - | - | - |
| Entitlement | | | | | | |
| AFDC | 87.3 | 78.7 | 74.4 | -9.9 | -5.5 | -14.7 |
| Food Stamps | 582.3 | 546.0 | 680.0 | -6.2 | 24.5 | 16.7 |
| Medicaid | 713.7 | 682.4 | 803.1 | -4.3 | 17.6 | 12.5 |
| Capital | | | | | | |
| Highways | 567.0 | 425.0 | 750.0 | -25.0 | 76.0 | -32.2 |
| Mass Transit (UMTA) | 76.0 | 78.0 | 23.0 | 2.6 | -70.5 | -69.7 |
| Community Dev. Block Grant (non-entitle.) | 50.3[b] | 56.9[b] | 14.5 | -1.2 | 13.1 | - |

(Table 6.1 con't.)

| Area/Program | Federal Aid | | | % Change in Aid | | |
|---|---|---|---|---|---|---|
| | 1981 | 1982 | 1983 | 81-82 | 82-83 | 81-83 |
| | ($) | ($) | ($) | (%) | (%) | (%) |
| Project Fund | - | - | 23.7 | - | - | - |
| Econ. Dev. | - | - | 5.9 | - | - | - |
| Planning/Capacity | - | - | 1.0 | - | - | - |
| Emergency | - | - | 5.7 | - | - | - |
| Program Admin. | - | - | 1.1 | - | - | - |
| Multi Yr. Funding | - | - | 19.5 | - | - | - |
| Emergency Jobs | - | - | 9.8 | - | - | - |

Notes:

- = nonapplicable or Texas did not opt into this program until FY 1983
* Program components may not sum to entire grant allocation due to omitted
  expenditures for administrative overhead and other non-service related
  activities.
a This includes an unknown amount of Emergency Jobs Bill Money
b Figure represents pre-block grant categorical expenditures

ning, child day care, and community services. These new priorities mirrored the preferences of the state's minority populations as expressed during state block grant hearings.[16]

Funding for the state's Preventive Health and Health Services Block Grant followed a similar pattern. The first year of the block grant produced a 13 percent reduction in funding from the 1981 categorical level of assistance. Funding for this block grant increased by 6 percent in 1983, partially restoring the cuts of the previous fiscal year. Changes in funding for this block grant produced changes in just two component programs, leaving a majority of the programs funded under the block unchanged. Federal aid cuts in 1982 resulted in the termination of the state's rodent control program, while a substantial portion of the partial restoration of 1982 cuts went to the state's health incentive program and emergency health services.

Funding for the Maternal and Child Health Care Block Grant experienced a dramatic increase of 50.9 percent in 1982 after a modest 8.5 percent drop in 1981, an increase due mainly to changes in the state's population size and substantial increases in eligible populations. Unsuccessful job seekers became eligible for assistance even while federal standards for program eligibility had become more restrictive, again because of the recession.

The state's allocation under the Alcohol, Drug Abuse and Mental Health Block Grant declined by 30 percent in 1982 as a result of the consolidation of categorical grant programs. In 1983 an 8.2 percent increase partially restored this cut. The mental health component received a higher funding level as a result of the state's decision to boost mental health services during the recession. Alcohol and drug abuse funding received only a modest 5 percent increase in 1983.

Another program adversely affected by consolidation was community services. Funding for the Community Services Block Grant dropped 26 percent in 1982 and an additional 7 percent in 1983. This cut represented the final death blow to the Great Society's anti-poverty and community action programs. Community action agencies had already acquiesced to this cut and sought replacement from other state-run social service block grants (for example, Title XX, Low Income Energy Assistance, and health grants).

The Education Block Grant was not implemented by the state until FY 1983. Even though funding levels were greater than under the categoricals, this cannot be considered a restoration of lost monies because the per-pupil allocations actually dropped in 1983. Rather, this increase was due entirely to an 8 percent increase in the state's pupil population. Current federal funding was only 1.6 percent ahead of 1981 levels, yet the state's pupil population had increased by nearly 12 percent. Finally, a higher proportion of these new pupils required special educational services.

Entitlement Programs. Entitlement programs such as Aid To Families with Dependent Children (AFDC), Food Stamps, Medicaid (characterized by direct aid to individuals as opposed to governments or nonprofit agencies) experienced the biggest federal aid cut during the period 1981-1983. However, cuts in some of these programs were partially replaced with federal funding increases during FY 1982-1983.

AFDC spending declined steadily between 1981 and 1983, dropping 9.9 percent in 1982. What makes this decline so impressive was the steady increase in AFDC-eligible recipients during the period. In spite of changes in eligibility standards that removed many recipients from AFDC rolls, many more families became eligible for assistance due mainly to the effects of the recession.

Replacement of earlier aid cuts was observed in the state's Food Stamp and Medicaid programs. A 24.5 percent increase in 1983 outlays reversed the 6.2 percent cut in the state's 1982 Food Stamps allocations. Changes in national eligibility standards and a significant increase in the population of eligible Food Stamps recipients explained this funding reversal.

The state's Medicaid allocation, which dropped 4.3 percent in 1982, increased 17.6 percent by 1983--an increase of 12.5 percent during the three-year period. Again increases in the state's eligible population accounted for the sharp increase in federal Medicaid allocations. But the economy was the reason for the increase in the number of eligible recipients, not Reagan's New Federalism policies.

Changes in Capital Improvement Programs Funding Levels

Federal funding for capital programs between 1981 and 1983 took another roller-coaster ride, especially in the area of highway construction and maintenance. Federal spending on the state's highway system increased 76 percent in 1983 after a 25 percent drop in 1982. The earlier cut was due in large measure to the national recession and to reduced federal gasoline excise taxes. The passage of the nickel-per-gallon federal gasoline tax helped bring about the increase. Finally, Texas is one of ten states guaranteed to receive proportionally more federal matching funds under a special provision in the new law for which Senator Lloyd Bentsen fought vigorously. The provision requires that each of these states receive at least an 85 percent return on their federal gas tax receipts. Before passing this provision, Texas had benefitted from only a 76 percent return rate.

The State of Texas did not assume responsibility for the capital-intensive Community Development Block Grant until 1983. Before then, federal support for community development--specifically, smaller non-entitlement cities--increased 14.5 percent in 1982 and declined slightly in 1983 (1.2 percent). The policy issues here were not fiscal but rather administrative: namely, which agency would run the program and how were the funds to be allocated to substate governmental units. The winner was a Hispanic-dominated state agency--the Texas Department of Community Affairs.

## Summary

Federal support for state operations decreased steadily between 1981 and 1983. Though there were modest and in some instances significant restoration of earlier federal aid cuts, sharp growth in the state's population of eligible recipients due to demographic and economic changes caused these increases. The more interesting story in Texas focused on administrative and responsiveness issues.

A CLOSER LOOK AT STATE RESPONSES TO FEDERAL AID CUTS AND BLOCK GRANTS

## State Response to Cuts:  Operating Programs

Block Grants. Faced with significant cuts in its Social Service Block Grant (SSBG) allocation, the Texas Department of Human Resources (TDHR) designed an equitable system to deal with cuts in federal funding. The TDHR state board chose to allocate cuts to priority areas based on program need, effectiveness, and efficiency. At its

August 1981 annual meeting the TDHR board established the following program priorities for allocating state and federal aid monies following a series of public hearings held across the state: (1) Protective services for abused and neglected children, (2) Community care for the aged and disabled, (3) Employment services, (4) Day care, (5) Family planning, (6) Family violence services, (7) Integrated community services.

Funding levels and changes in funding levels for 1982 and 1983 closely followed this ranking of program components. The one exception was spending for employment services, which increases 616 percent in 1983--a dramatic jump caused by the passage of the 1983 Emergency Jobs Act, which channelled $4 million through SSBG.

The most substantial federal funding reductions occurred in day care, family planning, and community services. However, instead of arbitrarily denying services to needy recipients, TDHR staff developed client priorities for these programs. Day care client priorities emphasized services to clients of AFDC families and clients of child protective services. TDHR eliminated funding for "extra meals" for day care centers and support for day care centers servicing only handicapped persons.

Child protective services have historically categorized clients according to degree of harm or threat to the client. Cuts in 1982 SSBG funding forced TDHR to drop funding for the lowest threat category of clients, producing a 5.2 percent drop in the number covered by the protective services program.

Community care services adopted an identical policy introducing new eligibility standards, including income, age, and need tests in 1982. These rules excluded and/or reduced support for persons with the resources to pay for services. They effectively targeted community care services to low-income and minimal-resource individuals, who otherwise could not afford in-home services.

TDHR was able to maintain client enrollments in the face of federal aid cuts by shifting SSBG-ineligible applicants to other aided programs. A relaxation in income tests for the Title XIX Primary Home Care Services program (Medicaid) allowed TDHR to shift clients who had formerly received SSBG family care services to Title XIX. Both programs provide for in-home health care, preventing costly institutionalization. Because there was no ceiling on federal Medicaid dollars available to the state, the number of clients that could be shifted was subject only to the limits of income tests. Between 1982 and 1984, 673 clients shifted from SSBG coverage to the Title XIX Medicaid program, 2.1 percent of total ineligible SSBG recipients.

Under pre-block grant federal regulations, day care and family planning vendors had to match a portion of their federal aid allocation with monies from their own jurisdictions. The current SSBG does not require a local match; however, state officials exercised this local match option and in 1983 raised the required matching level as a way to partially restore lost federal aid monies. TDHR and local providers negotiated the matching rates, based on available resources and need. The net effect was a more equitable and targeted restoration of federal aid monies.

Similarly client co-payments enhanced child protective and day care services. This method of revenue enhancement required clients to contribute directly to the costs rather than merely to pay a higher proportion of the costs of these services. Unlike user fees, a system of co-payments sought to maintain and augment existing services; it increased services by each additional dollar spent by clients. This system operated much like a matching grant, where the state increased services in an amount equal to the recipient's contribution.

Entitlements. The state's response to 1981-1982 cuts in federal entitlement programs was met by an increase in the state's matching expenditures for AFDC. The state's Board of Human Resources increased the state's contribution to AFDC spending by $12 million, producing a supplemental per child payment of $55 in January, 1983. This surpayment generated additional federal matching monies and allowed for a onetime increase of $75 per child. After heavy lobbying in 1981 by welfare rights groups, social service nonprofits, churches, and child welfare associations, the state legislature proposed a constitutional amendment to raise the ceiling on AFDC payments. To the surprise of many political observers, voters of the state adopted the consti-tutional amendment by a 2-to-1 margin. But to those aware of the changing character of the state's voters, it was expected.

Although state spending for AFDC increased, the number of aid recipients fell steadily with a 14 percent drop in total cases between 1981 and 1983. Declining enrollments were associated with lower per client expenditures and higher caseloads per caseworker. One regional welfare official suggested that this condition was due to rising administrative and overhead costs mandated by new federal regulations. Requirements for computerized eligibility screening and monthly reporting of client income levels forced the Texas Department of Human Resources (TDHR) to make large expenditures to implement these administrative activities.

The state's more visible response to cuts in both AFDC and, to a lesser extent, Food Stamps funding was to increase its monitoring of fraudulent applications and payments for assistance. It established a fraud hotline and contracted privately for special local prosecution of Food Stamp and AFDC violators. These efforts proved successful with a 20 percent reduction in fraudulent Food Stamp payments and a 48.7 percent reduction in fraudulent AFDC claims.

In spite of a signficiant restoration of 1981 Medicaid cuts, Texas officials took several steps to economize their operation of the state's federally funded health service programs for the indigent. A "lock-in" policy required excessive users of Medicaid to use only one physician and pharmacy, reducing costly screening fees charged for initial visits to physicians.

Moreover, 1983 brought new pressures for Medicaid to support experimental medical procedures, such as organ transplants. The state now supports only "established" medical procedures; however, increase political pressure to fund new experimental procedures will probably soon strain the state's Medicaid fund.

## State Responses to Cuts: Capital Improvement Programs

More important than funding cuts (with regard to the Community Development Block Grant) was the change in the state's control over administration and implementation of community development policy. The governor's decision to locate this block grant in the Texas Department of Community Affairs exemplified his concern to maintain control over the state's economic development policy. This is the only executive agency without a governing board and consequently is regarded as the "governor's" agency. TDCA spent a lot of time soliciting input from communities across the state on the design of the pro-gram. As a result, it produced an allocational formula that emphasized the targeting of assistance to distressed communities. One recent national study of the new block grant identified Texas as one of a few states effectively targeting substate allocations to communities with the greatest need [17] and potential for successful program implementation. [17] This confirms some observers' prediction that state-administered block grants would be more responsive to the needs of their state's communities.

The state's response to changes in federal funding for highway construction and maintenance was mixed. Initially, state officials lobbied hard for the federal gas tax increase and the 85 percent return rate rule. They were elated with the windfall of federal highway funds these produced in FY 83. At the same time the 90-10 matching provision requirement meant that the Texas Department of Highways and Public Transportation had to use some of its general revenue funds to meet the match. This required eliminating all 100 percent state-funded projects (farm-to-market roads), halting the practice of purchasing rights-of-way for local road projects, cutting in half the grass-cutting and trash pick-up programs, and implementing a hiring freeze. [18] Recognizing that without an increase in the state funding level the department would continue to fall behind in its efforts to build new highways and repair the 7,000 miles of roadway clasified by the federal governments as in "poor condition," highway officials began lobbying heavily for an increase in the state's gasoline tax. (The Texas Legislature met in special session that summer to consider the proposal; it passed).

In general, the state of Texas was much more responsive in terms of targeting newly-controlled federal funds than was expected. The same pattern was observable at the local level.

IMPACT OF NEW FEDERALISM POLICIES AT THE LOCAL LEVEL: THE HOUSTON CASE

Reflecting trends at the state level, Houston also experienced major economic and political changes prior to and during implementation of Reagan's New Federalism programs. These changes affected the reaction of Houston area governments to the new federal and programmatic policies.

Pressures on the Houston Economy

In a remarkably short period, descriptions of Houston as "Boomtown, USA," the "international city of the fast buck," the "golden buckle on the sunbelt," [19] were revised as the city's gold-and-glitter image began to fade. As

late as April 1982, unemployment was still under 5 percent, far below the national average. But by March 1983,
the jobless rate had jumped to 10.7 percent, and it
exceeded the national average by July 1983. Massive
layoffs occurred in Houston's oil-related industries, a
significant part of the area's economic base.

Meanwhile, the public sector suffered also. Instead
of their usual high-growth but no-tax-increase budgets,
many local governments had to lay off employees, raise
fees and taxes and delay planned capital improvements.
The city of Houston's perennial surplus of funds disappeared midway into FY 1983 (February). The mayor
proposed, and council adopted, a $25.1 million cut in the
city's $671 million general fund budget and a "one-time"
use of $20 million in federal revenue sharing money for
general operating expenses (as opposed to capital
equipment expenses). These actions were necessary to
balance the city's budget by June 30, 1983--the end of the
fiscal year. The shortfall had resulted from declining
sales tax revenues, which fell far below estimates made by
the beginning of the fiscal year.

Houston's public and private sectors had not fully
anticipated the depth of the recession. Like state
leaders, many community leaders had believed that
Houston's economy was immune from national trends--that
its "golden buckle" would not tarnish. In a speech before
many of these leaders, the city's comptroller warned
against such false assumptions in the future. He also
warned that "tough choices over taxes and city services
loomed ahead because of the recession and cuts in federal
aids."[20]

The city's intake of federal funds between 1981 and
1982 dropped by some $20 million. Although these cuts
amounted to only 2.3 percent of the city's total budgeted
expenditures for FY 1982, they obviously concerned the
city's financial officials.[21] They feared that federal
aid to municipalities would decline as long as Reagan was
president and the federal deficit so large. They also
predicted city revenue would continue to drop for another
year or two--until the area recovered fully from the
recession. One of the biggest worries was that the city
would have to delay its capital improvement activities,
endangering continued growth and expansion. At the same
time, a number of the city's elected officials anticipated
strong pressures from the minority community to absorb
some of the social service programs that had been
federally funded. This sensitivity to minority demands

was evidence of their growing numbers and political clout
as well as the more progressive attitudes of newcomers to
the city.

## Houston's Changing Political Culture

A substantial portion of the Houston area's growth
resulted from in migration by individuals from outside the
region, primarily from the Northeast and Upper Midwest
sections of the country and Mexico.[22] These newcomers to
Houston were "somewhat more likely than oldtimers to
criticize the quality of city services, law enforcement
and the general style of life."[23] Newcomers to the city
were also more likely to prefer tax increases and more
active state and federal involvement in improving the
quality and quantity of city services than "old timers"--
which explains some of the pressures on local officials to
increase public spending, especially in light of federal
budget cuts. The increased diversity of the city's
population made responsiveness a key political issue,
perhaps even more so than at the state level. Consequently, important questions regarding the New Federalism
changes from the local perspective were (1) the state's
responsiveness to local diversity and (2) the extent to
which state organizational structure would permit local
flexibility in policy making.

## Federal Aid Cuts and Responses: Houston Local Governments

In general three things happened. First, Houston
area local governments experienced fewer reductions in
federal funds for operating programs than capital
improvement programs. Second, the city proved to fare
better under the state block grant arrangement than was
intially anticipated, primarily due to demographics and
politics. Third, the city restored cuts in politically
sensitive federal programs in response to clientele groups
with considerable political clout. A closer look at the
extent of federal aid cuts and the city's reaction to them
will confirm these observations.

Current Operating Programs. The most significant changes
were in health, housing and education programs and to a
lesser extent entitlement programs (see Table 6.2.) The
city's Health department experienced losses in a number of
its federally funded health programs, particularly
categorical programs folded into the Maternal and Child

Table 6.2
Changes in federal aid for Houston Area: FY 1981-1983
(millions of dollars)

| Area/Program | Year | | | Percent Change | | |
|---|---|---|---|---|---|---|
| | 1981 | 1982 | 1983 | 81-82 | 82-83 | 81-83 |
| | ($) | ($) | ($) | (%) | (%) | (%) |
| Current Operating Programs | | | | | | |
| Social Services[b] Block Grant (Title XX) | 4.8 | 11.7 | 12.1 | 143.0 | 3.4 | 152.0 |
| Alcohol, Drug Abuse and Mental Health[b] | | | | | | |
| Block Grant | - | 0.714 | 0.583 | - | -17.9 | - |
| Alcohol | - | 0.195 | 0.156 | - | -20.0 | - |
| Drug | - | - | - | - | - | - |
| Mental Health | - | 0.519 | 0.429 | - | -17.3 | - |
| State Compensatory[c] Education | - | 4.2 | 4.7 | - | 11.9 | - |
| Education Block[c] | | | | | | |
| Grants | 15.1 | 14.3 | 13.9 | -5.3 | -2.8 | -7.9 |
| Chapter 1 | 11.9 | 12.8 | 12.3 | -7.5 | -3.0 | -3.33 |
| Chapter 2 | 3.2 | 1.5 | 1.6 | -53.1 | 6.6 | 50.0 |
| Community Service[d] Block Grant | 4.0 | 2.3 | 2.2 | -425.0 | -4.3 | -45.0 |
| Low Income Energy Assistance Block Grant [e] | 0.050 | 0.050 | - | - | - | - |
| CETA/Job Training Partnership [d f] | 25.0 | 15.5 | 8.2[a] | -38.0 | -47.1 | -67.2 |
| Preventive Health and Health Serv. Block Grant[d] | 1.9 | 2.7 | 2.6 | 42.1 | -3.7 | 36.8 |
| Rodent Control | 0.157 | .286 | - | 82.2 | - | - |
| Immunization | - | 0.109 | 0.109 | - | - | - |
| Health Incentive | 0.334 | 0.403 | 0.436 | 20.6 | 8.1 | 30.5 |
| TB | 1.5 | 1.5 | 1.6 | - | 6.7 | 6.7 |
| VD | - | 0.428 | 0.484 | - | 13.1 | - |

(Table 6.2 con't.)

| Area/Program | Year | | | Percent Change | | |
|---|---|---|---|---|---|---|
| | 1981 | 1982 | 1983 | 81-82 | 82-83 | 81-83 |
| | ($) | ($) | ($) | (%) | (%) | (%) |
| Maternal and Child Health Care Block Grant[b] | 2.8 | 1.8 | 2.1 | -35.7 | 16.7 | -25.7 |
| WIC | 0.350 | 0.419 | 0.599 | 19.7 | 42.9 | 71.1 |
| Block Grant | 1.2 | 0.959 | 0.959 | -20.1 | - | -20.1 |
| Family Planning[b] | 1.1 | 0.849 | 0.504 | -22.8 | -40.6 | -54.2 |
| EPSTD(XX)[d] | 0.022 | 0.019 | 0.019 | -13.6 | - | - |
| Entitlement[a] | | | | | | |
| AFDC | 21.0 | 20.0 | 27.8 | -4.8 | 39.0 | 32.4 |
| Food Stamps | 82.5 | 79.8 | 107.0 | -3.4 | 34.1 | 29.7 |
| Medicaid | 103.4 | 106.0 | 118.0 | 3.2 | 11.3 | 14.1 |
| Capital | | | | | | |
| Mass Transit[b] | 80.8 | 91.4 | 68.5 | 13.1 | -33.4 | -15.2 |
| CDBG (entitlement)[d] | 28.3 | 27.3 | 23.5 | -3.5 | -13.9 | -17.0 |
| Wastewater[d] | 40.2 | 39.6 | 38.2 | -1.5 | -3.5 | -4.9 |
| Econ. Dev.[d] | 0.081 | 0.037 | 0.037 | -7.4 | - | -54.3 |
| Housing[g] | 4.5 | 5.7 | 13.7 | 26.6 | 140.0 | 204.0 |
| Section 8 Exist. | 0.839 | 0.172 | 1.9 | -79.4 | 998.0 | 125.0 |
| Section 8 Const. | 0.165 | 0.220 | - | 33.0 | - | - |
| Section 8 Rehab. | 1.1 | - | - | - | - | - |
| Section 23 Leased Housing Rehab. | - | - | 0.303 | - | - | - |
| Section 23 Leased Housing Oper. | - | - | 0.256 | - | - | - |
| Low Rent Pub. Housing Operating | 2.4 | 3.4 | 3.6 | 42.2 | 4.9 | 49.1 |
| Modernization | - | 1.9 | 7.6 | - | 297.0 | - |

(Table 6.2 con't.)

Notes:

[a] Texas Department of Human Resources, Region XI.
[b] Harris County.
[c] Houston Independent School District.
[d] City of Houston.
[e] Gulf Coast Community Services Association.
[f] Funding is for the Job Training Partnership Act only. 1982 and 1983
    figures are for the CETA program.
[g] Housing Authority of the City of Houston.

Health Care Block Grant. In 1982 the city experienced a 35.7 percent decline in funding, followed by a modest and partial restoration in FY 1983. The restoration was due to advantageous state-level allocational decisions. Overall, however, the city lost 25 percent of its 1981 categorical allocation for maternal and child care health services, between 1981 and 1983.

Funding for the city's Preventive Health and Health Services Block Grant increased by 42.1 percent in 1982, largely because of a favorable allocation for the health incentive that which was the result of state reprioritizing. The city experienced a slight loss (3.7 percent) of block grant monies due to the elimination of the city's rodent control program at the state level.

The city replaced some of the cuts in health programs, such as rodent control, teen pregnancy, immunization, family planning, stray animal control, and lead poisoning, by increasing user fees and getting the city to absorb federally funded staff positions in its general fund budget. This strategy was more effective in the flush prerecession days of FY 1982 than it was in FY 1983, but then again the cuts were fewer in 1983.

Ironically, the federally funded health program that received the most publicity during this period also experienced funding increases--the Women, Infants, and Children (WIC) program. A bureaucratic struggle between the Personnel Department and the Health Department due to the Mayor's proposed spending cutbacks in mid-1983, caused the hassle over this program. The Health Department was targeted for personnel cuts under the cutback directive. City civil service regulations require temporary employees be laid off before permanent employees be laid off. Unfortunately, the city Health Department was using ten federally funded temporary employees to run its WIC nutrition program in four clinics serving 3,000 infants and pregnant women. Recognizing the problem, Health Department officials asked the Personnel Department to reclassify these slots as regular city positions--with little success, because they would represent future obligations to general fund monies. The issue came to a head when the four clinics were temporarily closed amidst much adverse publicity. The problem was resolved by promoting lower-ranking Health Department workers into WIC responsibilities.

Another unpopular decision surrounded the Health Department's 1982 rejection of a $535,000 federal family planning grant because of high administrative costs.

Federal regulations mandated a charge for services on a sliding-scale basis, which the Department regarded as cost-ineffective: it would increase collection costs and paperwork. When the money crunch hit the Health Department in 1983, this action was no longer commended as an efficiency move as it had been in FY 1982. Instead, it was attacked as shortsighted and irresponsible. Aggressive grantsmanship by the Health Department then became a high priority of the director hired in late 1983. His publicly stated goal was to increase the externally funded portion of the department's budget to 40 percent. He brought this grantsmanship philosophy with him from Chicago.

The Housing Authority of the City of Houston (HACH) actually increased its intake of federal funds between FY 1981 and 1983. Aggregate funding levels to the Housing Authority increased 28 percent between 1981 and 1982 and 139 percent between 1982 and 1983. These totals, however, obscure the shift away from new construction to rehabilitation or modernization activities, from new property acquisition to rent subsidies that recycle money through the private market. They also reflect HUD's growing sensitivity to the problems of big city housing authorities like Houston's. For example, the 1983 allocation for Section 8-existing actually included two new projects. One ($623,040) was a conversion of new construction monies originally planned for a new housing project. Another was amendment money ($1.9 million) to supplement funding level commitments made in the 1970s. These actions represent the effectiveness of the agency's staff, especially its director, in lobbying HUD officials in Washington.

Support for the change in the direction of federal housing programs, namely the move toward rent subsidies and housing vouchers, is growing. Houston's highly visible, high-density public housing project, Allen Parkway Village, has been plagued with problems. Its undesirability, even among the needy, was no more evident than in statistics collected at the height of the recession. While 3,000 families awaited placement in public housing facilities, 340 units in the unpopular large-scale Allen Parkway Village project were vacant.[24] In November 1983, the Board of Commissioners voted to close the 40-year-old project and make the 37-acre site available for private development pending city council and HUD approval. This move was not without controversy because it is adjacent to the city's Fourth Ward, an area with a heavy concentration of minorities. But a number of black leaders endorsed the sale of the Allen Parkway Village project and argued for replacing it with dispersed-site housing projects and rent subsidy programs.

The Housing Authority was aware that the Reagan administration had little affinity for operating subsidies for public housing projects. The rate of increase in funding levels for operating subsidies slowed considerably between 1982 and 1983 (4.9 percent as contrasted with a 42.2 percent increase between FY 1981 and FY 1982). Federal support for this program actually declined (10.3 percent) between FY 1983 and FY 1984. To cope with this decline the Housing Authority tried to increase its rent collection rate and become more efficient in its administration. The governor appointed a new board of directors in 1983, and the new board hired a new director to get the scandal-ridden agency under control.

Houston's Independent School District (HISD) did not experience a restoration of federal funds lost under the categorical grant consolidation. Its Educational Block Grant allocation continued to decline in 1983 but at a slower rate than in the previous year. The entire block grant allocation dropped 7.9 percent from its pre-block grant level of funding. The district's increased allocation under the state's compensatory education grant program partially offset this loss in educational block grant monies. The area's growth, especially among school-age children with special educational needs (for example, learning disabled and non-English speaking) accounted for this jump. Growth in the compensatory education program was steady between 1981 and 1983 (20 percent), partially offsetting the loss in Educational Block Grant monies.

Changes in federal funding for entitlement programs in the Houston area were deceptive (see Table 6.2.) They seem to suggest that the Houston area fared quite well during the initial rounds of the Reagan budget cuts and weathered the recession without any significant cuts in funding levels. Between 1981 and 1983, however, AFDC, Food Stamps, and Medicaid allocations all increased at rates higher than national or even Texas averages. This change was due solely to significant increases in eligible populations, especially food stamp recipients. The flood of job seekers to Houston and the late arrival of the recession in Texas produced a condition where many people were caught without any prospects for employment, in immediate need of general assistance. Higher aggregate funding levels did not necessarily mean an increase in the quality of services delivered. In fact, data on caseloads per caseworker for the Houston area suggested the opposite: they increased significantly.

Monies the TDHR regional office received did not go to increasing staffing or other personnel needs generated by an increase in the volume of clients. Administrative personnel claim that agency overhead had risen dramatically between 1981 and 1982. Federal requirements for an automated eligibility screening system and the rising cost of leased space worked to swell administrative overhead to nearly 30 percent of TDHR's operating budget. Officials expected this percent to increase for a few years before the agency reaped the savings from some of its investments (for example, automated eligibility screening system). Some TDHR officials feared that the agency would not be able to weather the interim period between aid cuts and the start-up of the new screening process.

Capital Improvement Programs. The Houston area has historically been more dependent on federal funds for capital rather than operating programs. For example, in 1978 federal funds for capital projects amounted to three-quarters of federal funds available to the city.[25] Consequently, changes in federal capital funding levels were of great concern to local officials.

Community Development. The capital-intensive program characterized by the sharpest reductions in funding levels was the Community Development Block Grant (FY 1981-1982, -3.5 percent; FY 1982-1983, -13.9 percent). Nevertheless the fiscal impact was minimal. The city had rarely been able to spend all its previous CDBG funds, and at the time of the cutbacks it had a large pool of unspent money.

The real impact of the cuts in this program was organizational. Contraction offered the mayor and her community development (CD) director the opportunity to try to get the program under control. (It had gotten very much out of control during the expansionary period.) HUD cuts served as the perfect rationalization for reducing the size of the CD staff, restructuring the citizen participation mechanisms, establishing new sub-contractor performance criteria and evaluation procedures, and semi-privatizing the housing rehabilitiation program.

There were relatively few examples of any use of the CDBG fund pool to replace lost federal, state, or local funds. The most notable example was the successful appeal by the Gulf Coast Legal Aid Foundation for a $180,000 subcontract to provide legal services to CD target-area residents interested in participating in the CD housing rehab program. This agency had lost over $300,000 in federal funds due to federal budget cutbacks. In addition, a few day care centers successfully petitioned city council to allocate more CD funds to replace lost state (federal pass-through) funds. Probably the biggest reason why more CD funds weren't substituted for lost local revenues was the general feeling that the long start-up time historically associated with CD contracts would not alleviate the city's fiscal stress before the economic recovery began.

Wastewater. A capital-intensive program of the city that has also experienced cuts was the Environmental Protection Agency (EPA) Wastewater Treatment program. Funding dropped gradually from $40.2 million in FY 1981 to $38.2 million in FY 1983 (-5 percent). For a city whose future had been banked on continued growth, but that had experienced a severe shortage in sewage capacity necessitating construction moratoriums, this drop in federal funding was considered serious. The problem became even greater in FY 1985 when the federal match dropped from 75 percent to 55 percent, and more stringent water quality standards had to be met.

Houston's city council responded to the actual and projected wastewater revenue shortfalls by raising severe rates and selling and passing an "alternative financing ordinance." The ordinance was designed to recoup all costs of new sewage treatment facilties by charging fees to private developers based on the the amount of sewage to be generated by their projects. This fee brought a lot of money into the city's Public Works Department almost immediately.

Economic development. The city of Houston had received an Economic Development Administration planning grant annually since 1979. While funding levels fluctuated, dipping considerably in FY 1982 (-67 percent) but rising in FY 1983 (+90 percent), the initial base was small ($75,000). The CDBG grant actually generated most of the city's recent federally funded economic development activity. Beginning in FY 1983, the CDBG division allocated 10 percent of its grant to economic development. This allocation was primarily in response to HUD's criticism of its FY 1982 program, which lacked a revitalization focus. The FY 1983 application included

$2.3 million for economic development and another $700,000 for renovation of non-profit social service agency facilities. This focus fit well with the Reagan administration's emphasis on public-private partnership and leveraging strategies. Further, it fit well with the mayor's inner-city redevelopment plan, a key plank in her re-election platform.

Houston's mayor called attention to the economic revitalization thrust by hiring a new Planning and Development Department director. The director's initial assignment was to prepare the city's first Urban Development Action Grant (UDAG) application. (A previous HUD audit of the CDBG program had recommended the city apply for a UDAG grant.) The request was for $3.15 million, which, along with $1.85 million in CDBG monies, would be used to leverage $13 million in private funds to construct El Mercado, a Hispanic-style shopping center in a blighted area near downtown. Unfortunately, the UDAG application was returned twice, each time because it lacked a clear demonstration of firm financial commitment from the private developer. When the city submitted it again in January 1984, few people expected it to be funded, and it was not. HUD's new impaction criteria made it almost impossible for pockets-of-poverty cities like Houston to compete with older declining cities. The city has continued to rely on more traditional mechanisms for funding economic development--the private sector and bonds.

Highways. Houston has two representatives on the three-member Texas Highway and Transportation Commission, including the chairperson. One was appointed in 1981, the other in 1983. It was no coincidence that the Houston area was a big winner under this arrangement. From 1971 through 1980, Houston received 9 to 11 percent of all state highway contracts. In contrast, between October 1982, and September 1983, 16 percent of the state's highway contracts were let in Houston, repre-senting 33 percent of all funds.[29] This situation was not considered unfair; if anything it was viewed as necessary--and still insufficient to meet the area's demand for additional capacity.

Houston has the most overloaded highway system in the state, if not the nation. The big boost in federal high-way funds (from the increase in the federal gas tax) was one factor that enabled the Highway Commission to respond to Houston's needs. However, local officials recognized that even with this increase the area's problems could not be resolved without local governments and the private sector. In 1983 the Houston Chamber of Commerce drafted a Regional Mobility Program, a $16.2 billion county-wide transportation project: nonlocal sources were expected to provide only 30 percent of this amount.

A common theme runs through this discussion of federally funded capital-intensive projects. Federal monies have played an important role in fueling Houston's growth. As these funds diminished, the scramble for their replacement began. One strategy was to utilize new federal jobs programs with strong economic development components. This strategy involved a great deal of lobbying at the state level, particularly in the program-design phase.

## THE NEW FEDERALLY FUNDED JOBS PROGRAMS

### The Emergency Jobs Bill

The state received an additional $62.7 million from Title I of the Emergency Jobs Bill of 1983. As dictated by federal statute, most of these "new" monies went into "old" programs, namely five block grants: Community Services, Social Services, Mental Health/Alcohol/Drug Abuse, Maternal and Child Health Care. Consequently, the same agencies charged with administration of the block grants controlled the allocation of these funds. Over 70 percent went to the CDBG program, administered by the Texas Department of Community Affairs (TDCA). The next largest recipient was Social Services (Title XX)--17 percent. Texas' approach was to use these funds as supplements to existing programs.

One real advantage of the infusion of Emergency Jobs Bill money under the CDBG grant was the opportunity to use up to 50 percent of the appropriation for public service activities. Funding for this activity had been limited to only 10 percent of the CDBG grant. The new job monies effectively relaxed this limit on social service spending. However, the potential for severe political repercussions may have deterred some communities from adopting this strategy. Some cities previously had a great deal of difficulty cutting back their CDBG spending on social services to the 10 percent level. The use of emergency jobs money for social services would have made this a recurring problem.

Some communities used these one-time supplements as

substitution monies for lost local revenues. For example, the city of Houston spent some of its $1.6 million emergency jobs program funds on an anti-litter project involving personnel in the city's Parks and Solid Waste Departments who faced layoffs because of spending cutbacks inside City Hall. Ironically, this was the only component of the jobs program that was without controversy. Critics said that allocating $1.3 million for off-duty police officers at crime-ridden public housing projects and $3 million to private contractors for street, storm sewer, and water main construction in low-income areas was "not reaching the unemployed." The CDBG director argued that they did stimulate the economy--the real intent of the law. City council resolved the problem by passing an ordinance requiring private contractors to make special efforts to hire the unemployed.

The irony of criticism of the use of emergency job bill monies for construction projects was that at the height of the recession this sector was particularly hard hit with layoffs. Perhaps critics simply could not see this bill as the countercyclical program that it was--in contrast with more traditional training-oriented jobs programs.

## The Job Training Partnership Act

The Job Training Partnership Act (JTPA), the replacement for CETA, is a more traditional jobs program. Its purpose is to train/retain individuals out of the work force rather than provide a quick fix for the short-term unemployed. Under CETA, the state's Department of Community Affairs had administered only the balance-of-state CETA program. Passage of JTPA made the state responsible for the entire jobs program--a major broadening of responsibility. Various state agencies (Texas Employment Commission, Texas Department of Community Affairs and the Texas Education Agency) competed among themselves as well as with the governor's Office of Planning for the right to administer the $119 million program. Ultimately, the governor recommended the program be placed in TDCA for three important reasons, all political. First, administering it from the governor's office would have resulted in a large increase in the size of the governor's staff, and Texans' opinions toward enlarged executive staffs (state and local) are negative. Second, by placing it in the TDCA, the governor maintained tight control over the program. (Again, TDCA is the only major state agency without a board or commission functioning in a policy-development and program oversight role.) The control over the jobs program, as over community development, was important; the governor had run on a platform promising to "bring more jobs to Texas." Third, the governor had to make amends to his Mexican-American constituency. As secretary of state, he had fought extension of the Voting Rights Act of 1975--an action he repeatedly had to defend himself against during his campaign. Once elected (with unexpected, but necessary heavy support from Hispanics), he needed to make amends. (The head of TDCA is Hispanic.) Predictably, this action offended a number of black leaders whom the governor ultimately appeased by appointing a black as director of the JTPA program itself.

In reality, a great deal of control of the JTPA program design still resides in the governor's Office of Planning, specifically the employment and training section. The Texas Job Training Partnership Act (HB 2251), passed May 30, 1983, formalized this rather unusual arrangement. The same act created a joint legislative committee charged with monitoring JTPA.

The major issues that evolved over state implementation of JTPA were designation of service delivery areas (SDAs), certification of Private Industry Councils (PICs), formation of the State Job Training Coordinating Council, and program design for Title II and Title III monies. Delays in settling each of the issues resulted in expenditure rates far below projections during the transition period (October 1, 1983 through June 30, 1984). The inexperience of the state staff, which tended to underestimate the time involved in gearing up at the local level, often caused the delays. Local SDAs began expressing fears of losing unspent monies, reminiscent of the old "spend it-or-lose-it" CETA days. This was particularly true of the Houston SDA.

The Houston City Council did not even approve a contract with TDCA to receive JTPA monies until December 13, 1984, and the first subcontract for training under the Houston JTPA program was not approved until January 4, 1984. Some holdups existed at the state level, but other SDAs faced similar problems and coped with them. TDCA criticized the city for having the poorest expenditure rate of all large cities during the first quarter. In spite of receiving the largest allotment in the state ($6.2 million), the Houston SDA served only 800 participants, while San Antonio served 1,400 with a $3.9 million grant and Dallas served 913 with $3.4 million grant.[27]

An initial struggle within the city took place between the CETA/JTPA director and business leaders on the one hand and old CETA subcontractors and minority city council members on the other. The question was whether the city or a nonprofit private sector entity should be designated the administering agency. Upon the urging of key minority city council members and established non-profits, the mayor finally decided to keep control of the program inside the city.

The private sector's initial influence on program design at both the state and local levels was significant, an expected finding for a state like Texas. Particularly beneficial was its role in identifying labor market needs and preventing a mismatch between training programs and real job opportunities. But the partnership was strained with regard to program implementation. Because many private sector PIC representatives had not dealt previously with federal jobs programs, a great deal of time was spent educating these individuals about federal regulations and procedures. Another problem was turnover. The initial enthusiasm of some of these representatives waned because of slowness and reversion to past policies. The pressure to get things moving has increasingly led to the awarding of subcontracts to established job service vendors. For example, the Houston PIC utilmately recommended that six of nine previous CETA subcontractors be funded for training programs in the nine-month interim period that ended June 30, 1984. One PIC member, particularly frustrated with this phenomenon, said that the act should have been named the "relief for people in the training business act."[28] On the other side, however, JTPA administrators throughout the state complained that the private sector hardly "rushed out to greet JTPA program participants with open arms" and in fact, remained fairly antagonistic, perceiving it as just another CETA program.

The lack of enthusiasm for Title II of JTPA (the traditional job training portion) is easier to understand than that for the Title III portion, aimed at assisting and retraining dislocated workers. In Texas, the decision was made to target Title III to areas of the state with serious worker dislocation problems. The money ($4.9 million) was allocated through four demon-stration projects rather than through SDAs. Following a thorough analysis of data supplied by the Texas Employment Commission, Texas Industrial Commission, universities, and business groups, three areas of the state were selected for assistance: the Gulf Coast (oil-related industries), East Texas (the steel industry), and the border (peso devaluation). The competition for these designations was keen--the recession was in full force, and a number of regions were suffering. But the state JTPA staff successfully convinced the state council of the need to target permanently dislocated workers--not the short-term unemployed. Even with the targets, implementation of Title III projects was slow.

The initial plan called for projects to start up in August 1983. As of January 1984, only two of the four projects were operating. (Two projects were funded in the Gulf Coast region.) Part of the difficulty was in drumming up interest among the dislocated workers themselves, who had not yet exhausted unemployment benefits that were higher than JTPA stipends. Thus, in spite of the state's well-intentioned efforts at targeting, implementational difficulties at the local level hampered program success of the Title II program. But, as we have shown, the majority of the state's targeting efforts were well received by its local governments.

CONCLUSION

This article examined the impact of Reagan's New Federalism policies on the state of Texas in the 1981-1983 period. The primary focus was on the extent of federal funding cuts and the consequences of shifts to a state block grant allocation structure. The results showed that there was very little short term change in funding levels or programmatic priorities attributable exclusively to the New Federalism policies. The major changes were more a consequence of mediating effects of marked long term economic, demographic, and political changes that characterized the state during this period. This was, of course, the real goal of the New Federalism decentralization strategy--diversity in reaction to federal funding cuts.

As of the end of FY 1983, there was a general consensus among local government and agencies through the state, but particularly in Houston, that things would be back to "business as usual" once the recession lifted and economic recovery took on steam. Many felt, however, that complete recovery was at least several years away. In the meantime, revenue enhancement, productivity, and privitization strategies were implemented to try to do more, or at least the same, with less.

There was one notable change affected by Reagan's New
Federalism programs that government officials were
happiest to deal with--the shift in the location of the
grantsmanship game. State officials were pleased to have
the responsibility for implementing policies more
sensitive to the state's regional diversities. Local
officials were happier to be dealing with the state. They
believed that their chances of winning the grantsmanship
game with fair officials was far greater on the Austin[29]
playing field than on the one in Washington. In
summary, state block grants were well received in spite of
reduced funding levels.

NOTES

1.   See Claude E. Barfield, Rethinking Federalism: Block Grants and Federal, State and Local Responsibilities (Washington, D.C.:   American Enterprise Institute, 1981); John Elwood, ed., Reductions in U.S. Domestic Spending: State and Local Governments (Rutgers, N.J.:   Transaction Books, 1982); John L. Palmer and Isabel V. Sawhill, The Reagan Experiment:   An Examination of Economic and Social Policies Under the Reagan Administration (Washington, D.C.:   The Urban Institute Press, 1982); Gregory B. Mills and John L. Palmer, eds.   Federal Budget Policy in the 1980s (Washington, D.C.:   The Urban Institute Press, 1984); Edward Gramlich and Deborah S. Laren, "Reagan's Proposals for a New Federalism,"   in Setting National Priorities:   The 1983 Budget (Washington, D.C.:   Brookings Institution, 1982); Richard Nathan and Fred Doolittle, The Consequences of Cuts:   The Effects of Reagan Domestic Programs On State and Local Governments (Princeton, N.J.:   Princeton University Press, 1983); Irene S. Rubin, Shrinking The Federal Government (New York:   Longman, 1985).
2.   See Barfield, Rethinking Federalism.   Daniel J. Elazar, American Federalism:   A View from the States, 3rd Edition, (New York:   Harper and Row, 1984); Advisory Commission on Intergovernmental Relations, Recent Trends in Federal and State Aid to Local Governments, M-118, Washington, D.C.:   July, 1980.
3.   See Susan A. MacManus and Robert M. Stein, "The Effect of Federal Budget Cuts on Houston," Texas Business Review, 56 (November/December, 1982):   281-284;   Ellwood, Reductions in U.S. Domestic Spending.   Nathan and Doolittle, The Consequences of Cuts; and Helen F. Ladd, "Federal Aid to State and Local Governments," in Mills and Palmer, Federal Budget Policy in the 1980s.
4.   See James W. Fossett, Federal Aid to Big Cities:  The Politics of Dependence (Washington, D.C.:   Brookings Institution, 1983); Susan A. MacManus, "Planning for Federal Cutbacks in Texas," Texas Business Review 56 (September/October 1982):   281-284;   MacManus and Stein, "The Effects of Federal Budget Cuts in Houston in Susan A. MacManus, ed., Federal Aid to Houston (Washington, D.C.: Brookings Institution, 1983).
5.   Office of State Comptroller, "The Texas Revenue Outlook, 1984-1985, Fiscal Notes, 83 (January 1983): 1-6.
6.   Office of State Comptroller, "Texas Oil Prices:  The OPEC Connection," Fiscal Notes, 83 (June 1983): 1-8.

7. Office of State Comptroller, "The Effects of the Mexican Peso Devaluations on the Texas Economy, Fiscal Notes, 83 (June 1983): 1-5.

8. Office of State Comptroller, "Hurricane Alicia Leaves Mark on Texas Coast and Texas Economy," Fiscal Notes, 84(July 1984): 1-7,20.

9. Susan A. MacManus, "Shifting to State Block Grants: The Priorities of Urban Minorities," Journal of Urban Affairs, (Summer 1985).

10. Office of State Comptroller, "Newcomers to Texas Swell Population Count, Fiscal Notes, 83 (December 1983): 15-17.

11. Stanley Lieberson, "Measuring Population Diversity," American Sociological Review (December 1969): 850-862.

12. Joe McQuade, "The New Texans: Part 3," Houston Chronicle, October 25, 1983.

13. Jim Simmon, "Pollsters Analyze White's Victory over Clements," Houston Post, November 7, 1982.

14. Felton West, "New Texas Senate Expected to be Slightly Less Conservative," Houston Post, November 4, 1982.

15. Office of State Comptroller, State of Texas: 1983 Annual Financial Report, Austin, Texas, 1983.

16. MacManus, "Shifting to State Block Grants."

17. Virginia P. Bergin, "An Implementation Analysis of the Use of Small Cities Community Development Block Grants As A Mechanism for Reaching the Most Distressed Communities," a paper delivered at the Conference on Allocative and Distributive Impacts of Reagan Policies, Sponsored by Virginia Polytechnic Institute at its Washington, D. C.-Alexandria, Va. Campus, April 20, 1984.

18. John Gavois, "Highway Officials Want to Avoid Funds Backlash," Houston Post, March 28, 1984.

19. Barbara McIntosh, "Houston: Boomtown, U.S.A.," Houston Post, September 24, 1978.

20. Speech before the Tax Research Association reported by Mike Snyder, "Lalor Says City Facing Retrenchment," Houston Post, February 23, 1983.

21. Susan A. MacManus and Robert M. Stein, "Government Fragmentation and Budgetary Responses to Cuts in Federal Aid," unpublished manuscript, 1982: 1

22. David Plane, "Where Do New Texans Comes From?" Texas Business Review, (November/December, 1982): 291-295.

23. Susan A. MacManus, "Managing Urban Growth: Citizen Perceptions and Preferences," in Steven C. Ballard and Thomas E. James, eds., Future of the Sunbelt (New York: Praeger, 1983): 142.

24. Janet Elliot, "Vacancies Plentiful, But Renters are Few for Allen Parkway," Houston Post, November 14, 1983.

25. MacManus, Federal Aid to Houston.

26. Laurie Paternoster, "2 Houstonians Don't Take Positions on Board Lightly," Houston Post, October 9, 1983.

27. Mike Snyder, "Houston Job Training Services Lag Behind Other Texas Cities," Houston Chronicle, March 29, 1984.

28. Mike Snyder, "Successful Executive Shifts Roles as Chief of Job-Finding Program," Houston Chronicle, January 29, 1984.

29. Delbert A. Taebel and Richard L. Cole, "Texas Cities and Federal Budget Cuts," Texas Business Review, 56 (March/April) 1982): 67-70.

# 7

# Small Cities' Policy Responses to the New Federalism

*Beverly A. Cigler*

Dwindling budgets, public concern over waste, growing service demands, and increasing calls for efficiency and effectiveness in government operations have had significant impact on all levels of government in the 1980s (Sbragia, 1983; Levine, 1980). The reduced scope and extent of federal programs and the transfer of responsibilities for local programs to state governments has had significant impact on state-local relations. As "creatures of the states," local governments are especially hard-hit by changes as they have fewer alternatives to increasing revenues. Local governments must live within their means because all states except Vermont have balanced budget requirements.

This chapter examines the policy responses to fiscal stress by small communities in one state. By studying the variety of options available for increasing local revenues, reducing expenditures, and implementing innovative management practices, the effects of many New Federalism programs on small communities are examined. This includes examination of the organizational environment in which privatizing strategies and users' fees, for example, are used, and of changes in grant-seeking behavior.

The chapter is divided into four sections: (1) a brief review of the research literature on fiscal stress; (2) an examination of the special problems faced by small, especially nonmetropolitan, governments, experiencing fiscal stress and New Federalism budget cuts; (3) a presentation of findings from a study of the policy responses to the New Federalism by small communities in North Carolina; and (4) policy suggestions emerging from the research.

## INCREASING INTEREST IN LOCAL FISCAL AUSTERITY

A large, urban-oriented research literature has addressed the recent fiscal squeeze on local governments, focusing especially on the relationship between changes in the local environment and changes in revenue reliance patterns (for example, Levine and Rubin, 1980; Bowman, 1981; Martin, 1982). The effects of external constraints on local government revenue-raising capacities, especially the limits on the use of taxes, has also gained increased research attention (for example, Ladd, 1978; Florestano, 1981; MacManus, 1981; Danzinger and Ring, 1982).

Concern with the quality, cost, and efficiency of local government service delivery has also spawned considerable research interest in strategies designed to improve management practices, as well as encouraging the development of many "how-to-do-it" materials (for example, Davis and West, 1985; Ammons and King, 1983; Greiner, Hatry, Koss, Miller and Woodward, 1981). Innovative management practices have the appeal of improved productivity: reducing fiscal stress and improving the climate of public opinion which affects the use of other options.

A key focus of the Reagan administration's New Federalism has been the use of a set of management practices focusing on the privatization of public services, including contracting out, load-shedding, volunteerism, coproduction of services and other alternative delivery arrangements (Savas, 1982; Poole, 1980). Although opposition has been vocal (Hanrahan, 1977), local governments have turned to these alternatives to traditional public bureaucracies for a wide variety of municipal programs and services (Straussman, 1981; Florestano and Gordon, 1980). Empirical research has been limited primarily to measuring the frequency and costs of alternative service provision (Fisk, Kiesling, and Muller, 1978; Florestano and Gordon, 1980). With few exceptions (Nelson, 1980; Wedel, 1976), the existing research overlooks the process of decisionmaking and evaluation involved in using alternative delivery arrangements, as well as overlooking the political and organizational context of such arrangements. The interface between expenditure/revenue patterns, innovative program management, and service delivery mechanisms has been neglected by researchers.

## FISCAL AUSTERITY IN THE SMALL GOVERNMENT SETTING

A case can be made that small, especially non-metropolitan, governments may be suffering the effects of fiscal crises more than their urban counterparts. Small communities have recently experienced two dramatic changes: (1) a resurgence in population and economic growth, and (2) increasing responsibilities for policy-making and service delivery, along with increasing mandates, as public functions are decentralized by successive presidential administrations heralding a New Federalism (Cigler, 1984). Just as these communities were beginning to deal with being thrust into the gamut of intergovernmental relationships, searching for ways to manage change, the effects of the modern three R's--revolt of the taxpayers, reduced federal aid flows, and recession with no federal bail out (Shannon, 1983)--were exacerbated by limited staff, expertise, and management resources.

In addition, the federal programs helping non-metropolitan areas have received the harshest treatment from the budget axe, with funds for water and sewer grants, farmers, job training, land and water conser-vation, highways, 701 planning, rural health and child nutrition, and the Appalachian Regional Commission either eliminated or drastically reduced. To date, state and local governments have lost an estimated 16 percent of their federal revenues from the initial Reagan adminis-tration cuts, with the local government loss estimated at $5.5 billion, or 22.7 percent. Beginning in 1986, three-year reductions in federal grants in aid could total an additional loss of $42.6 billion, according to data developed by the National Governor's Association and the National Conference of State Legislatures (Federal Funds Information for States, 1985). General Revenue Sharing would account for the largest losses.

What is striking about the research on the causes of and responses to local fiscal stress is the lack of attention to small and/or rural governments. It is unlikely that what is known from the urban-oriented studies is transferable to small and nonmetropolitan communities, because there is so little consensus on the theories, methodologies, and policy approaches regarding fiscal condition in general (Clark and Ferguson, 1983; Bahl, 1984). The extensive literature studying the relationships among urban size and costs, externalities, and benefits is ambiguous in findings, although suggestive of the need for increased attention to the differences between large and small communities (Miller, 1979; Puryear, 1979; Sokolow and Honadle, 1984).

A major technical problem is the lack of standardization in reporting, from community to community and state to state (Stinson, 1981; Honadle, 1983; Dillman and Hobbs, 1982; Browne and Hadwiger, 1981; Bryce, 1979), which limits systematic data collection. In addition, budget increases represent more problems for some communities than others (Clark and Ferguson, 1983; Kelso and Maggiotto, 1981). Conceptually, communities under greater duress are those that have fewer options available to them in resolving their woes (Weinberg, 1984). The options themselves are limited by such additional factors as state limitations on indebtedness, tax rates, aid alternatives, capitalization procedures, mandated programs, and others. Internal resources such as number of staff and staff expertise may be quite important. Capacity-building efforts by external agents such as state government, municipal and professional associations, consultants, and universities (Vocino, Pernacciaro, and Blanchard, 1979; Bender and Sellers, 1979; Cigler, 1981) may be necessary.

Small cities and rural governments have entered the intergovernmental arena at a time of increased concern for fiscal austerity. Their management capacity to effectively undertake the responsibilities of any chosen expenditure reduction, revenue enhancing, and/or innovative programmatic and service delivery arrangements is a key issue. A changing fiscal environment requires adaptive, not reactive responses. Honadle (1982, 1981) defines a government's capacity as its ability to anticipate and influence change; make informed, intelligent decisions about policy; develop programs to implement policy; attract and absorb resources; manage resources; and evaluate current actions to guide future actions. A number of recent works have addressed the general capacity of small governments to undertake their responsibilities (Banovetz, 1984; Green and Reed, 1981; Newland, 1981; Sokolow, 1981; Brown, 1980; Howitt, 1978) and generally have found limited capacity.

RESEARCH SETTING AND FINDINGS

The following study examines three aspects of the impacts of the latest New Federalism and changing fiscal environment on small governments in North Carolina: (1) the perceived impacts of recent federal budget cuts in relation to the nature of problems confronting small communities; (2) expenditure reduction, revenue enhancement, and innovative program management techniques employed to adjust to the New Federalism; and (3) local officials' perceptions of ways to improve local government capacity to effectively and efficiently respond to citizens in a changing fiscal environment. The data are drawn from the most recent survey of the North Carolina Local Policy Project, a continuing needs-assessment of small communities in that state initiated by the author in 1979 with cooperation from a variety of professional and governmental associations.[1] The findings are taken from the most recent survey effort, conducted between June and September 1983.[2] This involved sending questionnaires to 250 small governments in the state and receiving replies from 207, a response rate of 83 percent. All communities of population less than 50,000 with city managers and a computer-generated random sample of others received questionnaires. After eliminating questionnaires not completed by specifically designated respondents, managers and clerks, a usable sample of 198 communities resulted.[3]

The research occurred during a time of retrenchment. First, federal aid had actually peaked in fiscal year (FY) 1978. Second, California's ratification of Proposition 13 in 1978, limiting the growth rate of the property tax, had started a national trend toward tax limitation that had widespread effects nationwide. Third, public attitudes toward government became more negative due to rising tax bills, inflation, and growing federal deficits. It may be that citizens were not calling for less government, but for better government (Ladd, 1983). As such, the communities in this survey had for several years been in an environment in which citizens were asking for greater efficiency and effectiveness from government. Finally, by 1983, the full thrust of the Reagan administration's New Federalism proposals was a matter of public record, and many effects of the initial budget cuts had already been experienced by local officials.

Local governments' needs were determined by: (1) asking officials directly to describe their communities' problems and characteristics; (2) obtaining the officials' perceptions of the effects of the Reagan administration's programs on expenditure adjustments, revenue generation, and program/administrative process changes; (3) obtaining factual data on the sources of information most used and helpful to local officials; and (4) gathering officials' perceptions of problems in dealing with state government, a key capacity-builder in responding to the Reagan administration's New Federalism. The only variable that demonstrated differences in local community responses to the New Federalism was community size, with larger units responding in a greater variety of ways to their changing fiscal condition. So as not to confuse the major points made in this analysis, only frequencies are presented.

Effects of New Federalism

To gauge the impact of the New Federalism, the survey first asked the town managers/clerks to identify their communities' major problems. Given a list of seven types of concerns most often addressed in national surveys, officials most frequently mentioned their difficulties in attracting and supporting commercial facilities, with 65 percent of the sample communities citing the concern as their key problem. Forty-seven percent mentioned the need to retain existing jobs and 35 percent mentioned housing rehabilitation as a key problem. Other problem areas-- deterioration of the natural environment, insufficient new housing, blight and crime/drug problems--all drew a response rate below 30 percent. These figures indicate, as one might expect, that economic related issues (that is, commercial facilities and jobs) most concern small town officials in North Carolina.

The predominant concern with economic and financial matters dovetails with factual information obtained from community officials in highlighting concerns with community financial stability. Sixty percent of the communities reported having difficulty balancing their operating fund revenues against their expenditures, for example, and 59 percent were concerned about the stability of their credit or bond ratings. Clearly, these communities reported the need to adjust to the realities of shrinking budgets.

It is unlikely, moreover, that the near future will lessen the need for adjustment behavior, as attention to retrenchment policies will probably increase. Three-year grant-in-aid outlay reductions, beginning in 1986, show an estimated additional loss of 18.61 percent in federal funds (Federal Funds Information for States, 1985). Foremost among the cuts would also be General Revenue Sharing, but substantial cuts would be made in wastewater plants, public housing, community development, and the Appalachian Regional Commission. Four key rurally oriented programs would be especially hard-hit: Farmers

Home rural housing, rural cooperative funds, rural water and waste disposal programs, and the soil and water conservation programs of the U.S. Department of Agriculture. Of course, many other program cuts would substantially affect small and rural town residents: Medicare, Medicaid, Aid to Families with Dependent Children (AFDC), child nutrition programs, and job training.

The funding priorities of the Reagan administration have exacerbated the financial worries of the study communities. For example, survey respondents expressed a special concern about future losses of funds for several specific programs. Wastewater treatment plant funding was considered critical by 57 percent of the respondents, and funds for water lines were mentioned by 50 percent as a critical priority. Rather than dwelling on perceptions of critical needs or on specific programs, the survey sought to examine the adjustment behaviors used by the small governments in the state. As stated earlier, when spending requirements do not coincide with resources, local governments can maintain a healthy fiscal position if they take appropriate action to adjust to their changing fiscal environment. They may pursue expenditure reduction (spending control) strategies, revenue enhancement strategies, or a variety of related management techniques. A single state study can reveal trends in adjustment behaviors, keeping in mind the gamut of factors not controlled by local governments.

Data concerning the responses of North Carolina's small governments to stress were obtained through a series of questionnaire items that presented lists of possible strategies and methods, with open-ended responses possible. These responses are reported in the next subsection of this chapter. First, however, the managers/clerks were asked to rank their communities' three major "responses to the initiatives of the Reagan administration."

The typical North Carolina government uses expenditure reductions most often, then new revenue sources, and finally program or administrative process changes. More than half (51 percent) said their communities used expenditure reductions most frequently in responding to financial realities. Twenty-three communities sought new revenues more often than using any other coping behavior, and only 14 percent attempted to initiate program and administrative changes as their primary adjustment. Hypothesizing a relatively limited use of innovative programmatic and administrative tools and strategies, the survey also included a number of questions that sought to determine where local governments seek help in building their capacity to respond to stress, as well as questions aimed at determining local officials' perceptions of their utility. That information is presented in the section that follows a description of fiscal adjustment behaviors.

## Adjustment to Fiscal Stress: Expenditure Reduction Strategies

Managers and clerks were asked which activities aimed at adjusting expenditures have been pursued by their communities since 1980. (See Table 7.1). Sixty-seven percent of the communities tried to increase efficiency of existing programs, while 31 percent increased energy conservation efforts, and 28 percent cut back on existing programs or services. Although a great variety of other expenditure reduction strategies have been attempted, few communities are experimenting with these strategies. Private-public cooperation, for example, was mentioned by only 18 communities (9 percent); new joint provision of services with another government was mentioned by only 33 governments (17 percent); and only a fourth of the sample attempted to increase volunteerism. Still fewer communities (20 percent) began to contract out services to the private sector.

Responses to fiscal concerns by small North Carolina communities reveal a relative lack of harsh expenditure-reduction strategies. Only 6 percent of the communities studied claimed to have dropped programs entirely. While 20 percent mentioned terminating employees, the programs in which those employees worked were not eliminated.

Table 7.1 indicates that in cutting expenses, North Carolina communities relied more on traditional strategies such as efficiency, energy conservation, and cutbacks than on the new types of efforts that are receiving increased attention nationally. Volunteerism, for example, did rank fourth, but only one in four towns used that strategy. Other creative options ranked lower: in sixth place, was contracting out services to the private sector (20 percent); in seventh was joint provision of services with another government (17 percent); in eighth was shifting a program/service to another government (15 percent); and in tenth was public-private cooperation (9 percent). These rankings and percentages suggest some movement toward more

Table 7.1  Expenditure behavior of North Carolina communities

| Strategy | N= | Percent |
|---|---|---|
| Increased efficiency of existing programs | 132 | 67 |
| Increased efforts at energy conservation | 62 | 31 |
| Cut back existing programs or services | 55 | 28 |
| Attempted to increase volunteerism | 48 | 24 |
| Terminated employees but kept programs | 39 | 20 |
| Contracted out services to private sector | 39 | 20 |
| Joint provision of services with another government | 33 | 17 |
| Shifted some programs/services to other governments | 29 | 15 |
| Purchased services from another government | 22 | 11 |
| Private-public cooperation in formal programs | 18 | 9 |
| Dropped programs entirely | 12 | 6 |
| Other | 6 | 3 |

Responses to the question, "In adjusting expenditures, which activities have been pursued by your community since 1980?" (multiple responses yield totals over 100%)

innovative ways to cut municipal costs but also a general reluctance to turn to such strategies with great confidence.

## Adjustment to Fiscal Stress: Revenue Enhancement Strategies

The second most frequently used method of adjusting to the New Federalism, following spending control policies, involved attempts at revenue enhancement (Table 7.2). Significantly, users' fees, which constitute an important nontax revenue source that is relatively free of state-imposed restrictions, were found to be very popular new revenue. A majority of 55 percent of the communities surveyed cited users' fees as an expanding revenue source.

Despite the national government's continuing curtailment of grant funds, more than half of the communities (51 percent) claimed to have increased their search for new grants from other governments at all levels. This suggests the need for additional studies of why local officials have increased their grant-searching, in spite of the Reagan administration attempts to reduce the size and influence of government in domestic matters. Indeed, contrary to the objectives of new federalism, increased searching for new grants (51 percent) has been pursued by more than twice as many communities as increased volunteerism (24 percent). Also, another New Federalism strategy that reduces government's role, that of public-private ventures, has been pursued by only 9 percent of the study communities in response to the New Federalism.

Dovetailing with the general economic concerns of North Carolina officials, the search for new industrial/ commercial businesses was cited by 44 percent as an important coping strategy. As might be expected in a state with strong state-level review of local governments' finances such as North Carolina, new taxes (7 percent) and borrowed money (4 percent) ranked near the bottom of revenue enhancement strategies.

## Adjustment to Fiscal Stress: Program/Administrative Changes

Another series of questionnaire items measured local governments' innovation in adopting programmatic and administrative changes. According to survey respondents, this category was the least used response to fiscal realities. Table 7.3 reports generally low levels of use

Table 7.2  Revenue-seeking behavior of North Carolina communities

| Strategy | N= | Percent |
|---|---|---|
| Users' fees | 108 | 55 |
| Increased searching for new grants | 101 | 51 |
| Searched for new industrial or commercial businesses | 88 | 44 |
| Raised existing taxes | 63 | 32 |
| Annexation | 53 | 27 |
| New taxes | 14 | 7 |
| Other | 13 | 7 |
| Borrowed money | 7 | 4 |

Responses to the question, "Which one of the following responses has been most used by your community in adjusting to the New Federalism initiatives of the Reagan administration?" (multiple responses yield totals over 100 percent)

Table 7.3  Program/administrative innovation by North Carolina communities

| Strategy | N= | Percent |
|---|---|---|
| Personnel code/merit hiring procedures | 95 | 48 |
| Fiscal management or accounting system change | 91 | 46 |
| Personnel manual for employees | 85 | 43 |
| Long range capital improvement program | 66 | 33 |
| Performance, zero-based or PBS budget from a line item budget | 33 | 17 |
| Computerized management information system | 31 | 16 |
| Wordprocessing | 18 | 9 |
| Management by objectives system | 12 | 6 |
| Human relations training for employees | 13 | 7 |
| Sunset law | 6 | 3 |

Responses to the question, "Which of the following have been enacted by your community?"  (multiple responses yield totals over 100 percent)

of a range of measures judged to be innovative management initiatives. No item has been enacted by more than 48 percent of the study communities. Many innovative approaches which are currently receiving widespread media and academic attention in the field of public management, such as wordprocessing systems, computerization of information systems, new types of budgeting approaches, and participative employee relations strategies, have received little attention by the North Carolina communities studied.

The items listed in Table 7.3 are especially interesting in light of the fact that the study communities claim to use expenditure reduction strategies more than revenue enhancement strategies and that "increased efficiency of existing programs" is the most typical overall response to the New Federalism initiatives. Greater use of the program/administrative changes presented in Table 7.3 would be likely to help achieve increased program efficiency. This suggests a positive note in that much more can be done to increase the management capacity of the local governments in the survey.

The next chapter sub section takes a closer look at the dilemma faced by local officials who have increased program efficiency as a top priority, but who do not demonstrate wide participation in the use of generally accepted strategies for achieving that efficiency. Since the officials themselves have suggested their interest in a variety of adjustment behaviors to their changing fiscal condition, it is necessary to turn to the issue of where they can go for information and what their perceptions of this information's utility are.

## Information Sources and Their Perceived Utility

Beyond the primary concern with how officials have responded to the New Federalism, the survey also asked respondents about the sources of information that they use in their job. Asked to name the three most useful sources of new ideas, the managers/clerks most often identified the North Carolina League of Municipalities, with 63 percent of the officials citing it. The Institute of Government at the University of North Carolina was mentioned by 54 percent of the communities, followed by other local officials in-house (47 percent), other local governments (41 percent), and a variety of other informants such as in-house staff (31 percent), professional associations (27 percent), and regional governments (21 percent). State agency officials (19 percent) and national agency employees (1 percent) were ranked last as sources of new ideas for local government officials.

When respondents were asked about their sources of external assistance, state and regional agencies did somewhat better. Councils of government and other regional units ranked first, mentioned by 57 percent of the communities. Next mentioned were private consultants (45 percent). The state's Division of Community Assistance was mentioned by 38 percent of the sample communities; and other state agencies were cited by 23 percent of the communities. University extension programs, generally considered an important source of information in the state, were utilized by only 17 percent of the respondents for a last-place ranking among the six choices.

The respondents judged their best information sources in performing their jobs to be colleagues from other governments (cited by 58 percent of the respondents), the municipal council (mentioned by 54 percent of the respondents), and the North Carolina League of Municipalities (cited by 46 percent of the officials surveyed). Interestingly, not one official mentioned an agency of state government as a "best" source of information, despite 70 percent of the respondents claiming to have had face-to-face contact with state government personnel during the past year, 79 percent claiming contact through correspondence, and 85 percent claiming telephone contact with state personnel. Finally, 87 percent of the respondents claimed to be somewhat or very familiar with sources of state government assistance to local governments.

Familiarity with state government programs and local assistance efforts does not, however, lead to dissatisfaction. In fact, when asked direct questions about negative factors regarding state programs, most officials (60 percent) judged state programs to be adequate to meet local government needs. Still, a number of suggestions to state government for improving assistance to local governments emerged. In order of most often mentioned by local officials, there are needs for: more outreach through additional regional offices, fewer mandates, more technical assistance, greater effort at providing local governments printed matter regarding the availability of state programs, and a call for state agencies to list their telephone numbers on all correspondence.

POLICY DIRECTION EMERGING FROM NEEDS ASSESSMENT

This summary of the results of one effort at assessing the needs of North Carolina's local governments reveals a number of areas in which state government, professional and municipal associations, as well as other agents might improve efforts to aid local governments. The combined responses from the fiscal questions section and the sources of information section reveal a pattern of local government needs in North Carolina. Officials in small governments are in need of information regarding a wide variety of strategies for expenditure reduction, revenue generation, and especially, innovations in programs and administrative processes.

Simply using the number of communities already pursuing an expenditure reduction technique as a measure of information needed, the communities in this study need advice on ways to increase the efficiency of existing programs, on how to ensure energy conservation savings, and on how to practice cut-back management. Perhaps more importantly, the study communities may need basic information on the gamut of innovative strategies for stretching the municipal dollar that fall into the category of new modes of service production and distribution. The survey results do not reveal whether the study communities are aware of these strategies and simply have rejected them, or whether the communities are not cognizant of such options. Their low levels of use, compared to other states and the attention devoted to such strategies, however, suggests a lack of awareness.

Methods for utilizing citizen volunteers and/or neighborhood groups to coproduce government services, which may lead to increased tax savings, service effectiveness, and governmental efficiency, are much-neglected possible expenditure reduction techniques. Other neglected options are private-public cooperation, shifting of programs to other levels of government, purchasing services from other governments, and contracting out to the private sector. These solutions are especially important in light of some of the state's key problems, such as water resources development and the often-espoused need for regional cooperation.

Nationally, local governments are investing small amounts of public funds to attract large amounts of private money. In many cases, such public-private partnerships have created jobs, reduced unemployment, increased the tax base, and revitalized downtown areas.

Despite evidence of growing efforts to produce such partnerships in the larger North Carolina cities, this survey of smaller governments indicates that such partnerships have not come to North Carolina towns in large numbers.

The survey revealed that financial issues--jobs and attracting commercial facilities--most concern North Carolina town officials. The need to supply more information, increase technical assistance, and stimulate a more thorough dialogue on new innovative strategies for coping with expenditure options is clear.

There is a role for the key information sources used by local officials, such as municipal associations, to stimulate interest in the new service production and distribution strategies, as well as to develop evaluations of both their costs and benefits to local government. For others, such as state and regional agencies, the role may well be to continue offering technical assistance.

The state's communities appear to have a greater awareness of the variety of revenue-generating strategies. Still, it would be wise to identify the costs involved in users' fees before expanding their use. Local governments need information on pricing and efficiency concerns related to this device, such as the effects of development fees and exactions on growing communities. Historically, fees have been utilized for utility-type provisions such as water and sewerage. The increased interest and use of users' fees by North Carolina governments suggests more information should be offered on the use of this option for traditional local functions such as recreation, park development and various special services.

It is in the area of management improvement and program innovation strategies that the survey results reveal a glaring lack of initiative by most communities in the state to do things that would improve their efficiency in internal operations. It clearly is not too early to expect movement toward more professional management systems, capital improvement programs, innovative budgeting, use of new technologies, and employee relations programs. Dissemination of information about these concerns, more how-to-do-it materials, and technical assistance appears necessary.

Except for the mandate issue, North Carolina's local governments have few disagreements about policies directed toward them by state government. They are fortunate in having numerous sources of information to assist in translating their perceived needs into positive actions.

The survey results show that state government, however, could attempt a variety of new information strategies. Also, more time should be devoted to developing linkages among advisory groups and local officials, especially collaborative efforts in which municipal and professional associations first consult with local officials about their needs and then provide information. An important survey finding is that the state's local governments are not making use of innovative programs that could further enhance their ability to save and expand resources, thus providing even better services to citizens and increasing efficiency in internal operations. Needs assessments can enhance local policy and performance by providing the means for consultation among providers of information and their clients. The resulting dissemination of techniques and information would offer local officials a wider array of options for dealing with the impacts of the New Federalism.

Clearly, the Reagan administration's New Federalism has had major impacts on North Carolina's small communities, influencing their ability to undertake their responsibilities. The key finding of this research is that small governments may not currently have the capacity to deal with the wide variety of techniques for reducing expenditures, increasing revenues, and improving program management that are associated with the New Federalism. More attention is needed from external capacity builders (states, municipal and professional associations, and so on) and from researchers in developing an understanding of the political and organizational context in which alternative strategies operate.

NOTES

1.   The Project has produced seven separate surveys of
county and municipal officials since 1979.  Surveys have
included questionnaires completed by energy coordinators,
city and county managers, clerks, and finance officers, on
a variety of topics of concern to local government.
2.   Professor Terry Busson, Eastern Kentucky University,
will   replicate   the   survey   reported   here   for   small
communities in the state of Kentucky in 1985.
3.     The   study   sample   reflects   the   number   of   NC
municipalities   in   various   population   ranges,   as   shown
below.

| Municipal Population | No. of NC Municipalities | No. in Sample |
|---|---|---|
| over 50,000 | 8 | 0 |
| 25,000 to 49,999 | 10 | 7 |
| 10,000 to 24,999 | 26 | 21 |
| 2,500 to 9,999 | 96 | 61 |
| under 2,500 | 373 | 109 |
| Totals | 513 | 198 |

REFERENCES

Ammons, David, N. and Joseph C. King. 1983.
"Productivity Improvement in Local Government: Its
Place Among Competing Priorities." Public
Administration Review 42 (March/April): 113-120.
Bahl, Roy W. 1984. Financing State and Local Government
in the 1980s. New York: Oxford University Press.
Banovetz, James M. (editor) 1984. Small Cities and
Counties: A Guide to Managing Services Washington,
D.C.: International City Management Association.
Bender, Lewis and Robert Sellers. 1979. "University
Public Service Outreach to State and Local
Governments." State and Local Government Review 11
(January): 22-28.
Bowman, John H. 1981. "Urban Revenue Structures: An
Overview of Patterns, Trends, and Issues." Public
Administration Review 41 (Special Issue, January):
131-143.
Brown, Anthony. 1980. "Technical Assistance to Rural
Communities: Stopgap or Capacity Building?" Public
Administration Review 40 (January/February): 18-33.
Browne, William P. and Don F. Hadwiger (editors). 1981.
Rural Policy Problems: Changing Dimensions.
Lexington, Massachusetts: Lexington Books.
Bryce, Herrington J. 1979. Planning Smaller Cities.
Lexington, Massachusetts: Lexington Books.
Cigler, Beverly A. 1981. "Mandated Expertise:
Consultants and Local Capacity Building." Urban
Affairs Papers 3 (Winter): 23-32.
Cigler, Beverly A. 1984. "Small City and Rural
Governance: The Changing Environment." Public
Administration Review 44 (November/December): 540-
545.
Clark, Terry Nichols and Lorna Crowley Ferguson. 1983.
City Money: Political Processes, Fiscal Strain, and
Retrenchment New York: Columbia University Press.
Danzinger, James N. and Peter Smith Ring. 1982. "Fiscal
Limitations: A Selective Review of Recent
Research." Public Administration Review 42
(January/February): 47-56.
Davis, Charles E. and Jonathan P. West. 1985. "Adopting
Personnel Productivity Innovations in American Local
Governments." Policy Studies Review volume 4, number
3 (February): 541-549.

Dillman, Don A. and Daryl J. Hobbs (editors). 1982. Rural Society in the U.S.: Issues for the 1980s. Boulder, Colorado: Westview Press.

Federal Funds Information for States. 1985. Reported in Governors' Bulletin, number 16. Washington, D.C.: National Governor's Association.

Fisk, Donald, Herbert Kiesling, and Thomas Muller. 1978. Private Provision of Public Services: An Overview. Washington, D.C.: The Urban Institute.

Florestano, Patricia S. 1981. "Revenue-Raising Limitations on Local Government: A Focus on Alternative Responses." Public Administration Review 41 (Special Issue, January): 122-131.

Florestano, Patricia S. and Stephen B. Gordon. 1980. "Public vs. Private: Small Government Contracting with the Private Sector." Public Adminstration Review 40 (January/February): 29-34.

Green, Roy E. and B. J. Reed. 1981. "Small Cities Need Grants Management Capacity." Rural Development Perspectives 4: 28-30.

Greiner, John M., Harry P. Hatry, M. P. Koss, A. P. Miller and J. P. Woodward. 1981. Productivity and Motivation: A Review of State and Local Government Initiatives. Washington, D.C.: Urban Institute.

Hanrahan, John. 1977. Government for $ale: Contracting out-- The New Patronage. Washington, D.C.: American Federation of State, County and Municipal Employees.

Honadle, Beth Walter. 1981. "A Capacity-Building Framework: A Search for Concept and Purpose." Public Administration Review 41 (September/October): 575-580.

Honadle, Beth Walter. 1982. "Managing Capacity-Building: Problems and Approaches." Journal of the Community Development Society volume 13, number 2: 65-73.

Honadle, Beth Walter. 1983. Public Administration in Rural and Small Jurisdictions. New York: Garland Publishers, Inc.

Howitt, Arnold M. 1978. "Improving Public Administration in Small Communities." Southern Review of Public Administration 34 (December): 325-331.

Kelso, William A. and Michael A. Maggiotto. 1981. "Multiple Indicators of Financial Instability in Local Governments." International Journal of Public Administration 3 (2): 189-218.

Ladd, Everett Carll, Jr. 1983. "What the Voters Really Want." In James L. Perry and Kenneth L. Kraemer (editors). Public Management: Public and Private Perspectives. Palo Alto, California: Mayfield Publishing. 114-125.

Ladd, Helen F. 1978. "An Economic Evaluation of State Limitations of Local Taxing and Spending Powers." National Tax Journal 31 (June): 1-18.

Levin, Charles H. (editor). 1980. Managing Fiscal Stress; The Crisis in the Public Sector. Chatham, New Jersey: Chatham House Publishers.

Levine, Charles H. and Irene Rubin (editors). 1980. Fiscal Stress and Public Policy. Beverly Hills, California: Sage Publications.

MacManus, Susan A. 1981. "The Impact of Functional Responsibility and State Legal Constraints on the 'Revenue-Debt' Packages of U.S. Central Cities." International Journal of Public Administration 3 (1): 67-111.

Martin, Joan K. 1982. Urban Fiscal Stress: Why Cities Go Broke. Boston, Massachusetts: Auburn House.

Miller, Edward J. 1979. "Large Versus Small Cities: Does Size Make a Differnce." In Edward J. Miller and Robert P. Wolensky (editors). The Small City and Regional Community: Proceedings of the Second Conference on The Small City and Regional Community. Stevens Point, Wisconsin: The Foundation Press, Inc.

Nelson, Barbara J. 1980. "Purchase of Services." In George Washnis (editor). Productivity Improvement Handbook for State and Local Governments. Washington, D.C.: National Academy of Public Administration. 427-447.

Newland, Chester A. 1981. "Local Government Capacity Building." Urban Affairs Papers 3 (Winter): iv-v.

Poole, Robert W., Jr. 1980. Cutting Back City Hall. New York: Universe Books.

Puryear, David. 1979. "The Relevance of City Size." In Herrington J. Bryce (editor). Small Cities in Transition: The Dynamics of Growth and Decline. Cambridge, Massachusetts: Ballinger Publishing Company. 155-166.

Savas, E.S. 1982. Privatizing the Public Sector. How to Shrink Government. Chatham, New Jersey: Chatham House.

Sbragia, Alberta M. (editor). 1983. The Municipal Money Chase: The Politics of Local Government Finance. Boulder, Colorado: Westview Press.

Shannon, John. 1983. "Austerity Federalism--The State-Local Response." National Tax Journal 36 (September): 377-382.

Sokolow, Alvin D. 1981. "Local Governments: Capacity and Will." In Amos Hawley and Sara Miles (editors). Nonmetropolitan America in Transition. Chapel Hill: University of North Carolina press. 704-735.

Sokolow, Alvin D. and Beth Walter Honalde. 1984. "How Rural Local Governments Budget." Public Administration Review 44 (September/October): 373-383.

Stinson, Thomas F. 1981. "Fiscal Status of Local Governments." In Amos Hawley and Sara Miles (editors). Nonmetropolitan America in Transition. Chapel Hill: University of North Carolina Press, 704-735.

Straussman, Jeffrey D. 1981. "More Bang for Fewer Bucks? Or How Local Governments Can Rediscover the Potentials (and Pitfalls) of the Market." Public Administration Review 41 (Special Issue): 150-157.

Vocino, Thomas, Samuel J. Pernacciaro, and Paul D. Blanchard. 1979. "An Evaluation of Private and University Consultants." Public Administration Review 39 (May/June): 205-210.

Wedel, Kenneth R. 1976. "Government Contracting for Purchase of Service." Social Work 21 (March): 101-105.

Weinberg, Mark. 1984. "Budget Retrenchment in Small Cities: A Comparative Analysis of Wooster and Athens, Ohio." Public Budgeting and Finance 4: 46-57.

# 8

# New Federalism
# and Capital Budgets:
# The Case of Tulsa, Oklahoma

*Raymond A. Rosenfeld*
*and Alan W. Frankle*

Two of the principal issues facing urban governments today are the need for capital improvements to replace a decaying infrastructure or respond to rapid growth and the simultaneous uncertainty about the role of federal aid in financing these capital needs that has resulted from President Reagan's New Federalism agenda. New Federalism seeks to reduce the overall responsibility of the federal government in funding activities that it views as being the main responsibility of state and local governments. The extent to which New Federalism has affected the funding of local capital improvement projects in general, and specifically in Tulsa, Oklahoma, is the focus of this chapter.[1]

Because Tulsa is young, growing and economically healthy,[2] its situation probably is not indicative of urban United States in the 1980s, where fiscal strain in the face of a declining population and tax base and a deteriorating infrastructure is not uncommon. Yet, the fiscal problems of relatively healthy cities are a part of the urban landscape as well, and perhaps our case analysis will shed some light on this group of cities. Furthermore, if we discover a substantial capital needs problem as a result of New Federalism budget cuts, some inference can be drawn for other cities where the economic climate is not as positive as in our case example.

Most municipalities recently have realized a growing concern with managing the local capital budgeting process. Just as the railroad, automobile, and airline industries required massive public investment in order to fulfill their potentials, the growth and survival of many urban areas also requires substantial additions or renovations to public works if the expected quality of life in these municipalities is to be maintained.

In an era of tight budgets due to inadequate economic growth, demands for increased services, resistance to national tax increases, and President Reagan's New Federalism agenda of limiting and reducing the funding role of the national government in domestic affairs, there is a temptation to cut corners where it is most expedient from a short-term political viewpoint. Capital investment needs can be deferred and become invisible in terms of annual budgets, but ultimately, they must be seen as a hidden part of the fiscal squeeze faced by all local governments.[3]  William Gorham, president of The Urban Institute notes in his foreword to the series "American's Urban Capital Stock":

The attractiveness of relieving pressure on the budget by trimming capital expenditures is enhanced by the fact that bridges, sewers, and water mains--until they fail--rarely generate the same level of constituent concern as do cuts in the currrent services that cities deliver.[4]

There is little doubt that New York City's fiscal crisis was the direct result of management decisions to transfer operating expenses to the capital budget and consequently to defer improvements and additions to the infrastructure.[5]  In their important analysis of public works investments in the United States, Pat Choate and Susan Walter point to the declining net investment (gross investment less depreciation) in public capital improvements for all governments.

Despite unmistakable evidence of such deterioration, the nation's public works investments, measured in constant dollars, fell from $38.6 billion in 1965 to less than $31 billion in 1977--a 21 percent decline....

There are several reasons for these declines--a decrease in the nation's birth rate and the maturation of the "baby boom" have helped reduce the need for some kinds of investments.  But the greater part of the decline reflects the growing habit of government at all levels to cut back on construction, rehabilitation, and maintenance in order to balance budgets, hold down the rate of tax growth, and finance a growing menu of social services.[6]

In order for local officials to develop and manage sound and viable capital improvement plans and budgets, they must understand the impact of New Federalism budgets on their capital improvement programs. The following sections of this chapter describe the changes in federal aid for urban capital improvement programs under President Reagan's New Federalism and specifically illustrate the impact on Tulsa, Oklahoma. Finally, Tulsa's capital improvement agenda is presented, and several financing options are discussed as alternatives for managing the New Federalism.

## FEDERAL AID BUDGET CUTS

During the decade of the 1970s intergovernmental aid grew tremendously, and local governments became increasingly dependent upon these funds for operating expenses as well as capital improvements.[7] By 1980, it is estimated that 36.0 percent of state and local capital expenditures were paid for with federal aid.[8] Intergovernmental transfers became the lifeblood not only of older declining cities of the northeast and north central states but also of the rapidly growing cities of the south and southwest. The Urban Institute's case analyses of capital financing indicate that in 1979, fiscally strained New York City relied on federal aid for 43.5 percent of its capital expenditures;[9] Cincinnati, which appeared to have its capital plant under reasonable control, paid for 39 percent of its capital improvements from 1970 to 1977 with federal aid;[10] and economically healthy Dallas relied upon federal aid for 26.4 percent of its capital expenditures between 1975 and 1978.[11] From these examples, it appears that fiscal federalism prevented older cities from deteriorating more rapidly and enabled newer cities to keep up with the demands of growing populations.

The impacts of these intergovernmental transfers are not viewed as entirely positive. It is believed widely that urban renewal programs often accelerated urban decay and that the interstate highway system contributed to surburban sprawl.[12] Equally important and gaining support is the point of view that federal aid creates a dependency relationship, preventing or perhaps forestalling state and local governments from making decisions that address local problems under the constraints of state or local resources.[13]

After several decades of growth in intergovernmental aid ($6.0 billion in 1960 to $95.9 billion in 1981) and mounting criticism of its impact, the 1982 New Federalism budget cuts included a 9.4 percent decrease to $66.6

billion.[14]  In reality, the growth began to taper off in the late 1970's with 1977 being the year when grants calculated in constant dollars stopped growing.[15]  Thus, from the perspective of fiscal federalism, Reagan administration policies were a quickening of a trend rather than a new approach.

Furthermore, the 1982 budget decrease in grants-in-aid is due in part to the creation of several block grants through the consolidation of categorical programs in education, social services, health services, low-income energy assistance, and community services and community development for small towns only.  These block grants were budgeted for approximately 25 percent fewer funds than the replaced categoricals and do not affect urban capital improvement activities because they are largely in the area of human services.

In Table 8.1, the principal federal grant programs that fund or are eligible to fund capital improvements for state and local governments are listed.  Included are several programs that partially fund operating expenses but may be spent for capital improvements at local governments' discretion (Community Development Block Grants (CDBG), General Revenue Sharing, and Urban Mass Transportation Administration (UMTA), Capital and Operating Assistance Formula Grants).  Decisions to spend these latter grant moneys for operating expenses is indicative of the fiscal strategy of deferring capital needs in favor of more immediately pressing service demands.  While local officials could spend all of these grant funds on capital projects, they rarely do so.  Excluded from Table 8.1 for these three local option programs is the proportion of funds that national studies indicate are spent on operating or service expenses.  Thus, we have omitted 11 percent of CDBG funds, 30 percent of General Revenue Sharing, and 80 percent of UMTA Formula Grants.[16]

Overall, Table 8.1 illustrates a surprising 11.9 percent increase in federal capital improvement grants to municipalities during the initial period (1980 to 1984) of President Reagan's New Federalism agenda.  At the end of the 1982 federal budget process it appeared that New Federalism would indeed require local officials to devise new management initiatives to provide capital improvement dollars.  Yet the no-growth budget of 1981 and the substantial reduction that was achieved in 1982 were reversed in 1983 and 1984.  The much-discussed end of the growth in federal aid to state and local governments that

Table 8.1  Federal Grants Obligated for Capital Improvements[a] (in $ millions)

| Type of Grant | Fiscal Year | | | | |
|---|---|---|---|---|---|
| | 1980 | 1981 | 1982 | 1983 | 1984 |
| Economic Development Administration Grants for Public Works & Development Facilities | 192 | 220 | 130 | 7 | 170 |
| Housing and Urban Development | | | | | |
| Community Development Block Grant | 2,433 | 2,421 | 2,421 | 2,354 | 2,075 |
| Section 312 Rehabilitation | 214 | 85 | 49 | 84 | 86 |
| Urban Development Action Grants | 741 | 741 | 337 | 566 | 740 |
| Interior | | | | | |
| Outdoor Recreation | 225 | 175 | 26 | 91 | 108 |
| Urban Parks | 77 | 60 | 2 | 53 | 6 |
| Urban Mass Transit Administration | | | | | |
| Capital Improvement Grants | 1,700 | 1,925 | 1,680 | 1,561 | 1,096 |
| Formula Grants | 310 | 298 | 271 | 340 | 438 |
| Airport Development Aid | 640 | 443 | 411 | 816 | 811 |
| Federal Aid Highways | 8,077 | 8,799 | 8,003 | 12,111 | 13,057 |
| Environmental Protection | | | | | |
| Wastewater Facilities Construction | 4,376 | 3,900 | 2,117 | 300 | 3,032 |
| General Revenue Sharing | 3,197 | 3,200 | 3,200 | 3,197 | 3,197 |
| Total Grants For Capital Improvements | 22,182 | 22,267 | 18,664 | 21,480 | 24,816 |
| Percent Change from previous year | | (+0.4%) | (-16.2%) | (+15.1%) | (+15.5%) |
| Total Federal Grants | 91,500 | 95,900 | 86,800 | N.A. | N.A. |

Source:  1981 to 1985 Catalogue of Federal Domestic Assistance, Executive Office of the President, Office of Management and Budget.

(continued)

[a]Studies of CDBG, General Revenue Sharing and UMTA Formula grants indicate that approximately 89 percent, 70 percent and 20 percent respectively are spent for capital improvements or capital-improvement related expenses. See, U.S. Department of Housing and Urban Development, Sixth Annual Report on Community Development Block Grants (Washington, D.C.: U.S. Government Printing Office, 1981); Catherine Lovell, "Measuring the Effects of General Revenue Sharing: Some Alternative Strategies Applied to 97 Cities," in Revenue Sharing, edited by David A. Caputo and Richard L. Cole (Lexingnton, Mass.: Lexington Books, 1976), pp. 49-65; and Exectuve Office of the president, Office of Management and Budget, The 1982 Catalogue of Federal Domestic Assistance (Washington, D.C.: The U.S. Government Printing Office, 1982), p. 521.

New Federalism was to usher in did not materialize for capital improvement dollars.

It is important to point out, however, that although Congress by 1984 directed more funds to local capital improvements, inflation, particularly during the years of this period, continued to erode the new dollars' purchasing power. Adjusted for inflation, the 1980 to 1984 increase reveals a shrinkage of federal subsidies of approximately 6.4 percent.

As a result of the substantial decrease in federal aid for capital improvements realized <u>by 1982,</u> local officials were forced either to find new sources of revenue or defer more capital projects. This paper is concerned with local officials' responses after the initial federal cutback occurred, realizing, however, that because the 1981 and 1982 reductions were offset in 1983 and 1984, local strategies for managing New Federalism continue to change as New Federalism's fortunes change.

## THE LOCAL EXPERIENCE WITH FEDERAL AID

Like most major urban areas, Tulsa has been the beneficiary of substantial federal funds for its physical and social development.[17] Although governed by economically conservative mayors for several decades, Tulsa always joined its fellow cities in availing itself of federal funds whenever possible. During the last two decades, grants have been received for the full array of capital improvements including urban renewal, model cities, public housing, road construction, airport development, parks, neighborhood facilities, water and sewer improvements, and mass transportation.

In fiscal year 1980, Tulsa was awarded $42.1 million in federal grants that were spent on capital improvements (Table 8.2). The next two years saw a downturn to $36.6 million and $18.5 million respectively. Excluding funds for interstate highways and public housing modernization, which, in Tulsa, are not considered to be local responsibilites (absolutely no local funds are spent for these activities), Tulsa's federal aid for capital improvements climbed from $30.3 million in 1980 to $35.3 million in 1981 and fell to $12.8 million in 1982, a decline of 63.8 percent in the last year. Overall, from 1980 to 1982, Tulsa's federal grants for capital improvements declined by 57.9 percent.

It should be noted that three of the programs listed in Table 8.2 give Tulsa officials the option of spending

Table 8.2  Federal Grants Used for Capital Improvements in Tulsa

| Type of Grant | FISCAL YEAR | | |
|---|---|---|---|
| | 1980 | 1981 | 1982 |
| Economic Development Administration | 2,100 | 0 | 485 |
| Port Authority | 0 | 452 | 0 |
| Housing and Urban Development | | | |
| Community Development Block Grants | 5,009 | 5,000 | 4,728 |
| Urban Renewal Closeout | 6,481 | 0 | 0 |
| Section 312 Rehabilitation | 143 | 27 | 0 |
| Urban Development Action Grants | 240 | 0 | 0 |
| Interior | | | |
| Outdoor Recreation | 126 | 186 | 0 |
| Urban Parks | 0 | 0 | 0 |
| Urban Mass Transit Administration | | | |
| Capital Improvement Grants | 351 | 0 | 968 |
| Formula Grants | 0 | 0 | 0 |
| Airport Development Aid | 3,535 | 7,260 | 0 |
| Federal Aid Highways | | | |
| Interstate* | 11,597 | 907 | 1,160 |
| Other | 8,031 | 2,740 | 2,108 |
| Environmental Protection | | | |
| Wastewater Facilities Construction | 528 | 14,441 | 1,096 |
| General Revenue Sharing | 3,800 | 5,200 | 3,400 |
| Public Housing Modernization | | | |
| Comprehensive Improvement* | 0 | 0 | 4,504 |
| From Operating Subsidy* | 168 | 353 | 77 |
| Total Awards | 42,109 | 36,566 | 18,526 |
| Total excluding interstate highways and public housing* | 30,344 | 35,306 | 12,785 |
| Percent change from previous year | | (+16.4%) | (-63.8%) |

grant funds for capital or operating expenses. We have included only those funds that were budgeted for capital needs. For Community Development Block Grants, between 10 and 12 percent of the total grant was devoted to social services, which is consistent with the national aggregate data cited above. None of Tulsa's Formula Grant from the Urban Mass Transportation Administration was devoted to capital improvements, although nationally, 20 percent of these funds are spent for capital projects. Finally, in 1980-1982 Tulsa budgeted 51, 75, and 48 percent respectively of its General Revenue Sharing grants for capital improvements, again less than the national figure of 70 percent. Had Tulsa officials chosen to spend all of these grant funds for capital improvements, the 1982 decline in federal aid would have been 52.9 percent rather than 63.8 percent.

This 1982 reduction in funds for Tulsa is far greater than the national figures cited earlier. This is in part because Tulsa was awarded sizeable discretionary grants in 1981 for airport development and wastewater treatment facilities and in 1980 for highway construction and urban renewal. These grants were the result of several factors occurring simultaneously, namely, the implementation stage of local capital improvements planning, the availability of funds, and federal or state discretion with funds. Even where federal funds are distributed to the states by formula, the city is not guaranteed to receive the same amount or proportion of these moneys each year. For example, the State Department of Transportation and the State Health Department may pass through large grants for federal highways or wastewater treatment facilities intermittently, with large grants one year and small grants the next.

The 1982 New Federalism budget reductions suggested that Tulsa's prognosis for additional federal grants would be bleak. At that time, it appeared that when Tulsa's "turn" for a large dollar grant arrived again, the size of the pie would be smaller. This was the modus operandi for managing the New Federalism in 1982 and 1983. In fact, as we have seen, President Reagan's 1982 New Federalism budget for local capital improvement grants was reversed in 1983 and 1984.

## TULSA'S CAPITAL PROGRAM

Tulsa's capital needs were identified through a 1974-initiated systematic capital improvements policies and

procedures program that follows the well-accepted guidelines outlined by Moak and Killian in their manual,
Capital Programming and Capital Budgeting.[18]  The city
developed a capital project request form and implemented a
public official and citizen review process to compare and
rank competitive projects by predetermined criteria.  In
addition to the funded projects, Tulsa identified capital
projects expected to be funded during the 1982 to 1985
period as well as estimates of the capital needs for each
five-year period until the turn of the century.  This
"wish list" is constantly changing as new information and
needs are identified and assessed.

This capital program applies to the activities under
the city's direct control and is supposed to apply to the
trusts and authorities as well.  Yet where the trusts and
authorities have their own revenue base (such as the
Airport Authority) and ability to sell revenue bonds and
do not rely on the city for capital funding, capital
programming may not be coordinated through the city's
process.

Tulsa's 1981 capital wish list included $128 million
in projects that were funded by a five-year 1 percent
sales tax that began in 1981.  Unfunded projects on this
list for 1982 to 1985 amounted to $283 million for which
Tulsa hoped to identify new funding sources.

Capital outlay for each year differs substantially
from the aforementioned budget figures since funds are not
expended until construction of each project occurs.  The
annual capital expenditure budget of Tulsa and its various
trusts and authorities has been increasing at a rapid
pace.  In 1980 capital expenditures totalled $57.2 million
and increased to $65.3 million in 1981 but dropped to
$61.5 million in 1982.[19]  The 1981 increase reflects a
growing demand for an expanded public infrastructure and
the allocation of new sales tax funds for capital
improvements.

When the federal grants that Tulsa receives are
juxtaposed against this capital expenditure pattern,
federal aid, excluding interstate highway and public
housing modernization funds, equals 53.0 percent of 1980
capital expenditures and 54.1 percent of 1981 expenditures, but only 20.8 percent of the 1982 outlays.  This
illustrates the size of the federal commitment in
relationship to the total capital program.  The figures
changed substantially in 1982 when the federal funding
commitment declined by almost two-thirds, and the local
commitment increased due to the additional sales tax

revenue.

As a result of New Federalism budget cuts, the state's administration of federal funds, and Tulsa's own capital programming, Tulsa officials saw a substantial decline in federal aid for capital improvements in 1982. The 1980 five-year sales tax which was designed to enable the city to catch up on its capital needs was generating $20 to $30 million a year, leaving Tulsa in an overall "no loss" situation. In the aggregate, local revenue was replacing federal revenue, and the city was continuing to fall behind in funding its capital needs. This may have been the minimum impact, as 43 percent of Tulsa's capital expenditures from 1981 to 2000 were expected to be water and sewer projects while 45 percent were street and highway related. Both of these categories received considerable federal support during the last two decades. As a result of New Federalism policies, improvement or expansion of these facilities over the next two decades may receive less federal support than was once anticipated. Even with the increased federal gasoline tax, relatively few funds are expected to be spent for urban roads. Thus, the local funding problem is compounded by the fact that many municipalities like Tulsa did not pursue an optimum capital budget when subsidies were high and have belatedly recognized these pressing needs as available federal moneys are curtailed.

## TULSA'S REVENUE ALTERNATIVES

Local governments have limited options for reacting to New Federalism cutbacks. One alternative is to do nothing and fall further behind. Such a course of action will stunt the growth of newer cities and cause further economic deterioration in older cities. Another approach is to limit the growth of the city to the capacity of the existing infrastructure with currently funded improvements. With few exceptions, it is unlikely that elected officials, particularly in the conservative sun belt, will pursue policies to limit growth. Tulsa tried to develop such a program in the mid-1970s and all officials associated with the effort resigned or were removed from office. It appears that the political culture is not conducive to government policies that limit individual initiative. Thus, to say that Tulsa and similar cities can limit their appetite for capital improvements by limiting their growth, is wishful fancy. Likewise, the approach of placing a greater portion of the infrastructure burden on developers is also difficult for political reasons. There is a perception that to do so beyond certain "limits" will discourage continued growth.

Because Tulsa officials in 1982 were committed to continued rapid growth, the only feasible option was to look for new public revenue sources to offset the decline in federal subsidies. Conceptually, it is ideal to raise the needed funds for capital improvements from those who benefit from the improved municipal service. This entails matching the nature and life of the projects to the source of the financing. While optimal in theory, this strategy is not always available due to legal, constitutional and political constraints within state and municipal governments. Tulsa had five revenue sources that could be tapped for capital projects. One source was a sales tax increase, already employed in 1980. Other alternatives included a payroll tax, an occupation tax, a bond issue to be retired by an ad valorem tax increase, and an increase in water and sewer fees. These were the alternatives that were presented to city officials in 1982 as a working basis for managing the New Federalism. The authors of this paper, along with others, were involved in analyzing the city's revenue options for capital improvements.

Table 8.3 summarizes the level of tax or fee increase that would be required to overcome the loss of $20 million of annual federal aid that Tulsa realized by 1982 in comparison to its grant level in the late 1970s and in 1980. The citizens of Tulsa would be subject to one of these increases just to maintain a capital spending program equivalent to those of the 1970s, without any increases for catch-up or improvement. It was most likely that a combination of these revenue sources at lower levels would be employed, thus matching water and sewer fees, for example, to such capital improvements.

The payroll and occupation taxes will not be described further because they were dismissed by city officials as being politically infeasible in Oklahoma due to the need for enabling legislation. Not only does the State of Oklahoma share little revenue with its municipalities, but it has not been generous in giving urban Tulsa additional authority to govern its own affairs.

The first option is an additional 66 percent sales tax.[20] The advantages of a sales tax are that it is inexpensive to administer, it places a portion of the overall tax burden on nonresidents who also benefit from the capital improvements being funded, and nationally it has a high level of public support.[21] Because sales taxes

Table 8.3  Revenue Options for Tulsa

| Revenue Source | Rate Needed To Generate $20 Million Annually |
|---|---|
| Sales tax | $ .66 |
| Payroll | 0.50% |
| Occupation | 1.12% |
| Ad valorem | $1.57 per $1000 assessed value* |
| Water and sewer fees | 61.00% |

*This tax rate will generate $20 million at one time and will remain in effect for twenty years. It represents a 17.8% increase over the current city tax rate but only 2.1 percent of the total city/county/special district tax rate. In order to generate $100 million to be spent over five years and to be paid back by ad valorem taxes over 20 years, a tax rate of $7.85 (88.8 percent city tax increase or 8.3 percent total tax rate increase) will be needed. Finally, in order to generate $20 million annually, four $100 million bond issues, spaced five years apart would require a permanent ad valorem tax increase of $31.40 or 355 percent increase over the current city tax rate and 41.4 percent over the current total tax rate.

are usually paid in very small increments, they are not particularly onerous to most citizens. The disadvantages are that it can result in some displacement of economic activities if the new tax rate is not equivalent to that of the surrounding areas. Also, sales taxes are generally considered to be regressive, particularly when food and medicines are taxed. In Oklahoma, food is taxed while medicines are not. Tulsa's five-year 1 percent sales tax includes a rebate policy that is designed to overcome the regressive nature of the tax, although Tulsa's 2 percent local option sales tax (which is the principal revenue source for operating expenses) does not include such a provision. A sales tax increase in Oklahoma requires a majority vote of the people.

The second tax option is to increase ad valorem or property taxes. In Oklahoma this requires a citizen-approved bond issue since the state constitution prohibits city use of ad valorem taxes except to repay bond issues for capital improvements. The Oklahoma Constitutuion also requires three-fifths voter approval for streets and road bond issues and limits the total outstanding debt for such purposes to 10 percent of the taxable property in the city. Other public utility bond issues require a simple majority vote and have no ceiling.

Tulsa's outstanding debt covered by the ceiling was about $25 million, which was only 2 percent of the assessed valuation of $1.166 billion.[22] Estimating the decrease in federal subsidies to be $20 million per year from 1982 to 1986, the municipality could market a $100 million bond issue to maintain status quo through 1986. Assuming a twenty-year maturity, an average interest cost of 8 percent, and a constant principal and interest repayment pattern, the five-year decrease of $20 million per year would cost over $2 million per year if amortized over a twenty year period.[23] If the cutback in federal aid is permanent, which it was expected to be in 1982 and 1983, the city would have to market a $100 million bond issue every five years just to stay even with the 1981 subsidy. (The constitutional ceiling on streets and road bond issues could prevent this kind of debt even if the citizens of Tulsa were willing.) For every $100 million bond issue, the increase in ad valorem taxes would be 88.8 percent of the city's tax rate, but only 8.3 percent of the total city/county/special district tax rate. The 1981 city tax rate was $8.85 per $1,000 assessed value, while the total tax rate was $75.88 per $1,000.[24] In fifteen years, the taxpayers' burden would become constant with

four $100 million bond issues outstanding at one time,
increasing the 1981 city ad valorem tax burden by an
astronomical 355 percent but involving an <u>actual</u> tax
increase of 41.4 percent over the total current burden.
It is unlikely that any citizenry can be expected to vote
$100 million bond issues every five years, but this is
what it would take to manage the New Federalism as it
appeared in 1982.

A third option for Tulsa is to increase its water and
sewer fees. As a user fee, costs and benefits are closely
linked, making this option particularly attractive if it
is used only for water and sewer improvements. Its
administrative costs are particularly low because a
collection system already exists. The principal disadvantage is the difficulty in devising a fee structure that is
not regressive to small residential users and does not
discourage large industrial users from locating or
remaining within an area. Finally, some might argue with
the idea of using water and sewer revenues to pay for
other types of capital improvements.

There is no compelling reason why these funds must be
spent for the water and sewer system. Prior to 1981 such
revenue went into Tulsa's general fund to defray the cost
of government expenses beyond the water and sewer department. In fiscal year 1981, these fees generated $32.771
million for Tulsa.[25] A fee increase of 61 percent would
be needed to generate the additional annual $20 million in
revenue. Unlike the above tax increases, water and sewer
rates do not require a vote of the people.

TULSA'S CHOICES

With the strong leadership of the City Commission, in
1983 Tulsa citizens approved a variety of revenue-options
to pay for $123.3 million in capital improvements and to
make up for the 1982-projected New Federalism grant
reductions. The new revenue funded less than half of
Tulsa's $283 million captial budget identified for the
1982-1985 period.

General obligation bonds totaling $94.0 million were
approved by voters for capital improvements to the street,
sewer, and park systems. The ad valorem tax increase
required to retire the bonds was to be phased in over five
years (as the bond money is needed for capital projects).
In the fifth year, the tax increase would be 68.9 percent
of the city's 1981 tax rate but only 8.9 percent of the
total combined ad valorem tax rate.[26] Because a variety

of existing bonds were to be retired in the first five years, Tulsa's total ad valorem tax rate will not exceed the 1981 rate as a result of the new bonds.

In addition, the Tulsa Metropolitan Water Authority approved increased water and sewer rates for the metropolitan area. By 1985 the new rates reflected a 32.5 percent increase over then-existing rates. The authority planned to sell $29 million in revenue bonds to pay for one-half the cost of sewer improvements and all of the cost of planned water improvements.

In addition to the ad valorem taxes and the water and sewer fees that were increased in 1983 to fund capital improvements, Tulsa was already relying heavily upon the 1981-approved five-year sales tax increase. Before the sales tax expired in December 1985, it was reauthorized by the voters for an additional five years and projected to generate an additional $230 million for capital improvements.

## SUMMARY AND CONCLUSIONS

The concepts behind President Reagan's New Federalism suggest an ideal of solving local problems with local funds. The planning, control, and funding of improvements in municipal services was to be returned to state and local governments. The question addressed in this study is the actual effect of such a policy shift on local decisionmakers and taxpayers.

On the national level, we documented a substantial loss of funds in 1982, the year of first New Federalism budget. When the Office of Management and Budget prepared projections for fiscal year 1983 fund obligations, they anticipated an additional reduction of 11.3 percent (see the 1983 Catalogue of Federal Domestic Assistance). In fact, the funds expanded substantially in both 1983 and 1984, resulting in a net increase of 11.9 percent in federal funds available for local capital improvement grants between 1980 and 1984. Adjusted for inflation this reflects a 6.4 percent loss.

The case analysis of the City of Tulsa estimates a loss of more than $20 million per year in federal sub-sidies for capital improvements between 1980 and 1983. This initial loss in federal moneys meant that a one cent sales tax enacted in 1981 as a method of catching-up on capital improvements would only keep Tulsa in line with previous years' capital spending when federal subsidies were higher. Local officials were forced in 1983 to identify new funding sources to offset the loss in federal aid.

In 1982 and 1983 municipalities throughout the country began to review funding sources in the anticipation that President Reagan's New Federalism budget cuts marked the beginning of the permanent loss of federal aid. These cuts created a climate that forced local governments to begin the process of weaning themselves from the federal money machine. In 1983 Tulsa substantially increased water and sewer fees and approved a $94.3 million general obligation bond issue to meet capital expenditure plans with locally generated revenues. While these new revenues offset the aggregate reduction in federal aid, they did not generate an immediate net increase in capital funds. One positive result from the local perspective, however, was that Tulsa officials gained complete control over policymaking for capital projects in which no federal funds are involved. This is exactly the situation the New Federalism agenda sought.

In 1983 and 1984 the national picture of federal grants for capital projects improved substantially. The size of the federal pie grew again, making more aid available for cities such as Tulsa. Meanwhile, the climate of New Federalism continued, perhaps contributing to making Tulsa voters more amenable to new local taxes and higher fees for services. In 1985 Tulsa voters extended the extra one cent sales tax for five years to generate an additional $230.8 million for capital improvements. One cannot help but suggest that the rhetoric of New Federalism helped create the environment in which Tulsa voters did what was "expected" of them. The end result appears to be a net increase in the funds, local and federal, that are targeted for capital improvements in Tulsa.

Had the New Federalism budget cuts continued beyond the sizeable success of 1982, many cities including Tulsa would have been hard-pressed to keep capital fund budgets at viable levels. Tulsa had a low overall tax rate in 1982, making new taxes not particularly onerous. But what of the effect on the declining, highly taxed cities in the northeast and north central region of our country? With already high tax burdens and decaying infrastructures, the decline of federal subsidies could be catastrophic. In addition, the shift from federal subsidies to local taxes or fees results in a shift from progressive to regressive taxes. The exception would be funds raised by local payroll or income taxes that would closely parallel federal moneys. However, in most cases, the burden of capital expenditures in the older cities will fall on the ever-increasing proportion of poor which make up the population of these cities.

NOTES

1.   This research is part of a larger project that is reported in Michael D. Joehnk, et al., Alternative Funding Sources:   Meeting the Capital Expenditure Needs of the City of Tulsa (Tulsa, OK:   Office of Business Research, College of Business Administration, University of Tulsa, 1982).    This   project   was   funded   by   the   Economic Development Commission of the Metropolitan Tulsa Chamber of Commerce.

2.   By almost all standards, Tulsa would be characterized as a healthy city.   In the ten-year period of 1973 to 1982, Tulsa's population grew by 8.6 percent to approximately 368,000, while its net bonded debt per capita declined by 40.6 percent to a meager $227.   During the same time period, the per capita income grew by 179 percent   to   approximately   $15,000.    Although   Tulsa's unemployment rate was as much as half of the national average during most of this decade, the 1983 oil glut contributed to rising joblessness.   By the middle of 1983 Tulsa's unemployment rate rose to almost ten percent, still below the national figures.   Commercial construction permits in 1982 totaled $305 million, 164 percent more than a decade earlier.   Finally, 1982 bank deposits were $4,920 million, an increase of 174 percent over the 1973 figures.   See City of Tulsa, Oklahoma Annual Financial Report June 30, 1982, Auditing Department, City of Tulsa, pp. 68-69.

3.   George   E.   Peterson,   "Transmitting   the   Municipal Fiscal Squeeze to a New Generation of Taxpayers:   Pension Obligations and Capital Investment Needs," in Cities Under Stress:    The   Fiscal   Crises   of   Urban   America,   edited   by Robert   W.   Burchell   and   David   Listokin   (New   Brunswick, NJ:    The   Center   for   Urban   Policy   Research,   Rutgers,   The State University of New Jersey, 1981), pp. 249-276; "State and Local Government in Trouble," Business Week, October 26, 1981, pp. 135-181.

4.   Nancy Humphrey, George F. Peterson, and Peter Wilson, The Future of Cincinnati's Capital Plant (Washington, DC: The Urban Institute, 1979), p. xi.

5.   David A.  Grossman, The Future of New York City's Capital  Plant  (Washington,  DC:    The  Urban  Institute, 1979), p. 5.

6.   Pat Choate and Susan Walter, American in Ruins:   The Decaying   Infrastructure   (Durham,   NC:    Duke   Press Paperbacks, 1983), p. 7.

7.   George E. Peterson, "Capital Spending and Capital Obsolescence:   The Outlook for Cities" in The Fiscal Outlook for Cities, edited by Roy Bahl (Syracuse: Syracuse University Press, 1978), pp. 53-54; Michael J. White, "Capital Budgeting" in Essays in Public Finance and Financial Management:   State and Local Perspectives, edited by John E. Peterson and Catherine Lavigne Spain (Chatham, NJ:   Chatham House Publishers, Inc., 1980), pp. 42-52; Catherine H. Lovell, "Evolving Local Government Dependency," Public Administration Review 41 (January, 1981), pp. 189-202; and James W. Fossett, Federal Aid to Big Cities:   The Politics of Dependence (Washington, DC: The Brookings Institution, 1983), pp. 52-53.
8.   Rochelle L. Stanfield, "The Users May Have to Foot the Bill to Patch Crumbling Public Facilities," National Journal 14 (November 27, 1982), pp. 2016-2021.
9.   Grossman, New York City, p. 23.
10.   Humphrey, et al., Cincinnati, p. 44.
11.   Peter Wilson, The Future of Dallas's Capital Plant (Washington, DC:   The Urban Institute, 1980), p. 36.
12.   Jane Jacobs, The Death and Life of Great American Cities (New York:   Vintage, 1961); Herbert J. Gans, "The Failure of Urban Renewal:   A Critique and Some Proposals," Commentary 39 (April 1965), pp. 29-37; Charles N. Glabb and A. Theodore Brown, A History of Urban America, second edition (New York:   Macmillan Publishing Co., Inc., 1976), pp. 295-296.
13.   David B. Walker, Toward a Functioning Federalism (Cambridge, Mass.:   Winthrop Publishers, Inc., 1981), pp. 188, 201-204.
14.   David B. Walker, Albert J. Richter, and Cynthia Cates Bolella,   "The   First   Ten   Months:      Grants-in-Aid, Regulatory,   and   Other   Changes,"   Intergovernmental Perspective 8 (Winter 1982), p. 6.
15.   Walker, Toward, p. 7.
16.   See, U. S. Department of Housing and Urban Development Sixth Annual Report on Community Development Block Grants (Washington, DC:   U.S. Government Printing Office, 1981); Catherine Lovell, "Measuring the Effects of General Revenue Sharing:   Some Alternative Strategies Applied to 97 Cities," in Revenue Sharing, edited by David A. Caputo and Richard L. Cole (Lexington, MA:   Lexington Books, 1976), pp. 49-65; and Executive Office of the President, Office of Management and Budget, The 1982 Catalogue of Federal Domestic Assistance (Washington, DC:   The U.S. Government Printing Office, 1982), p. 521.

17. It should be noted that all of these federal grants are not awarded directly to the municipalities or controlled by elected city officials. Federal funds have a wide variety of avenues to reach an urban area. In the case of Tulsa, federal highway funds are spent by the State Department of Transportation and never cross the city's ledgers. Because Oklahoma's constitution does not allow local governments to sell revenue bonds but does allow public trust authorities to do so, a variety of urban activities are parcelled out. This includes the Inland Port of Catoosa, urban renewal, some park areas, mass transportation, airports, water and sewer, and public housing. In some cases, federal grants for these activities are received by the public trust authority, bypassing the City Commission and avoiding centralized control of capital expenditures.

18. Lennox L. Moak and Kathryn W. Killian, A Manual of Suggested Practice for the Preparation and Adoption of Capital Programs and Capital Budgets by Local Governments (Chicago: Municipal Finance Officers Association, 1964).

19. Letter from the Deputy City Auditor to the authors, December 2, 1982.

20. City of Tulsa, Oklahoma Annual Financial Report June 30, 1982, p. 30.

21. Advisory Commission on Intergovernmental Relations, 1982 Changing Public Attitudes on Governments and Taxes, S-11 (Washington, DC: U.S. Government Printing Office, 1982), p. 4.

22. Joehnk, et al., Alternative Funding Sources, p. 90.

23. For a detailed discussion of new municipal bonding devices, see, Randy Hamilton, "The World Turned Upside Down: The Contemporary Revolution in State and Local Government Capital Financing," Public Administration Review 43 (January/February, 1983), pp. 22-31.

24. City of Tulsa, Oklahoma Annual Financial Report, June 30, 1982, p. 63.

25. Ibid., p. 31.

26. Tulsa Tribune, May 9, 1983, p. 1B+.

# PART THREE

# The Policy Impacts
# of the New Federalism

The changes brought about by President Reagan's New Federalism impact not only on the operations and administration of state and local governments, but also on specific policy areas that must be administered at various levels within the federal system. Attempts to centralize or decentralize decision making in a particular policy area, for example, can have implications on the implementation of critical programs and projects. This section examines how initiatives under the New Federalism have impacted on three national policy areas.

Charles Moore and David Sink examine the changes that have occurred in the national housing policy since 1981. The authors outline the definitional, programmatic and funding changes in national housing policy that impact on conventional home buyers as well as selected groups such as the elderly. After outlining the overall changes in housing policy, Moore and Sink focus on the specific effects that these changes have had on one community-- Birmingham, Alabama.

Another policy area that has been dramatically affected by Reagan's New Federalism has been water pollution programming. With a fifty state overview, Pinky Wassenberg outlines the various approaches that the states have employed in order to cope with federal program cuts. Wassenberg also assesses the overall impacts of these actions on the national policy to reduce water pollution.

The final two chapters in this section focus on the Community Development Block Grant Programs affecting small and large communities. In Chapter 11, Dale Krane discusses the state takeover of the Small Cities Community

Development Block Grant program (SCCDBG) in the State of Mississippi. Krane reports that in spite of dire predictions to the contrary, the state has handled SCCDBG quite responsibly. Correspondingly, in her analysis of the Community Development Block Grant program in Houston, Susan MacManus points out that several programmatic and managerial changes which have resulted from the change to state control and budget cutbacks. In the case of Houston, budget cutbacks become the catalyst for significant programmatic and organizational reform.

# 9

## A Diminished Federal Role in Public and Assisted Housing Under Reagan

*Charles H. Moore*
*and David W. Sink*

As with other national government issues discussed in this volume, housing and community development represent a basic test of the priorities of the Reagan administration and the underlying values of our economic system as modified by government policies. That housing and community development should be a subject of significant governmental interest is not at issue except for those at each extreme of our ideological spectrum. Rather, the point is the nature and degree of governmental intervention.

Specifically, the Reagan administration has sought to diminish greatly the role of the federal government in housing and community development. In their concise review of federal housing policy, Struyk, Mayer, and Tuccillo conclude that the Reagan administration has sought to greatly reduce the federal government's role in housing assistance and finance, and decentralize to local governments the control over federal community development monies (1983, Chaps. 6-8, passim).

This chapter addresses the question of what impact federal housing policy has had or will have on local housing policy, on its constituents, and instrumentalities. Such a discussion addresses two major theses of the Reagan administration, namely that (1) reduction of the federal government's role will "unleash" the private sector, and (2) devolution of policy responsibility to state and local governments will stimulate new resources and policy innovations to meet local needs. In turn, achieving these goals would help target scarce resources and find more efficient and effective ways of delivering public goods such as housing and community development. With respect to housing for low and moderate income persons and families, have these theses been borne out?

To begin to answer these questions, we present a case study of housing needs and policy in Birmingham, Alabama. This case will focus on the interaction between recent federal policy changes, local housing needs and conditions, plus local intergovernmental policy responses to these circumstances. The nature of these interactions is the heart of the New Federalism story. The story is also an urgent message.

To set the context for this case study, a brief overview of recent federal housing developments and their philosophical underpinnings may be useful.

## CUTTING AT A QUICKENED PACE

Now in his second term, President Reagan has stepped up the systematic erosion of housing assistance, financing, and housing programs through the Community Development Block Grant (CDBG). During the first term, a shift from the more expensive construction of new units under Section 8 of the Housing and Community Development Act of 1974 to rehabilitation of existing units reflected an economy and efficiency objective. Opponents of such a shift argue that despite the increased cost, 750,000 new units are needed each year to make housing allowance programs workable and meet minimum needs (Dolbeare, 1984). Others contend a much higher number is necessary (Schechter, 1984).

Such a debate appears moot at this writing because the Reagan administration's FY 1986 budget for assisted housing proposes a two-year moratorium on any additional assistance for lower income, elderly, and handicapped housing. These cuts, from a FY 1985 appropriation of $10.8 billion in new budget authority to a proposed FY 1986 level of $499 million (a 95 percent reduction), would cap the total number of households assisted through Department of Housing and Urban Development (HUD) programs at approximately 4.1 million.

Beyond this moratorium, the Reagan administration has proposed a continuation of cuts in public housing operating subsidy funds, an end to the Farmers Home Administration housing programs, an end to the Urban Development Action Grant (UDAG) program including its housing provision, a 10 percent cut in CDBG funds, plus discontinuation of the CDBG loan-guarantee program and Section 312 home rehabilitation loans. Congress is certain to fight several of these measures, though likely will succeed in saving but a few, most likely UDAG.

To understand these budget reductions and program discontinuations, we must consider them in light of mounting budget deficits and Reagan's strategy to reduce them. Though the President's FY 1986 budget will be altered by Congress, as were previous budgets, Reagan has managed to shift the debate away from tax increases to spending reductions. In effect, he is using the deficit, presently estimated in excess of $200 billion per year, to convince Congress to further curtail government's domestic activities. Though Congress will include defense budget reductions in the deficit-fighting package, domestic program cuts will be deep. Along with the proposed end of revenue sharing, housing and community development curtailments will severely cripple efforts by cities such as Birmingham, Alabama, to upgrade housing stock.

PROGRAMMATIC TRENDS IN HOUSING ASSISTANCE

An overview of the Reagan administration policy on assisted housing may be discussed in five major topics:

1. a reduction of government's housing role and a desire to return public housing to the free market;
2. whether the housing problem of the poor is now primarily one of affordability or of housing quality;
3. the adequacy of "trickle down," the availability of standard housing for the poorest, and the number of units needed;
4. the extent of state and local control over CDBG housing programs;
5. drastic reductions in the federal housing budget as contrasted with tax expenditures.

In general, the administration has redirected U.S. housing policy toward the free market, attempting to inject supply-and-demand as the determinant of both the affordability and supply of housing for low- and moderate-income persons and families.

Free Market Public Housing

The Republican platform on which President Reagan ran successfully for reelection clearly stated its free-market orientation to replace subsidies with housing vouchers, public ownership with home ownership, and a housing policy with macroeconomic policy. Such an underlying philosophy may be detected in efforts to replace housing subsidies by modifying the Section 8 existing program with "family housing payments," or cash vouchers with which poor people could shop for their own housing. Based on the generally favorable experiences of the Experimental Housing Allowance Program (EHAP), the cash voucher plan is proposed to replace subsidized housing. Congress has authorized a small number of vouchers but has been reluctant to endorse a wholesale shift to the system.

In a highly controversial demonstration project, HUD has proposed to sell 2000 units of public housing to their tenants on the premise that home ownership will eventually lead to economic self-sufficiency. Such a program, in larger dimensions, may well threaten the already short supply of available housing and penalize the very poor with annual incomes under $5,000.

## Affordability or Quality

At the urging of the Reagan administration, Congress has de-emphasized new construction and substantial rehabilitation in favor of utilizing the existing stock of housing. The main justification for this radical shift is efficiency, because using existing housing is far cheaper than building new units. What is unclear is whether there is sufficient housing for low income nonrecipients in the absence of new construction programs (Struyk, Mayer, and Tuccillo, 1983).

Further, the administration has consistently argued that the housing problem of the poor is more one of being able to afford standard housing, rather than its availability. It is on this very basic issue that critics of Reagan's housing policies are most vocal. Both sides agree that housing quality in this country has markedly improved. Yet need for standard housing is great. The lowest, responsible current estimate of low income housing need (Report of the President's Commission on Housing, 1982) is that there are some 7.5 million renter households plus an undetermined number of the 10 million owners with incomes below 50 percent of median income who need housing assistance (Low Income Housing Information Service, 1983). "Emphasizing the affordability problem in program implementation, while structuring housing assistance to serve a fixed number of recipients using the existing stock, can be expected to have little impact on housing quality" (Struyk, Tuccillo, and Zais, 1982, p. 409).

## An Adequate Supply of Housing

President Reagan has proposed a sharp curtailment of federal housing programs by imposing a two-year moratorium on new, subsidized housing. Leading to this halt has been a steadily reduced number of housing starts in favor of a shift in emphasis to existing stock. In addition, he proposes dropping rental housing development grants, a new program to provide money to local governments to build rental housing.

An extension of the affordability-availability argument is the prevailing assumption of the administration that as new housing is built for middle- and upper-income home buyers that the oldest and lowest-cost housing becomes available to the poor. Given abandonments, condominum conversions, and annual losses in the supply of housing, it is estimated that the total annual requirement for new conventionally built housing would be 1.9 million units (Schechter, 1984, p. 43). New housing starts in the first Reagan administration have fallen far short of this need.

## Decentralized Control over CDBG

The Reagan administration has initiated a large number of measures to reduce federal control over the CDBG program (Struyk, Mayer, and Tuccillo, 1983 p. 81). In the process, the program has been vulnerable to charges that HUD has been less than diligent in enforcing grant rules, especially those that concern targeting of low- and moderate-income groups. Under President Carter, HUD stressed that projects should benefit the poor. As a result, the program shifted markedly toward housing rehabilitation and social services. Since Reagan took office, the emphasis has swung more toward economic development and public works projects.

As with any of the block grants, CDBG implementation has struggled with balancing local discretion and flexibility with adherence to the intent of the federal legislation. Through reduced HUD oversight and deemphasis on targeting strictly to low-income neighborhoods, the current administration appears to be severely altering the direction and intent of the CDBG program.

## Budget Cuts and Tax Expenditures

Reagan and the Republican party repeatedly have

reaffirmed their belief in homeownership by supporting federal tax deductibility of mortgage interest payments. The proportional importance of sharp reductions in the federal housing budget becomes apparent when contrasted with housing-related tax expenditures. Primarily consisting of homeowner mortgage interest, homeowner property tax deductions, deferral of capital gain on the sale of a home, and exclusion of capital gain on the sale of a home, tax expenditures will have increased by 100 percent (from $26.5 billion in 1980 to an estimated $53 billion by the end of 1985). Interestingly, currently proposed tax reform urges repeal all but one of the four major sources--property tax deductions. Any serious reform of this imbalance is probably unrealistic, given the political popularity in both the Congress and the administration in maintaining the homeowner mortage interest deduction.

## Federal Policy and Local Implementation

As a means of investigating the real and potential effects of Reagan's housing policy, we have examined assisted housing problems and programs in Birmingham. The case study that follows includes a review of demographic changes, unemployment and structural shifts in the economy, housing conditions, housing availability and construction activity, and public housing. The chapter concludes with a summary of the relationships between federal and local housing policy.

## THE SITE: BIRMINGHAM, ALABAMA

In the last 25 years, Birmingham has been, and still is, a city of transitions--demographic, economic, political. Well-known for its intra sigence and, therefore, its pivotal role in the civil rights movement, Birmingham now has a black mayor, Dr. Richard Arrington, and a majority black population. Located in the heart of the sunbelt, Birmingham grew as an industrial city. Known as the "Pittsburgh of the South," it developed because of the presence of all the natural resources necessary for the making of steel. As an industrial city in the Sunbelt, Birmingham has not been immune to major national demographic and economic forces. In fact, it is prototypical of Sunbelt urban distress.

The president's 1980 National Urban Policy Report developed a classification of the nation's larger cities by relative degree of community need (a taxonomy of urban distress) and population change (The President's National Urban Policy Report, 1980). Birmingham was in the "population decline--high degree of resident need" category in 1980. The Report summarizes the most needy declining large cities as "typically locked in, physically and fiscally, by their suburbs; have steadily lost middle income and non-minority residents; face diminished resources for public services; struggle to maintain an aging infrastructure; have a growing pool of unskilled workers; and suffer housing and commercial abandonment. In many cases employment has declined even more rapidly than population" (The President's Report, 1982).

Much of this general categorical description fits Birmingham, a description thought to be more accurate for frostbelt than sunbelt cities. Birmingham was a high need, distressed city even before the 1982-1983 recession sent city unemployment sky-rocketing. During the recession, Alabama suffered the second-highest unemployment rate among the 50 states for almost a year. Birmingham's official unemployment rate hit almost 17 percent and has declined currently to about 10 percent. (Estimating under-employed and discouraged workers puts the city's true unemployment rate between 15% and 20%.) Because of its heavy industrial infrastructure, Birmingham and its region now are suffering substantial structural unemployment. The city has experienced severe permanent job loss in the industrial and manufacturing sector of the local economy, which historically has provided over one-third of all unemployment in the city and its Metropolitan Statistical Area (MSA). Steel plant closings have had a serious ripple effect in the entire local economy.

Thus, Birmingham's economy--like the nation's--is in a long-term transition from a manufacturing base to something else. Allied health sciences anchored by the University of Alabama Medical School complex, and other hospitals, have grown. Local economic development efforts have focused on downtown central business district (CBD) renewal, with an emphasis on white-collar service occupations: education, finance, banking, insurance, government, communications, research.

Population trends affecting central cities nationally are also found in Birmingham. While the city's population between 1960 and 1980 decreased from 341,000 to 286,000, the actual number of households increased from 101,855 to 107,500 over the same time. Due to growth in one- and two-person elderly households, of female-headed households with children, and of young couples postponing having children, the average household size dropped from 3.3 persons in 1960 to 2.6 persons in 1980.

Most significant in this population change has been the increase in the number and proportion of low and moderate income households in the city. These households were those with an annual income in 1980 of $14,800 or below (80 percent of MSA median income). In 1970, there were 41,000 low and moderate income households in Birmingham, 39 percent of all households. In 1980, 61,490 households, 57 percent of all in Birmingham, were in the low and moderate income category. Prior to the severe recession, in ten years, the number of low and moderate income households (using HUD's CDBG definition) increased by almost 20,500. Of these 61,490 households, 52,322 are low income (below 50 percent of MSA median).

The increase of these households is attributable in large part to the growth of female-headed households and elderly households. In 1980, 36,884 of the 107,500 households in the city had a female head. Two-thirds of these (19,550) were elderly, and one-third (11,500) were families with children. As for the elderly, 30,000 of the 107,500 households had heads over age 65 (Birmingham Comprehensive Housing Plan, 1982; Rohling, 1985).

HOUSING CONDITIONS IN BIRMINGHAM

Among the major factors influencing housing and housing needs in Birmingham have been (1) city population changes, (2) the deteriorating condition of existing housing, (3) the availability of sound housing; and (4) the cost of housing.

Many low and moderate income households are forced to live in substandard housing because the availability of standard housing, even if it were affordable, is in short supply. Table 9.1 shows the results of a city survey in 1980 of the structural conditions of the housing stock (Birmingham Plan, 1982).

Structural Condition of All Units

Table 9.1 shows that the 20,700 low income families in need of moving out of substandard conditions, if they could afford it, would be competing for 2,908 units of housing in sound condition.

Birmingham's vacancy rate, particularly for rental units, is very low: between 2 percent and 3 percent over

Table 9.1  Structural Condition of All Units

|                                                          | Occupied Units | Vacant Units | Total Units |
|----------------------------------------------------------|---------------:|-------------:|------------:|
| Units in sound condition                                 |         75,025 |        2,908 |      77,935 |
| Units needing routine maintenance                        |         11,451 |          731 |      12,182 |
| Units substandard, but could be rehabilitated            |         20,095 |          820 |      20,915 |
| Units unfit, and could not be rehabilitated              |            929 |        2,187 |       3,114 |
| Total                                                    |        107,500 |        6,646 |     113,146 |

Structural Condition by Income

|                                                          | Low-Income | Others | Total   |
|----------------------------------------------------------|-----------:|-------:|--------:|
| Units in sound condition                                 |     25,857 | 52,078 |  77,935 |
| Units needing routine maintenance                        |      8,740 |  3,442 |  12,182 |
| Units substandard, but could be rehabilitated            |    18,140* |  2,775 |  20,915 |
| Units unfit, and could not be rehabilitated              |     2,567* |    547 |   3,114 |
| Total                                                    |     55,304 | 58,842 | 113,146 |

*The bottom line is that 20,707 low income households are currently living in substandard or unfit units-that's approximately 50,000 citizens locked into substandard conditions.  The magnitude of this problem is very serious, and is indeed not only a matter of public policy but also a matter of social justice.

the last decade. This is below the 5 percent average for central cities found in the President's 1980 National Urban Policy Report (pp. 5-15). This means there is not enough stock to "trickle down" to those searching for inexpensive shelter, and those in substandard conditions are further locked into their present situation.

## Cost of Housing

The average cost of a new single family home in Birmingham is approximately $70,000. Given current interest rates, a family would need an income above $40,000 a year to afford such a house. The 1980 census found the median Birmingham family annual income to be $15,235. Clearly the overwhelming majority of city residents do not earn sufficient income to purchase the average new home. Indeed, most families are unable to purchase existing homes at the 1982 average sales price of $52,000.

## Rehabilitation

Most of the 20,095 occupied housing units needing some level of rehabilitation are low income housing, either single family or duplex rental units. Providing sound housing for low income renters has been very difficult because their numbers have grown, condominium conversion has occurred, and some landlords have not responded to building code enforcement efforts or have simply "milked" the profits from housing or land while the shelter deteriorates (Birmingham and Alabama have no basic landlord--tenant legislation governing rights and duties of both parties).

## New Construction and Rental Assistance

There is an obvious need for additional housing of all types in the Birmingham market. The need is greater for low-income families, especially among renters. The Birmingham Comprehensive Housing Plan projects the need for 12,000 new housing units to meet the growth in the number of new households, 8,000 of which must be for low-income households (or some 800 units annually). In terms of rental assistance, in 1980 there were an estimated 20,000 households in need of rental assistance, a situation grown worse with the recession of 1982.
The private market has not responded to these

needs. Birmingham was tardy in using the inventory of federal housing programs (except for conventional public housing). But by the 1970s, while three of every four new housing units built were multifamily and duplex units, most of these were built under federally subsidized low-income programs such as Section 235, Section 8, Section 202, and conventional public housing. Two other measures of Birmingham's housing problems are germane.

## Conventional Public Housing

The Birmingham Housing Authority (BHA) provides 6,700 conventional public housing units and 1,700 Section 8 Certificates, thereby housing about 26,000 persons, 10 percent of Birmingham's population. These assisted housing programs are utilized at a 100 percent rate with thousands of families on growing waiting lists. In both public and Section 8 housing, attrition rates are dropping to less than 10 percent annually. The 3,600 families on the public housing waiting list, grown from 500 eligible families in 1980, increases at 1,200 families a year. The Section 8 waiting list, about 1,100 eligible families, has been closed since December 1981.

The average annual income of the 6,700 households in conventional public housing is just over $4,000. This is important, first, because BHA is housing low-income persons and, second, because of a Reagan administration initiative to sell the public housing stock to tenants or on the open market. Selling public housing has been an administration goal since 1981 for all 2,500 public housing authorities having 2.3 million families nationally. A demonstration program to do this is now underway. One question occurs (public philosophy aside): even assuming a subsidy for an initial purchase of a public housing unit, how will families--now owners--on an average $4,000 a year income be able to afford routine maintenance and utility bills--if, in fact, they are not displaced by developer speculation and conversion attempts?

## Homelessness

Homelessness has dramatically increased in Birmingham, and the nation, over the last four years. Joblessness has produced homelessness for some of the previously housed. Unemployment has put a larger pool of people and families at risk of homelessness. A close study of the homeless in Birmingham in 1984 (Moore, 1984) found an annual estimate of 12,000 homeless people in Birmingham, with almost 1,000 homeless persons on any given day and night during the year. These 12,085 homeless consist of (1) 3,257 chronic, traditionally homeless, (2) 400 persons deinstitutionalized from mental health facilities, and (3) 8,428 newly homeless. Startlingly, about 70 percent of the homeless are newly so, people suffering severe economic dislocation, over-whelmingly of local origin. Mostly these are local families, not chronic transients. The 1984 HUD national study of homelessness (for which Birmingham was one of the sample points) underestimated the severity of homelessness in Birmingham by better than 50 percent per day by almost entirely ignoring the category of the newly homeless. Even with recent efforts at emergency shelter, Birmingham falls short of having enough emergency shelter beds by more than 600 per night.

This is a quick, aggregate portrait of Birmingham's housing conditions and housing needs at present and for the near future. What are some public policy implications of this picture?

HOUSING POLICY: NATIONAL AND LOCAL

The city government of Birmingham became involved in housing during the 1970s, and then only under the stimulus of federal government programs--most importantly, the Community Development Block Grant (CDBG) begun by the Housing and Community Development Act of 1974. Prior to this time, the Birmingham Housing Authority (BHA) had been the only public provider of low-income housing. The city of Birmingham worked with BHA in the late 1960s and early 1970s as a partner in typical urban renewal projects (BHA had the redevelopment authority in its state charter), which resulted in the clearance and demolition of low-income housing on land for commercial reuse, but no replacement housing or new construction resulted from these project activities.

In the last decade, the cast of actors engaged in local housing policy has greatly increased. It now includes Mayor Richard Arrington, who has appointed two task forces on housing in the last three years; the City Community Development Department with its Office of Housing, which combines traditional planning staff and functions and building code inspection and enforcement services with newer CDBG-funded housing programs; the

Birmingham Housing Authority and its subsidiary, the Birmingham Housing Development Corporation; several multi- or single-neighborhood community development corporations; major interest groups like the Urban League (a housing counseling agency); Birmingham Area Board of Realtors; Greater Birmingham Association of Homebuilders; several urban mission agencies and churches and other non-profit agencies. The latter have sponsored individual housing developments (usually Section 202 assisted) or maintained emergency shelters. Recently, many have come together in two new organizations: (1) cooperative downtown ministries (CDM), which operates two emergency shelters and soup kitchens, and (2) Health Care for the Homeless Coalition, which successfully obtained a nationally competitive grant for a multi-year program for that purpose. The number of actors involved in housing policy has increased, along with the diversity of their efforts, in the last decade.

What has been accomplished in recent years in assisted housing, and what of the likely future? Table 9.2 adapted from the City's Comprehensive Housing Plan, summarizes the types of housing programs, both federal and local, that have been utilized in Birmingham in the last decade. Some commentary on Table 9.2 will point out important developments.

Table 9.2 provides telling clues to what is happening in local housing policy. First, out of twenty-seven different public program types or categories, only one-- Housing Code Enforcement--is financed only or pre- dominantly by local, own-source revenues. All of the other local programs (labeled Local CDBG) come from federal CDBG funds. Second, almost all the programs providing assistance to renters were federal in origin, not local.

Table 9.2 illustrates the depth of penetration of federal resources into a typical local housing market. It is clear in this case that severe reduction and/or termination of federal housing programs will throw the city back on its own resources, private and public. The general question is if Birmingham suffers from critical low and moderate income housing needs even with federal resources from previous decades, what will the housing needs become without federal resources? A brief summary of housing policy efforts is in order.

The City's CDBG program has spent about 40 percent of its annual entitlement since 1974 on public works--capital improvement projects that indirectly support residential

Table 9.2  Summary of Federal and Local Government Housing Programs in Birmingham

| Type of Program | Assistance | Tenure | Income Level | Assistance |
|---|---|---|---|---|
| Section 8 | New Construction Rehabilitation/ Financial | Renter | Low/Moderate | No New Construction or Substantial Rehabilitation Planned |
| Section 202 | New Construction | Renter | Low/Moderate | Estimated 51 Units Planned |
| Public Housing | New Construction/ Rehabilitation Financial | Renter | Low/Moderate | Limited to 110 Units Future Construction Questionable |
| Section 236 | New Construction/ Financial | Renter | Low/Moderate | Program Terminated |
| Section 221 (d) 3 | New Construction/ Rehabilitation | Renter | Low/Moderate | N/A |
| Section 221 (d) 4 | New Construction/ Rehabilitation | Renter | No Maximum Income Limits | N/A |
| Section 203 | New Construction/ Acquisition | Owner | No Maximum Income Limits | N/A |
| Federal National Mortgage Association | Acquisition/ New Construction | Owner | No Specific Limits | N/A |
| Government National Mortgage Association | Acquisition New Construction | Owner | No Specific Limits | N/A |
| Federal Home Loan Mortage Corporation | Acquisition/ New Construction | Owner | No Specific Limits | N/A |
| Section 234 | New Construction | Owner | No Maximum Income Limits | Planned for Termination |
| Section 235 | New Construction | Owner | Low/Moderate | Planned for Termination |
| Alabama Housing Finance Authority | Acquisitiion/ New Construction | Owner | Non-Low | 500 Units Annually |
| Urban Development Action Grant | New Construction | Owner | | Currently Planned for Termination although New Application Pending |
| Section 312 | Rehabilitation | Owner | Low/Moderate | Program Terminated |

## Birmingham Local CDBG-Funded Programs

| Program | Type | Beneficiary | Income | Units |
|---|---|---|---|---|
| Cash Rebate | Rehabilitation | Owner | Low/Moderate | 1,000 Units Annually |
| Rehabilitation Grant Program | Rehabilitation | Owner | Low/Moderate | Included Within Cash Rebate |
| Deferred Payment | Rehabilitation | Owner | Low/Moderate | 100 Units Annually |
| Non-Profit Sponsor | Rehabilitation | Owner/Renter | Low/Moderate | 12-15 Units Annually |
| Relocation-Rehab-Sell Program | Rehabilitation | Owner | Low/Moderate | 30-50 Units Annually |
| Spot Renewal Program | Rehabilitation | Owner | Low/Moderate | 12-15 Units Annually |
| Owner Occupant Variable Interest Rehabilitation Loan Program | Rehabilitation | Owner/Renter | Low/Moderate | 80 Units Annually |
| Renter-Rebate Program | Rehabilitation | Renter | Low/Moderate | 100 Units Annually |
| Multi-Family Loan Program | Rehabilitation | Renter | Low/Moderate | 100 Units Annually |
| Relocation Services | Financial | Owner/Renter | No Specific Limits | 100 Units Annually |
| Housing Counseling Program | Housing Counseling | Owner/Renter | No Specific Limits | N/A |
| Housing Code Enforcement | | Owner/Renter | No Specific Limits | N/A |

conditions. Another 40 percent has gone for direct housing assistance, mainly for rehabilitation of low- and moderate-income owner-occupied dwellings to prevent further deterioration of the housing stock. These expenditures have generally not been targeted to predominantly low-income neighborhoods, nor have they been coordinated with other expenditures like the city capital improvements budget. Still, about $4 million a year up to FY 1982 helped. Since the Reagan budget cuts began, Birmingham's annual share of CDBG funds has shrunk from $12 million to $8 million. The President's proposed FY 1986 budget calls for another 18 to 24 percent cut in CDBG funds to be ended in two years.

In the area of new construction assistance, Birmingham has, in the last four years, used two Urban Development Action Grants (UDAG) and a Section 235 set-aside to write down land or interest costs and thereby reduce the cost of new housing for several hundred moderate income residents. These successes, even though not targeted to low-income households, appear to be one-time-only occurrences.

Private, for-profit efforts to increase the supply of low- and moderate-income housing have not been significant. Private developers have recently linked up with public programs like Section 235 and UDAG to produce a modest number of single family dwellings for moderate income families. In a few cases, entrepreneurs have successfully developed low-income housing for the elderly using Section 8 and Section 202 federal assistance.

However, it has been the private, non-profit sector, primarily through local church sponsorship, and its ability to gain federal Section 202 and Section 8 assistance that has been the basis for a significant contribution to housing for the elderly in recent years. However, non-profit organizations have been even less successful in developing needed housing resources for other low-income households. A few projects have been successful in partnership with the Birmingham Housing Authority and Housing Development Corporation, but success does not match the growing need.

Ironically, Birmingham's Comprehensive Housing Plan anticipated recommending, when research on it was begun in 1980, maximum utilization of the entire array of federal housing programs. By the time the plan was finished in 1982, it concluded in part: "The decision of the federal government to reduce its role in housing, coupled with the limitations placed on the use of funds available to the city for housing purposes, indicates that the needs of a substantial number of the projected 22,000 households that will be in need of financial assistance by 1990 will be difficult to meet." The same conclusion is true for present and projected goals for new construction and rehabilitation. The city plan finishes by noting:

A number of existing activities and measures will continue to improve its housing conditions. Some of these include: the utilization of land write-downs to developers; modification of building codes; changes in zoning classifications; and the provision of public improvements, utilities, and services, as a means to facilitate housing construction. The latter, along with housing code enforcements, demolition assistance, and relocation assistance, should continue to be useful tools through which the city will be able to improve residential redevelopment and neighborhood revitalization.

What is significant about this list is that it enumerates the traditional tools cities have used to improve housing; all the activities come out of local, own-source revenues embodied in the city's general fund and capital improvements budgets, and there are no significant resources for investment in housing production or rehabilitation. The city is reduced to a low-cost, indirect (support activities) strategy of housing improvements without any federal resources.

## THE FUTURE FOR CITIES LIKE BIRMINGHAM

What impact has federal housing policy during the five years of the Reagan administration had on local housing policy? What is the future for housing programs in cities like Birmingham? In brief, the answer is grim: given the age, deterioration, and shortage of assisted and public housing in Birmingham, a future of cutbacks, moratoria, and recessions effectively halts local efforts to provide additional decent housing for those residents who cannot secure it on their own.

Birmingham, as an aging, central city with a declining tax base and increasingly dependent population, is not atypical. Many central MSA cities, especially in the northeast and midwest, are experiencing an absolute decline in the quality of living for their indigent populations. Higher than national average unemployment rates exacerbate the problem. Given these rates of unemployment, a major proportion of which is structural in nature and unlikely to be reduced in the short term, the demand for additional units of housing provided by the Birmingham Housing Authority through various federal programs will only increase. Faced with a two-year moratorium on assisted housing, and a local shift of CDBG monies (after percentage cuts) away from housing local housing policymakers can only apply "Bandaids" to deepening scars.

Birmingham and Alabama are revealing examples of several systemic verities: (1) states and locales have varying degrees of ability and wherewithal to replace federal housing budget cuts with local funds; (2) states and locales exhibit considerably different levels of willingness to make up the shortfall; and (3) Birmingham's local authorities are captives of a political subculture that discourages governmental aggressiveness in enlarging its role of providing human services such as housing. In short, not all states will assume devolution of policy discretion equally or well. Instead of bettering government by distributing decisionmaking authority closer to the people, the Reagan administration has threatened to impoverish government by delegating equal protection for adequate housing to levels of government not necessarily equipped to guarantee it.

The private sector, made up of real estate interests, developers and contractors, homebuilders, construction and management firms, is constrained by "return on investment" concerns from building and maintaining substantial amounts of low-cost housing for low- and moderate-income residents. Homebuilders and developers, even while talking about "downsizing" the average size of a new home and hoping for regulatory relief from the constrictions of local building codes and other housing quality standards, have not produced significant numbers of low-cost units without public subsidy for many years.

One option on the private sector side being explored in Birmingham and other cities is the formation of a pool of construction and mortgage money by a consortium of lenders--banks and savings and loan companies. The pool would serve two purposes: first spread the risks of default among the partners so that no one institution would be greatly exposed and, second, act as a revolving loan fund to encourage growth in participation. So far, lending agencies have not shown great enthusiasm for such an idea but may be encouraged with "seed money" from non-profit agencies such as churches and CDC's. Pursuing such options may become the only major direction to go in seeking sufficient resources for new construction and substantial rehabilitation.

Some states have active, well-endowed Housing Financing Agencies that can help pick up some of the slack of lost federal funds. Alabama is not such a state. The Alabama HFA provides relatively negligible amounts of funds, and, to date, none of the funds provided by it have been targeted to low- and moderate-income families.

Ultimately, the difficulty for cities like Birmingham is the question of initiating and sustaining subsidies for shelter costs for low- and moderate-income families. Even if construction and rehabilitation money could be found, the income structure of the population shows affordability is also a problem. A shelter cost subsidy program (no matter how structured) is a long-term, open-ended proposition. Throwing cities back on their own resources, at a time of multiple constraints on urban fiscal policy, renders the likelihood of cities substituting their own shelter subsidy programs for a terminated Section 8 or PHA subsidy extremely problematic. The states--particularly the poorer ones--will be of only limited help. Many cities and states will search for alternate sources of housing funds, but the search now is "ad hoc" in character and less systematic in approaching the totality of housing needs in the nation and the nation's cities.

224

REFERENCES

Birmingham Housing Authority. (1982). Birmingham comprehensive housing plan, 1982.

Dolbeare, C.N. (1984). Treasury tax proposals pose dilemma for housing advocates. Unpublished manuscript.

Downs, A. (1983). The coming crunch in rental housing. The Annals of the American Academy of Political and Social Science, 465: 76-85.

Easterbrook, G. (1983, July). Examining a media myth. The Atlantic, pp. 10, 14, 16, 20, 24.

Grigsby, W.G. & Corl, T.C. (1983). Declining neighborhoods: problem or opportunity? The Annals of the American Academy of Political and Social Science, 465: 86-97.

Hartman, C. (1984). Shelter and community. Society, 21, 18-27.

Kain, J.F. (1983). America's persistent housing crises: errors in analysis and policy. The Annals of the American Academy of Political and Social Science, 465, 136-148.

Kinsley, M. (1983, January). Who's the fairest of them all? Harper's, 9-11.

Low Income Housing Information Service. (1983, February). The 1984 Reagan budget and low income housing. Washington, D.C.: Low Income Housing Coalition.

Nenno, M.K. (1984). Housing allowances are not enough. Society, 21: 54-57.

Office of the President of the United States. (1980). National urban policy report. Washington, D.C.: U.S. Government Printing Office.

Peirce, N.R. & Guskind, R. (1985, January 5). Reagan budget cutters eye community development block grant program on its 10th birthday. National Journal, pp. 12-16.

President's Commission on Housing. (1982). The report of the President's commission on housing. Washington, D.C.: U.S. Government Printing Office.

Rohling, A. (1985). Basic material needs. Birmingham, AL: Community Resource Associates.

Rothman, R. (1984, February 4). Expanded voucher program sought for housing the poor. Congressional Quarterly Weekly, p. 34.

Schechter, H.B. (1984). Closing the gap between need and provision. Society, 21: 40-47.

Sternlieb, G. & Hughes, J.W. (1983). Housing the poor in a postshelter society. The Annals of the American Academy of Political and Social Science, 465: 109-122.

Sternlieb, G. & Hughes, J.W. (1984). Structuring the future. Society, 21: 28-34.

Struyk, R.J., Mayer, N., & Tuccillo, J.A. (1983). Federal housing policy at president Reagan's midterm. Washington, D.C.: The Urban Institute.

Struyk, R.J., Tuccillo, J.A., & Zais, J.P. (1982). Housing and community development. In J.L. Palmer & I.V. Sawhill (Eds.) The Reagan experiment. Washington, D.C.: The Urban Institute.

U.S. Congress. House. (1984). Committee on Banking, Finance, and Urban Affairs. Making affordable housing a reality. Hearing before a subcommittee of the House Committee on Banking, Finance, and Urban Affairs, 98th Cong., 2nd sess., 1984.

U.S. Congress. House. (1984). Committee on Banking, Finance, and Urban Affairs. Urban development action grants. Hearing before a subcommittee of the House Committee on Banking, Finance, and Urban Affairs, 98th Cong., 2nd sess., 1984.

Wiesenthal, E. (1985, May 1). Tenants, critics eye HUD housing sale. Public Administration Times, 1: 5.

# 10

## State Responses to Reductions in Federal Funds: Section 106 of the Federal Water Pollution Control Act Amendments of 1972

*Pinky S. Wassenberg*

INTRODUCTION

Many contemporary federal environmental policies created during the 1970s were designed to operate within an intergovernmental framework. Congress delegated the responsibility for the formulation of pollution abatement regulations to the United States Environmental Protection Agency (EPA). The EPA, in turn, could pass the authority to implement these programs to the state governments. This delegation of implementation authority to the states was accompanied by federal funds to offset, at least partially, the costs of state participation.

Since 1981, the Reagan administration has emphasized the desirability of, and the need for, extensive state participation in the implementation of federal environmental programs (see Portney, 1984; Vig and Kraft, 1984). However, it has also reduced the amount of federal funds available to participant states to offset program-related costs Council on Environmental Quality (CEQ), 1982. For example, under the Reagan administration water quality funds were reduced by 42 percent and air quality funds by 19 percent from 1981 through 1983 (Portney, 1984: p. 148).

This study examines this aspect of the Reagan administration's New Federalism by focusing on state government responses to reductions in federal aid under the Federal Water Pollution Control Act Amendments of 1972. First, a brief history of intergovernmental relations in the area of water pollution policy is presented, including a discussion of the major features of the 1972 amendments. Second, the patterns of state and federal funding under the act are described. Finally, state responses to reductions in federal funding are analyzed.

## INTERGOVERNMENTAL RELATIONS AND WATER POLLUTION POLICY

The history of water pollution control policy in the United States can be divided into two eras, pre-1972 and post-1972, distinguished by the enactment of the landmark 1972 amendments. Although there had been a trend toward increasing federal power, prior to 1972, state governments were the primary architects and implementers of water pollution control policy. After 1972, the federal Environmental Protection Agency (EPA) assumed primacy.

### The Pre-1972 Era

Federal entry into the arena of water pollution regulation occurred in 1948 with the enactment of the first Federal Water Pollution Control Act (FWPCA) (62 Stat. 1155). Initially, the federal role was limited to support of and assistance to the states (Senate Report, 1972: p. 3669). This support included financial, technical, and planning assistance to state governments. The federal government's enforcement authority, granted in 1956 amendments, was limited to cases of interstate pollution (70 Stat. 498).

In 1965, the federal role was increased to include oversight of state pollution control regulations. The 1965 amendments ordered states to develop water quality standards and submit these standards to the newly created Federal Water Pollution Control Authority (79 Stat. 903). States retained the primary authority for the development and enforcement of these standards (Baldwin, 1969; Wenner, 1971).

Growing dissatisfaction with this arrangement combined with political conditions in the early 1970s to provide impetus for a landmark restructuring of the entire FWPCA in the 1972 amendments (Lieber, 1975). Complaints about the long, complex federal enforcement process and the inadequacy of the pre1972 water quality standards were accentuated by the publication of government and independent research indicating that both the incidence and severity of water pollution in the nation were increasing (CEQ, 1973: p. 168; Lieber, 1975: pp. 21-23). Lieber argues that these perceived problems with the pre-1972 FWPCA were aggravated by the confluence of three political factors (pp. 15-19). The early 1970s saw the birth and growth of environmentalist interest groups in the national political arena. Democratic presidential candidates, with their sights set on the 1972 campaign, were interested in capitalizing on popular concerns by emphasizing environmental issues. In addition, the creation of the EPA in 1970 provided a bureaucratic constituency favoring reform of existing pollution control laws to increase its own jurisdiction and confirm its centrality to national pollution policy.

Some critics of the pre-1972 FWPCA blamed the states for the increase in water pollution since the states had the responsibility for development and initial enforcement of the water quality standards. Advocates of an increased federal role in environmental policy argued that the continuing degradation of national waters was evidence of the states' inability to carry out their responsibilities (Zwick and Benstock, 1971; Dworsky, 1972). This inability was linked to the states' lack of financial and technical resources. Additionally, it was argued that states were unwilling to set stringent water quality standards for fear of losing polluting industries to states with looser standards. Supporters of the states argued that their programs had not been in existence long enough to have an impact and that the lack of financial and technical resources could be remedied through increased federal support (Lieber, 1975: pp. 36-37; Jolly, 1982: p. 116).

## The 1972 Amendments

The 1972 amendments radically altered the structure and content of national water pollution control efforts. The changes introduced by the 1972 amendments can be divided into three groups: 1) changes in policy goals, 2) changes in programmatic structure, and 3) changes in the division of authority between the federal government and the states. The pre-1972 goal was to ensure that national waters remained sufficiently unpolluted to conform with their major use classifications. These classifications were made through a two-step process. First, all watercourses were categorized according to their major use, for example, industrial, recreational, agricultural. Then discharge limitations were calculated to ensure that a body of water would continue to be useful for its designated purpose (CEQ 1973). For example, more pollutants could be dumped into a watercourse designated for industrial use than could be dumped into water used for recreation. Classification was difficult, controversial, and time-consuming, creating an obstacle to implementation. Also, it was argued that these standards implied a right to pollute permitting continued degredation of national waters (Senate Report 1972, p. 3675).

The 1972 amendments adopt a more ambitious set of goals:

1. it is the national goal that the discharge of pollutants into the navigable waters be eliminated by 1985;
2. it is the national goal that wherever attainable, an interim goal of water quality which provides for the protection and propagation of fish, shell fish, and wildlife and provides for recreation in and on the water be achieved by July 1, 1983 (P. L. 92-500, §101(a)).

These new goals were to be achieved by the use of strict effluent limitations in addition to existing water quality standards (Senate Report, 1972: p. 3675).

The programmatic structure of the 1972 amendments concentrated pollution control activities into two major programs--the nonpoint source pollution program (Section 208) and the point source pollution program (Section 402). Section 208 mandates a control program designed to eliminate pollution that comes from sources which are difficult to isolate and identify individually. These are called nonpoint sources. Agricultural runoff, for example, is a non point source. The second program, Section 402, is the point source pollution program. This program regulates discharges that come from identifiable points, such as factories or municipal sewage treatment outlets. The division of authority between the federal government and the states changed in the 1972 amendments. This change, however, was not apparent from the statement of goals at the beginning of the 1972 statute. Among those goals was the following:

It is the policy of the Congress to recognize, preserve, and protect the primary responsibilities and rights of States to prevent, reduce, and eliminate polution ... (P. L. 92-500, §101(b)).

The body of the statute sets up quite a different division of authority. The 1972 amendments shift primary authority for the development and enforcement of pollution

regulations away from the states to the federal government, specifically, the EPA (P. L. 92-500, §§301, 302,
306-308, 402, 403). States are given the opportunity to
obtain the authority to implement these uniform national
standards set by the EPA, but the EPA retains authority to
review and, if necessary, revoke state use of that
authority. In the absence of state participation, the EPA
enforces the regulations within the state.

Lieber explains that the apparent contradictions
between the goal quoted above and the structure of the act
were the result of an attempt to placate two conflicting
sets of demands (1975). As discussed earlier, dissatisfaction with the results of existing state programs made
it unlikely that state primacy would continue. However,
the move to federal control was not without opposition.
President Nixon was pursuing his New Federalism,
advocating a return of regulatory responsibility to the
states. State governments strongly opposed the change in
the division of authority. Also, it was hoped that
implementation would occur more quickly if the work could
be spread out to state governments. Obviously, the forces
favoring centralization had more success than did those
favoring retention of state control.

Even though the FWPCA was scheduled for reauthorization in 1982, the Reagan administration has not
presented a proposal for major revision of the act
(Portney, 1984: p. 150). Reagan administration efforts
under the FWPCA have focused on encouraging states to
apply for the authority to implement specific programs
under the act while at the same time persuading Congress
to reduce the funds available to reimburse states for
their participation in these programs (CEQ, 1982).

## Federal Funding Under the 1972 Amendments

Two types of federal assistance are available to
states under the 1972 amendments. States are eligible for
grants to finance the construction of sewage treatment
facilities required to meet the water quality and effluent
standards set by the EPA (§205). States also receive
funds under Section 106 to reimburse them for "the
reasonable costs ... of developing and carrying out a
pollution control program ..." (§106). These Section 106
funds are the focus of this study. Table 10.1 lists total
state and federal expenditures under Section 106 for
fiscal years 1975 through 1983.

As illustrated by Table 10.1, the total amount

Table 10.1   Total State and Federal Section 6 Expenditures for Fiscal Years 1975–1983*

| Year | Federal | State |
|------|---------|-------|
| 1975 | $39,232,581 | $62,569,291 |
| 1976 | 40,502,900 | 65,719,215 |
| 1977 | 40,502,900 | 57,324,569 |
| 1978 | 42,447,000 | 65,671,620 |
| 1979 | 42,447,000 | 71,288,634 |
| 1980 | 39,480,000 | 67,933,359 |
| 1981 | 41,460,000 | 67,253,039 |
| 1982 | 41,460,000 | 72,234,283 |
| 1983 | 40,257,000 | 76,936,540 |

*Unpublished data provided by the United States Environmental Protection Agency

available to states under Section 106 increased slightly from 1975 ($39,232,581) through 1983 ($40,257,000). This apparent $1,024,419 increase only represents a 3 percent increase over a period of eight years during which the inflation rate for any one year was greater than three percent. When these dollar figures are adjusted for inflation, it becomes apparent that from 1975 through 1983 there was, in fact, a 49 percent reduction in funds made available under the program.

Aggregate state expenditures under the program also appear to have increased from 1975 through 1983. The total for state government expenditures for Section 106 increased 23 percent ($62,569,291) during those eight years. In reality, however, aggregate state expenditures decreased by 38 percent when inflation is taken into account. One cannot generalize about individual state responses to reductions in federal funds by examining aggregate figures. State responses to the incremental reduction in federal funds under Section 106 of the FWPCA are examined through the use of data for each state in the following section.

STATE RESPONSE TO SECTION 106 FUNDING CUTS

The comparative state policy analysis literature indicates that the availability of federal funds acts as an incentive for the development of state policies (Morgan and Lyons, 1975; Strouse and Jones, 1974; Welch and Thompson, 1980). Klingman presents a framework for the analysis of state responses to reductions in federal funds in his analysis of block grant funding (1984). He suggests three possible state reactions: 1) states may choose to withdraw from participation in the federal program; 2) states may choose to continue participation but scale back their efforts under the program in proportion to the reduction in federal funding; or 3) states may choose to continue participation and existing levels of operation by replacing the lost federal funds with funds from state sources.

State responses to the reduction in Section 106 funds from the federal government have been examined to ascertain which of the three responses appears dominant. Data on federal and state expenditures for forty-three of the fifty states were available. (These forty-three states are listed in Table 10.2 according to their EPA region). Therefore, it should not be assumed that the results of this analysis apply to all fifty states.

Only two programs under the FWPCA make state participation in their implementation optional--the point
source pollution program (§402) and the dredge-and-fill
program (§404). From 1972 through 1984, thirty-five
states applied for and received program authority under
Section 402 (Wassenberg, 1985). No state has withdrawn
from participation in this program. From 1972 through
1983, no state had received program authority under
Section 404. Therefore, Klingman's first suggested state
reaction does not seem to fit: states have not withdrawn
from participation in federal water pollution control
programs due to a reduction in Section 106 funds.

The second possibility is that states are continuing
participation and replacing the lost federal funds with
funds of their own. The data on state and federal expenditure levels under Section 106 have been analyzed to
determine whether this is a credible description of state
responses. This analysis involved examining the
correlation (Pearsons r) between the federal and the state
expenditures for each fiscal year from 1975 through
1983. If states are replacing lost federal funds with
own-source funding, these correlations should be negative
indicating that as the level of federal funding decreased,
the level of state funding increased. The correlation
coefficients representing the relationship between state
and federal funding levels for each fiscal year are
presented in Table 10.3. Throughout the nine-year period,
the relationship between federal and state 106 expenditures remains strong and direct. The lowest correlation
occurs for fiscal year 1983 (r = .56). Therefore, states
do not appear to be reacting to a decrease in federal
expenditures under Section 106 by increasing their own-
source contributions to the program.

The process of elimination leaves us with the
proposition that state governments are reacting to reduced
federal funding by remaining in the programs and adjusting
state operations to meet the reductions in available
funds.

A second avenue of analysis was pursued to determine
whether the pattern suggested by the yearly correlations
persists when one examines the relationship between state
and federal expenditures over multi-year periods. There
could be a lag-time between the reduction in federal funds
and observable state reactions. The changes in levels of
state and federal funding were computed for: 1) the
period 1975 through 1983 (all years in the dataset); 2)
1975 through 1981 (the years prior to the first Reagan

Table 10.2  States Included in the Analysis Listed by EPA Region

REGION I
Connecticut
Maine
Massachusetts
New Hampshire
Rhode Island
Vermont

REGION II
New Jersey
New York

REGION III
Delaware
Maryland
Pennsylvania
West Virginia

REGION IV
Alabama
Florida
Georgia
Kentucky
Mississippi
North Carolina
South Carolina
Tennessee

REGION V
Illinois
Indiana
Michigan
Minnesota
Ohio
Wisconsin

REGION VI
Arkansas
Louisiana
New Mexico
Texas

REGION VII
Iowa
Kansas
Missouri
Nebraska

REGION VIII
Colorado
Montana
North Dakota
South Dakota
Utah
Wyoming

REGION IX
Arizona
Hawaii
Nevada

Table 10.3  Correlations Between State and Federal Section 106 Expenditures
Fiscal Years 1975-1983

| Year | r* |
|------|------|
| 1975 | .83 |
| 1976 | .85 |
| 1977 | .76 |
| 1978 | .74 |
| 1979 | .78 |
| 1980 | .65 |
| 1981 | .66 |
| 1982 | .70 |
| 1983 | .56 |

*All correlations listed are significant at the .001 level. However, since
the dataset represents the entire population being analyzed, technically
statistical significance is not a consideration. However, the practice in the
literature at this time is to include it for reference.

administration budget); and 3) 1982 through 1983 (the first two Reagan administration budget years). For each period, change in levels of both state and federal expenditures was defined as the increase or decrease in dollar amounts from the first year of the period through the last year. Correlations between the change in state levels and the change in federal levels were computed for each period. Again, if states are resorting to replacement funding, negative correlations should be produced because as the level of federal spending declined, the level of states' spending would increase. These figures are reported in Table 10.4

The only period for which a notable correlation is found is from 1975 through 1981, the pre-Reagan period. During that period, there was a modest positive relationship (r = .32) between changes in levels of federal and state expenditures under Section 106. During the Reagan administration years and over the entire nine-year period, no such relationship is evident. The correlations, while minute, remain positive, suggesting that the conclusion from the year-by-year analysis holds when the data is grouped into multi-year periods. States do not appear to be replacing lost federal funds with increased state expenditures under the program. In general, the reduction in federal funds for the program has been matched with a reduction in state expenditures, though the aggregate figures indicate that the overall reduction in state funds from 1975 through 1983 (38 percent) has been less than the reduction in federal funds (49 percent). This indicates that states are absorbing an increasing proportion of the costs of the implementation of federally designed and mandated water pollution control programs.

## STATE CHARACTERISTICS AND THE LEVEL OF FEDERAL 106 FUNDING

The administrator of the EPA is instructed to divide the total amount of Sectuib 106 money allocated by Congress in a given year among the states according to the population of the state, the severity of the water polution problem within a state, and the amount of state funds allocated to water pollution control (106(f)). The next question addressed was whether changes in the level of Section 106 funding received by a state could be related to possible indicators of these three characteristics. Are all states being hit equally by the reduction in federal funds, or are states that meet these statutory

Table 10.4 Correlations Between Changes in State and Federal Expenditures
Under Section 106

| YEARS | r | p* |
|-------|-----|-----|
| 1975-1981 | .32 | .02 |
| 1982-1983 | .09 | .31 |
| 1975-1983 | .01 | .49 |

*Because the dataset represents the entire population being analyzed,
technically statistical significance is not a consideration. However, the
practice in the literature at this time is to include it for reference.

criteria being hit less hard than the other states?

The data analysis presented in this section is an exploratory rather than a confirmatory analysis. It does not proceed from theoretically derived hypotheses. Rather, it is an attempt to discover whether the factors determining the amount of aid received by a state change from the pre-Reagan years to the first two years of the Reagan administration and whether these factors are similar to the factors specified in Section 106 of the 1972 amendments.[1]

The impact of four independent variables was explored: 1) state expenditures for Section 106 during the period for which the dependent variable was measured; 2) state population density in 1970; 3) the year in which the state passed its first water pollution control statute; and 4) the average yearly state government revenue from state sources during the period for which the dependent variable was measured. State Section 106 expenditures indicate the level of state financial commitment to the program and, as discussed above, are related to the level of federal funding received by the states in each year included in the dataset. A change in one produces a change in the same direction in the other. State population density is included as an indicator of the severity of water pollution within the state. Areas of population concentration are major contributors to both point and nonpoint source pollution (CEQ, 1976: p. 15). State commitment to water quality control is also indicated by the number of years the state's major pollution control law has been in effect. The year the major water pollution control law was enacted in each state was reported by Wenner (1971).

Finally, the amount of state revenue from state sources was included because two contradictory arguments can be made for expecting a relationship between this variable and a change in the level of federal funds received by a state. First, an economically healthy state should be better able to afford to maintain its participation in federal regulatory programs than would a state with financial problems. Alternatively, the EPA could assume that economically pressed state governments were in greater need of federal assistance to carry out the nonoptional state programs under the FWPCA. Either way, there should be a relationship between state revenue levels and federal aid. The average amount of state revenue for each state was computed for each of the three periods examined (1975-1981, 1982-1983, and 1975-1983).

Table 10.5 presents the results of the three regressional models. The four variables discussed above explained 46 percent of the variation in change in the level of federal aid received during the period 1975-1981. The two most powerful independent variables in the model are the year in which the state's first water pollution control law was passed (beta = -.65) and the state's population density (beta = -.63). The older the state's water pollution law, the smaller the cut in federal aid to that state. This suggests that states with older, established water pollution control programs maintained higher levels of federal aid under Section 106 during the pre-Reagan years. The lower the density of the population, the higher the state's level of federal funding. This observation is difficult to reconcile with the statutory mandate to give greater consideration to states with severe pollution problems given the relationship between urban concentration and the severity of water pollution.

The next most powerful independent variable was the average state revenue from state sources for the period (beta = .45), indicating that the higher the state revenue, the higher the level of federal funding for the state. The alternative contention that the EPA would protect financially strapped states in need of funds to carry out their programs is not supported by the evidence. The least powerful explanator of the four considered is the actual level of state Section 106 expenditures (beta = .37). The direct relationship between level of state funding and level of federal funding remains even when controls are added to the model but it is not the greatest determinant of the level of federal funding received.

The second linear model examined the relationship between these four dependent variables and the level of federal Section 106 funding received by the states during the first two Reagan administration budget years, 1982-1983. None of the four independent variables proved useful in explaining the level of federal funding received by the states during this period. All four variables combined accounted for only 10 percent of the variation in federal funding.

The third model tested the relationship between the four variables and the level of federal funding during the entire period covered in the dataset, 1975-1983. Only one variable proved to be a strong determinant of funding over this extended period of time--population density (beta = -.59). The relationship with the dependent variable remained inverse. Population density it explained 8

Table 10.5  Results of Multiple Regressions

1975-1981

| Independent Variables | B | Beta | p* |
|---|---|---|---|
| Population density | - 569.36 | -.63 | .002 |
| State 106 spending | .67 | .37 | .013 |
| Average own-source revenue | 1110.83 | .45 | .004 |
| Year of major law | -8296.09 | -.65 | .001 |

$R^2$ = .46    p =  .001*

1982 - 1983

| Independent Variables | B | Beta | p* |
|---|---|---|---|
| Population density | - 761.25 | -.38 | .125 |
| State 106 spending | .67 | .10 | .597 |
| Average own-source revenue | 54.47 | .01 | .959 |
| Year of major law | -4488.92 | .16 | .500 |

$R^2$ = .10    p = .557*

1975-1983

| Independent Variables | B | Beta | p* |
|---|---|---|---|
| Population density | -1282.96 | -.59 | .015 |
| State 106 spending | -.51 | -.12 | .472 |
| Average own-source revenue | 1257.38 | .21 | .237 |
| Year of major law | -11630.76 | -.38 | .095 |

$R^2$ = .21    p = .142*

*Because the dataset represents the entire population, technically statistical significance is not a consideration. However, the practice in the literature at this point is to include it for reference.

percent of the variation in the level of federal funding.

Thus, the four independent variables that survived the initial analysis proved to be reasonably strong determinants of the level of federal funding received by a state only for the pre-Reagan administration era. These variables appear to be logical indicators of the three factors that the FWPCA requires the EPA to take into consideration when dividing the available Section 106 moneys among the state; yet, after 1981, they seem to be unrelated to the level of funding actually received by the states.

## CONCLUSIONS

The Reagan administration has not made a major legislative attempt to alter the structure of the existing FWPCA even though that statute sets up a division of authority between the state and federal government that is clearly antithetical to the aministration's New Federalism initiatives. The existing FWPCA places the federal EPA in a clearly dominant role and centralizes both standard-setting and enforcement powers at the federal level.

The Reagan administration has advocated returning this authority to the states yet has also advocated decreasing the amount of federal support for the state efforts. This returns federal water pollution control strategy to the pre-1972 era in which state governments were the primary architects and enforcers of pollution control standards. The federal government is relegated to providing limited financial and technical aid for those efforts.

The administration may have achieved the decentralization it desires without waging a battle in Congress to alter the intergovernmental distribution of powers under the FWPCA. In the previous section, an examination of the correlations between levels of state and federal spending under Section 106 of the FWPCA indicate that states are not responding to reduced levels of federal aid by increasing spending from state sources. Neither are they abdicating the responsibility for the administration of federal programs under the FWPCA. That leaves the logical conclusion that states are attempting to administer existing programs on decreasing budgets. They must either reduce their implementation efforts to fit within a tighter budget, or they must increase their efficiency so that they can pursue the same level of implementation with fewer resources.

A recent survey of twenty state governments indicates that state refusal to engage in replacement funding is not limited to the Section 106 program (Lester, 1985). Lester asked state officials to indicate whether their states were providing replacement funding to offset recent reductions in federal funds for a number of environmental programs. Only seven of the twenty states that responded to his survey indicated that they engaged in some replacement funding (p. 13). Most replacement funding occurred in programs designed to control the disposal of hazardous wastes (p. 14). Three states indicated that legislation to authorize additional state funding for environmental programs was pending in the state legislatures.

Lester points out that his results may be time-bound (1985, p. 20). States do not appear to be responding to federal aid cuts by increasing state support for environmental programs. However, the state policymaking process takes time. Perhaps state governments are merely reacting slowly, and a reexamination of the question of state response to federal budget cuts in intergovernmental programs at a later date may find an increase in replacement funding by state governments.

The FWPCA gives the EPA the authority to supervise state implementation of federal water pollution control programs. However, EPA's ability to do so has been limited by a series of budget cuts, the elimination of data-gathering programs, and reductions in personnel (Portney, 1984). Therefore, it is unlikely that the EPA retains the resources needed to determine how state agencies are adjusting their implementation efforts to meet the reduction in financial resources. The EPA may be unable to determine whether states are responding to budget cuts by increasing their efficiency or by decreasing their diligence. Which alternative a state pursues will depend on the state government's desire to pursue aggressive regulation of water pollution. States will have regained, in practice, the autonomy they had under the FWPCA prior to 1972--an autonomy of action explicitly denied them in the 1972 amendments.

A return to the pre-1972 era may conform with the administration's theory of federalism; however, it ignores the problems with pre-1972 federal water pollution policy that lead to the adoption of the 1972 amendments. Advocates of centralized water pollution policymaking authority argued that the states lacked the capacity to carry out comprehensive pollution regulation and that environmentally conscious states would be penalized by the loss of industry to states with looser standards (Rowland 1982). The Reagan combination of increased state respon- sibility with decreased federal funds gives state critics of federal domination in pollution control part of what they advocated in the debate over the 1972 amendments-- increased state autonomy. However, it deprives them of the increased federal assistance that they sought to increase the administrative and technical capacity of state programs.

This study also discovered that indicators of state fiscal and legislative involvement in water quality regulation, state population characteristics, and the severity of the water pollution problem in a state are related to the level of Section 106 funding received by a state only from 1975 through 1981. During the first two years of the Reagan administration, these factors cease to explain the variation in federal assistance to states. This finding is interesting because the statute authorizing the federal grants explicitly directs the administrator of the EPA to apportion Section 106 funds among the states according to severity of pollution, state regulatory effort, and state population size. It is difficult to reconcile these statutory specifications with the empirical evidence that suggests that following 1981, the Reagan administration apportioned Section 106 funds among the states on a basis other than that mandated by the statute.

Appendix A:  Independent Variables Included in Initial Anayses of
             Changes in Levels of Federal Aid to States Under Section 106

Seriousness of Water Pollution in State
Percent of stream and shore miles polluted in state's EPA Region
Estimated cost of industrial water pollution abatement in state
Population density
Population size
Percent of state population employed in manufacturing
Per capita value added by manufacturing in state

State Involvement in Water Pollution Control Efforts
State participation in optional program under Section 402 of the FWPCA
Year in which state enacted its first major water pollution control law
Level of state spending under Section 106 of the FWPCA

State Economic Well-Being
Average per capita state revenue from own sources
Average per capita income
Average percent unemployed

NOTES

1. Initially, a number of dependent variables representing the seriousness of a state's water pollution problem, its population size, and its economic condition were entered into three multiple regression models. These variables and their operationalizations are listed in Appendix A. One model was tested for each of three dependent variables. In the first model, the dependent variable was the change in the level of federal funding received by a state from 1975-1981, the pre-Reagan years. In the second model, the dependent variable was the change in the level of federal funding received by a state during the first two years under Reagan administration budgets, 1982-1983. In the third model, the dependent variable was the change in the level of federal funding received by a state during the entire period from 1975-1983.

Based on initial data runs, the number of independent variables for each model was reduced by eliminating those independent variables that contributed the smallest amounts to the percentage of variation explained by the linear model.

REFERENCES

Baldwin, Frank B. (ed.). 1969. Legal Control of Water Pollution. Davis, California: University of California, Davis.

Council on Environmental Quality. 1973. Environmental Quality: Fourth Annual Report of the Council on Environmental Quality. Washington, D.C.: U.S. Government Printing Office.

------. 1976. Environmental Quality: Seventh Annual Report of the Council on Environmental Quality. Washington, D.C.: U.S. Government Printing Office.

------. 1982. Environmental Quality: Thirteenth Annual Report of the Council on Environmental Quality. Washington, D.C.: U.S. Government Printing Office.

Dworsky, L. 1972. "Toward an Effective and Credible Program for Water Pollution Control". In Phillip O. Foss (ed.) Politics and Ecology, pp. 86-97. Belmont, California: Duxbury Press.

Jolly, C. 1982. "State and Federal Roles in National Water Cleanup." State Government 55: 115-118.

Klingman, David. 1984. "A Framework for Analyzing State Responses to Federal Block Grants." Paper delivered at the 1984 annual meeting of the Midwest Political Science Association, Chicago, Illinois.

Lester, James P. 1985. "Reagan's New Federalism and State Environmental Policy." Paper delivered at the 1985 annual meeting of the Midwest Political Science Association, Chicago, Illinois.

Lieber, Harvey. 1975. Federalism and Clean Waters: The 1972 Water Pollution Control Act. Lexington, Massachusetts: Lexington Books.

Morgan, D. and W. Lyons. 1975. "Industrialization and Affluence Revisited: A Note on Socioeconomic Dimensions of the American States, 1970." American Journal of Political Science 19: 263-276.

Portney, P. 1984. "Natural Resources and the Environment: More Controversy Than Change." In John L. Palmer and Isabel V. Sawhill (eds.) The Reagan Record: An Assessment of America's Changing Domestic Priorities, pp. 141-176. Cambridge, Massachusetts: Ballinger Publishing Company.

----- (ed.). 1984. Natural Resources and the Environment: The Reagan Approach. Washington, D.C.: The Urban Institute Press.

Rowland, C. K. and Roger Marz. 1982. "Gresham's Law: The Regulatory Analogy." Policy Studies Review 3: 572-580.

Strouse, J. and P. Jones. 1974. "Federal Aid: The Forgotten Variable in State Policy Research." Journal of Politics 36: 200-207.

United States Senate. 1972. Senate Report Number 92-414. Washington, D.C. U.S. Congressional and Administrative News, pp. 3668-3739.

Vig, Norman and Michael Kraft (eds.). 1984. Environmental Policy in the 1980s: The Impact of the Reagan Administration. Washington, D.C.: Congressional Quarterly Press.

Wassenberg, P. 1985. "The Implementation of Intergovernmental Regulatory Policy: A Rational Choice Perspective." Paper delivered at the 1985 annual meeting of the Midwest Political Science Association, Chicago, Illinois.

Welch, S. and K. Thompson. 1980. "The Impact of Federal Incentives on State Policy Innovation." American Journal of Political Science 24 (November): 715-729.

Wenner, Lettie M. 1971. Enforcement of Water Pollution Laws in the U.S. Ph.D. dissertation, University of Wisconsin.

Zwick, David and Marcy Benstock. 1971. Water Wasteland. New York: Grossman Publishers.

# 11

## State Government Control of Small Cities' CDBG Awards: The Case of Mississippi

### *Dale Krane*

Title III of the 1981 Omnibus Budget Reconciliation Act shifted primary responsibility for the U.S. Department of Housing and Urban Development's Small Cities Community Development Block Grant program (SCCDBG) to the states. This transfer of the small cities CDBG program from federal authority to state control was grounded philosophically in the "states' rights" belief that state governments understood and could serve the needs of their localities better than the national government. Devolution of the SCCDBG program involved not only an attempt to implement a new vision of American federalism, it also involved the transfer of control over an important set of financial resources. Since its modest beginnings in 1975 as an appendage to the community development entitlements to large cities, the small cities program has emerged as the second largest source of federal aid to nonmetropolitan areas.[1] By permitting state officials to award federal dollars to community development projects in their respective states, the intergovernmental transfer of SCCDBG meant that state officials were no longer "bypassed" for the first time in the program's history. Because of its unique features, the small cities CDBG program was labeled as "the truest test" of President Reagan's "New Federalism" initiatives.[2]

Legislative debates over the proposed devolution raised a number of questions about the program's implementation and impact. For example, opponents of the transfer, such as the National League of Cities, argued that the states did not possess sufficient managerial capacity to operate the CDBG program. A second serious allegation was voiced by citizen groups like Rural America that contended that state officials would not maintain the federal government's commitment to the low- and moderate-income beneficiaries identified in the congressional mandate. Other fears articulated during the debates included worry about the imposition of state priorities on local jurisdictions, concern over the possible politizations of awards, and suspicions about the emergence of a new layer of bureaucracy between the national government and eligible communities.[3]

This chapter examines the Mississippi experience with state government control of the small cities CDBG program by describing and analyzing the state's responses to the managerial problem of program "take over," the development and implementation of the state's award process, and the pattern of SCCDBG awards made by the state agency responsible for SCCDBG administration. Mississippi serves as a natural laboratory for a test case of the program's devolution because (1) the state contains the largest proportion of targeted citizens and one of the largest proportions of targeted jurisdiction among the fifty states and (2) the state only recently has begun to adopt modern and professional forms of public management common in many other states.

## HUD ADMINISTRATION OF THE SMALL CITIES CDBG PROGRAM

The small cities program evolved out of the Nixon-Ford Administration's campaign to transform the plethora of Great Society categorical grants into "blocks" of assistance for discrete functional areas.[4] Small cities and nonmetropolitan areas (that is, under 50,000 population) were included in the original 1974 Housing and Community Development Act (HCDA) simply because these jurisdictions already were receiving aid under the old categorial grants, especially urban renewal. Besides these "hold harmless" provisions, small cities could compete for the 20 percent balance of the CDBG appropriation earmarked for nonmetropolitan areas.[5] The 1977 amendments ended the "hold harmless" feature and required all cities under 50,000 that desired federal community development aid to compete for a share of the monies designated for the nonmetropolitan program. By contrast, large cities (that is, 50,000 and above in population) received CDBG funds as an entitlement via a HUD-devised formula.[6]

Instead of the automatic entitlements given to large cities, small cities faced the challenge of interjurisdictional competition for limited funds. Success in the small cities competition was much harder to gain when compared to the large cities entitlement process.[7] For example, HUD granted awards to less than half of the small cities that applied for SCCDBG funds; on the other hand, HUD provided funds to over 90 percent of the large cities that filled out the required application forms.[8] Decisions on small cities discretionary allocations were made step-by-step through HUD's organizational levels; however, "the bulk of the review and decision-making for most applications occurred in HUD's 39 area offices."[9]

Equally important, HUD used its authority over the discretionary aid to small cities to push these localities in the direction of housing rehabilitation. "HUD was determined," Walter Williams reports, "to integrate its community development and housing programs into one grant."[10] Small cities soon discovered that success in the CDBG competition depended on making housing rehabilitation their top priority. Simply put, HUD continued its old urban renewal program under the guise of the small cities program.

As heirs to twenty-five years of policy aimed at "community development," the separate CDBG programs for large and small cities sought to "create viable urban communities" in order to assist "the nation's cities, towns, and smaller urban communities face critical social, economic, and environmental problems."[11] Congress, in drafting the 1974 HCDA, mandated seven objectives by which HUD was to evaluate applications for CDBG dollars. Reagan and Sanzone pointed out: "most important (and controversial) is the requirement that CDBG monies be used for 'the elimination of slums and blight and neighborhood and community facilities of importance to the welfare of the community principally persons of low and moderate income'".[12] The operationalization of HCDA objectives into HUD's award criteria has created a steady source of debate throughout the program's history. A prime example of this conflict can be found in the 1977 frostbelt-sunbelt battle over whether the "low and moderate income" language of the 1974 Act permitted income-targeting versus slum elimination as an appropriate strategy for community development.[13] Another issue directly related to the small cities program was the contention that HUD awards within the nonmetropolitan category usually went to the relatively larger jurisdictions, while the smaller cities and towns (for example, under 5,000 population), where "need" often was the greatest, lost out in the project competition.[14]

Criticisms such as these moved the Carter administration to experiment with the feasibility of state government management of the small cities program. The 1980 "demonstration project" using the states of Kentucky and Wisconsin produced such favorable results--58 percent of Kentucky and 70 percent of Wisconsin localities preferred state management to HUD management--that the Reagan Administration touted the "demonstration project" as evidence that state governments could "take over" many of the federal assistance programs identified by the Reagan Administration as contributing to "overload" at the national level.[15] State-administered SCCDBG drew heavy opposition from interest groups that sought to continue the direct linkage between Washington and the local jurisdictions. However, with the support of a president philosophically committed to the devolution or "turnback" of assistance programs to the states, the 1981 Budget Act transferred authority over Small Cities funding to the states and effectively ended HUD's role in distributing federal discretionary aid to small cities.[16]

MOVING FROM DECISION TO OPERATIONS: THE PROBLEM OF STATE "TAKE OVER"

The 1981 act specified that states must elect to administer the SCCDBG program by (1) "accepting the option known as 'buying in' by a state making a 10 percent cash or 'in-kind' match[17] and (2) preparing "a statement of community development objectives and its proposed use of funds."[18] Thirty-six states and Puerto-Rico "bought in" to state-administration of SCCDBG in fiscal year (FY) 1982. The transfer of the small cities program from HUD to state control created an implementation problem for each state that decided to "take over" the program. Implementation, of course, involves more than routine administrative actions; it involves an interaction process among individuals and organizations aimed at putting a program into effect. Bardach has characterized policy implementation as a "process of assembling numerous and diverse program elements" in order to turn out some product or service.[19] Because control and discretion are linked closely in the assembly process, political discretion and supervision enter into many aspects of program delivery to the intended recipients. Consequently, successful implementation depends upon the ability "to penetrate through bureaucratic/political layers in trying to reach a final set of actors--those who manage the treatment or service, those who deliver it, and those who receive it."[20]

The extent to which operational policy reflects the legislative mandate will depend on the tradeoffs made by the administrative decision-makers as they try to balance their choices along the major dimensions of implementation. Five distinct strands of agency activity must be knit together in order to create an effective implementation strategy. First, whether the policy decision is placed in a new unit or an existing unit, the responsible agency must "gear up" for the new program. That is, personnel must be hired or reassigned, budgets prepared, new standard operating procedures established, and the rest of the everyday activities that accompany normal administration of any program must be initiated. Second, the agency must devise a technical solution to the problem(s) that provoked the policy decision. For example, if one problem (among others) with the small cities program was HUD's lack of responsiveness to the smallest cities then the state agencies faced the task of designing an award process that did not disadvantage the smallest cities. Third, the agency in charge of a new program must seek to institutionalize the policy by putting it into place in a reasonable time frame. Money must be moved, recipients served, errors corrected, and progress reported often in one year. Fourth, the agency must seek compliance with the legislative mandate. This can entail ordinary enforcement actions or it may require more subtle bargaining or public marketing in order to obtain the desired participation by the intended targets of the policy. Finally, the implementing agency must build a political base for the new program. Quite simply, a sufficient number of "satisfied" clients who will support the agency and its program during the next legislative appropriations cycle must be cultivated.

Each of the states that assumed responsibility for the small cities CDBG program faced these implementation problems posed by the "take over" process. That is, each state agency had to "gear up" an organization, devise an award process, institutionalize their policies into a functioning program, obtain participation and compliance from localities used to working with HUD, and build political support among the small cities while not making the same mistakes that led to the removal of the small cities program from HUD control.

Assessments of state capacity to administer the small

cities program must be based on analyses of state experience with the transferred program. A principal purpose of
implementation analysis is "to identify factors which
affect the achievement of statutory objectives."[21]
Managerial and political choices that contribute to
assembling the necessary program elements can be expected
to have significant consequences not only for the
effectiveness of the program but also for the type of
impact the program makes. The rest of this chapter
utilizes implementation analysis to examine several issues
associated with state "take over" of the small cities CDBG
program by the State of Mississippi. In addition to
relevant federal and state documents, the views described
in the following sections are drawn from interviews with
the staff of HUD's area office in Jackson, Mississippi,
the staff of the Governor's Office of Federal-State
Programs (GOFSP), and various local officials and private
grantsmen around the state. A brief presentation of
contextual information about Mississippi will facilitate
the analysis of this state's operation of the small cities
CDBG program.

## MISSISSIPPI: THE LARGEST "COMMUNITY DEVELOPMENT" TARGET

If the primary objective of the small cities CDBG
program is community development activities designed to
"create viable urban communities" that benefit "principally persons of low and moderate income" residing in
jurisdictions with populations under 50,000 then the state
of Mississippi constitutes one of the largest (if not the
largest) targets for the small cities CDBG program.
Measured by any standard, Mississippi is extremely poor.
The state ranks fiftieth in per capita income with a 1981
state average income of $7,408, or 70.6 percent of the
national average ($10,491). Approximately 35 percent of
the state's residents live on federal assistance and in
thirty-two of the state's eighty-two counties, the
principal source of income is federal transfer payments.

Although Mississippi has changed slowly from a purely
agricultural economy to one that includes significant
manufacturing and service components, the state remains
very rural with a widely dispersed population. Compared
to the national average of 73.7 percent urban population,
Mississippi's urban population is only 47.3 percent (only
Vermont and West Virginia are more rural). Seventy-seven
percent of all county seats, usually the largest munici-
pality in a county, have a population of less than

10,000. Only three standard metropolitan statistical area exist wholly within the state and only one city has a population in excess of 50,000. Federal dollars to Mississippi localities typically have been used for infrastructure improvement or for social services. The reason is obvious: the state still lacks many of the basic public goods and services common in more affluent parts of the nation. For example, as of 1981, sixty-six towns, or 23 percent of the state's incorporated areas did not have sewer and water systems.[22] Similarly, 27 percent of the state's dwellings are substandard (fifth worst in the country). With "needs" like these, one can easily understand why Mississippi is a natural laboratory for testing community development strategies.

Mississippi also serves as a test site for the allegation that many states lack the managerial capacity to operate the SCCDBG program because Missisippi, starting in the 1970s, slowly has entered a phase of governmental modernization and professionalization.[23] For example, the merit system for state employees is less than ten years old and executive preparation of the state budget began in a tentative fashion in 1984. Similarly, open meetings, open records, and ethics codes for public officials have gained grudging acceptance within the last five years. The governor is ranked among the five weakest in the nation,[24] earning interest on public money is hailed as modern cash management, and enforcement of laws regulating purchases by local jurisdictions were applied in a comprehensive manner for the first time only three years ago. Sigelman's study of administrative quality in the fifty states puts Mississippi in the "low quality" category.[25] Thus, just as the state is the largest community development target in the nation, Mississippi also is the state closest to the old pre-professional model of administration that many opponents of CDBG's transfer to state authority feared.

## STATE "TAKE OVER" OF THE SMALL CITIES CDBG PROGRAM IN MISSISSIPPI GEAR UP THE ORGANIZATION

Because Mississippi was one of the thirty-six states to "buy in" to a state-administered SCCDBG program, the HUD area office "was instructed to help the state identify and decide on which agency would take over the program."[26] Although some thought was given to the Mississippi Department of Economic Development, the governor assigned responsibility for the small cities CDBG program to the

Governor's Office of Federal-State Programs. Finding a proper home for SCCDBG caused little political or administrative difficulty in Mississippi because prior to FY 1982 the GOFSP maintained a staff of twenty-six that serviced HUD programs such as 701, EDA, and small cities. In effect, Federal-State Programs had a "territorial" claim to SCCDBG.

Fortunately, intergovernmental conflict between HUD and the governor's office was minimal in Mississippi. A psychological factor that potentially could have ignited federal-state hostility was the depressed morale of HUD area office personnel who faced Reduction-In-Force (RIF) notices as a result of SCCDBG's transfer to state control. For example, the state of North Carolina informed HUD that it would manage the transfer on its own and the HUD area office did little to assist. But in Mississippi "things went very well." The area office "didn't wait until the state decided to take over the program, area staff were sent to D.C. for training in the new regulations," and provided "lots of help" to the state.[27] The governor's office even went so far as to offer positions to the RIFed HUD personnel.

A second type of intergovernmental conflict also avoided in Mississippi was a clash between local jurisdictions and the state agency in charge of SCCDBG. In Tennessee, for example, the state program apparently was designed with very little local input. Consequently, even two years into the state CDBG program, some local grant administrators in Tennessee remain alienated from the state operating agency.[28] By contrast, the CDBG task force established in Mississippi to design the state's program included representatives from cities, towns, and counties throughout the state and served to identify and gain consensus on the state's objectives for the small cities program.[29] This representation of local interests on the GOFSP's task force combined with the task force's use of multiple public hearings clearly made a difference in minimizing program misunderstandings between state and local officials at the very beginning of the "take over" process.

## DEVISE A TECHNICAL SOLUTION

The crucial component of state "take over" is each state's award process. HUD permitted states to copy the department's old award criteria or to design their own as long as the state process complied with congressional mandates and HUD regulations. HUD's 1982 rules (24 CFR Part 570.498) gave "maximum feasible deference to State interpretation of the statutory requirements."[30] As a result of this carte blanche from HUD, the thirty-six states that elected to manage the SCCDBG in FY 1982 adopted award mechanisms that can be grouped into three basic cateories: (1) competitive systems, (2) funding formula systems, and (3) substate allocation systems.[31]

Mississippi, like 88 percent of the states in FY 1982, adopted a competitive system for small cities CDBG awards. A conscious effort was made by GOFSP staff members to avoid living up to the state's perceived administrative stereotype. Recall that two principal fears of state-administration were the capacity issue-- could the states professionally manage the block grant?-- and the fidelity issue--would the states award SCCDBG dollars in accordance with the congressional mandate? Mississippi was suspect on both counts by HUD adminis- trators. As a key member of the governor's office vehemently stated (a year after the transfer was made), "they (the federal officials) didn't think we could do it (operate CDBG) and we did it."[32]

Rather than recount all of the steps that led to the state's award process, two decisions critical in molding its final shape merit discussion. First, out of a series of statewide public meetings conducted by the GOFSP's CDBG task force, four guidelines or "targets" for state- administration emerged: (1) provide access to these funds by small communities; (2) provide for maximum flexibility for local governments to develop projects that meet their own particular needs whether they be housing, infra- structure, economic development, or other needs that are eligible for assistance; (3) provide for the maximum use of these funds to address the critical needs of Mississippi; and (4) avoid any possibility of political- ization of the award process.[33] In contrast to HUD's exclusive emphasis on large-scale housing rehabilitation and slum-removal projects in urban areas, Mississippi made a conscious decision to broaden both the functional and jurisdictional spread of small cities CDBG funds.

Second, the CDBG task force, operationalized these political directives into a specific program design and applications process that was approved after another round of public hearings and workshops. Applications were rated following an elaborate ranking system that awarded points not only for the quality of the project and the number of "targets" served by the project (for example, number of

low and moderate income beneficiaries, total jobs
created), but also for the applicant's administrative
capacity and institutional commitment to the project
(for example, general taxing effort, project conformance
with adopted comprehensive plan). Multiple members on the
GOFSP staff rated each application and verified it by an
on-site visit.[34]

Mississippi's award process differs in several
important respects from that used by other states. Unlike
states that allocate the majority of their SCCDBG money to
project categories that reflect the state's priorities
before they made specific funding decisions (for example,
Kentucky and Michigan), Mississippi "decided to let the
applications drive the award system." That is, "funds
were not set aside for each of these program areas (that
is, the three targets of housing, public facilities, and
economic development) prior to the receipt of applications. The needs expressed in each of the three target
areas determined the amount of state funds set aside for
each area."[35] Also unlike other states (for example, Iowa
and Utah), Mississippi decided not to allocate its funds
on the basis of geographic location or to assign applications to categories that combine jurisdictional type
with project type (for example, Alabama). Similar to
states like Delaware, Iowa, Massachusetts, and Utah,
Mississippi's award mechanism embodied a competitive
process that made all applications compete against each
other.[36] One important aspect of Mississippi's award
system deserves special mention--the award of points based
on a project's leveraging ratio of CDBG dollars versus all
other dollars. That is, projects received points for the
ratio of other dollars (public and/or private) that the
jurisdiction agreed to commit or to contract to the
project. The director of the governor's office best
summarized the Mississippi SCCDBG award mechanism when she
said, "Federal decisions were typically a go/no go
decision. Ours is a more complex scoring system, so that
no one factor will win or lose an award."[37]

Institutionalizing The Policy

The third aspect of implementation bears a
complementary relationship to the technical solution and
the degree of program compliance. Both an agency's
ability to sustain a program on an effectively functioning
basis over time and its ability to gain compliance with
program directives are linked to "the complexity of joint

action," which in turn is grounded in the preferences of
the different participants in a policy.[38]   Program rules
can foster rapid institutionalization of a policy as well
as compliance with the policy.  For example, HUD commonly
allocated money to a given jurisdiction on a multi-year
basis.  While HUD had to close out its accounts annually,
there was an assurance that the locality would continue to
receive funds.  By contrast, Mississippi has adopted a
project-year approach that requires local officials to set
the expected time period (for example, twelve, eighteen,
or twenty-four months) for project completion.[39]   This
seemingly simple difference in decision rules leads to
important consequences.  HUD's rules let grant recipients
apply every year, even if their project had shown little
progress toward completion.  Mississippi, on the other
hand, only permits applications from recipients that have
completed 90 percent of a funded project (or have no
current SCCDBG project underway).   The 90 percent rule
encourages steady progress toward project completion and
reduces application and paperwork burdens on the state
aency.   The award of points for "leveraged" money also
acts to foster project completion.  As a former GOFSP
director pointed out:   "Leveraging is the key to our
program.  We want the cities to put up other funds to help
finance the project and to increase local commitment.
Bank participation therefore can serve more cities
now."[40]   By rewarding applications from communites that
"leverage" other monies, the governor's office gains
assurance of local determination to finish the project.
Another benefit of "leveraging" is that it increases the
overall pool of money available for community development
projects.  For example, first year SCCDBG funds of $21.3
million attracted $27.76 million other funds, an increase
of 130 percent.[41]

GAINING COMPLIANCE

Policy implementation poses no greater challenge to
agency personnel than the problem of compliance.  Because
compliance involves the relationship between a governmental agency and its external constituencies, agency
staff often must modify the behavior of not always willing
targets of a policy.  Typically, compliance in an assistance program is "purchased" with financial "carrots."[42]
In the face of recalcitrance, agencies will, if necessary,
use "sticks" in a ratchet-like manner using more and more
serious sanctions.[43]   Because both of the compliance

strategies can become very costly, a third and sometimes less expensive form of compliance-inducement used by agencies is education and persuasion.[44]

Responsibility for monitoring SCCDBG compliance in Mississippi rests with the Grantee Services Division, Department of Community Development, Governor's Office of Federal-State Programs. Compliance with SCCDBG rules is achieved through the standard techniques of (1) briefings at contract meetings, (2) project implementation work-shops, and (3) field monitoring. More important than the necesssary administrative actions are the political realities surrounding the governor's office that push it to seek compliance via prevention rather than via appre-hension. A former GOFSP director explained:

The 'I Gotcha' attitude of HUD is not our first task. Creating successful projects is in our and their (jurisdictions') interest. What a city does reflects on our office and on the governor. it is in our best interest to help the cities work out their problems before they become too big.[45]

Because of these political realities, the basic compliance strategy used by the Grantee Services Division depends on efforts to educate local officials about state and federal regulations and to provide recipients with services that minimize the changes of mismanagement (for example, model budget forms and filing systems).

BUILDING POLITICAL SUPPORT

Every program must build a political base to survive. In a very real sense, policy survival is the litmus test of successful implementation. "Unless a program generates favorable political support from its clientele, the program will face a shaky and uncertain future."[46] Devolution of the small cities program, as expressed in a letter by the National Governors Associa-tion, presumes that "elected state officials will assure more direct accountability for use of these funds and will produce funding decisions that are more responsive to local needs."[47] As in the issue of compliance, the basis of comparison is with previous HUD practice.

Local officials in Mississippi expressed anxiety about state administration during the early days of the transfer process. Their concerns included the possibili-ties of "even more red tape with state government strings over and above those imposed by the federal government" and that "politics will become a major issue and there will be no equitable distribution of programs."[48] GOFSP managers express an awareness of these legitimate worries of local officials: "our applicants want a fair shake-- the perception of mistreatment needs to be eliminated."[49] Furthermore, state agency administrators are fully cognizant of their political location between the governor and local officials:

In my meetings with state legislators, mayors, county supervisors, the rating system file can be shown to the individuals. Once we show an individual why their city has not received an award, they learn how to improve their application for next year and to enhance their chance for success. There is an appreciation for the objectivity going into it (the award mechanism). They can see how the system works. It doesn't change every year like federal guidelines did. Now a city knows what it is striving to achieve and each year it can upgrade the quality of its application.[50]

From the above quotes, it becomes obvious that a relatively objective and rational decision system yields several mutual benefits to the state agency and the local officials: (1) it serves as communication and educational medium between the state agency and local jurisdictions, (2) it permits the state agency to develop standard operating procedures that require minimal annual modification, (3) the stability of the award process permits advance planning on the part of local officials, and (4) it serves as an insulator from charges of political favoritism for the state agency and to some extent for the jurisdictions that "won" awards.

This review of SCCDBG's transfer from HUD to state administration in Mississippi suggests that certain advantages accrue from state control of this federal assistance program. For example, a common complaint about federal administration was the frequency of regulatory rule change. Local managers of community development projects remember the constant need to modify their own budget and record-keeping systems in response to modifications in federal rules. State administration can be more stable provided the SCCDBG unit is relatively insulated from electoral change. More continuous and "sensitive" technical assistance is another benefit likely to flow from state control. Although HUD did issue technical assistance contracts and also allowed grantees to hire consultants, HUD never could overcome the "distrust" factor inherent in federal-local relations, especially when HUD technical assistance was intermingled with the compliance monitoring function.[51] While the Mississippi governor's office likewise provides technical assistance and monitors for compliance, the disposition of the staff makes a significant difference. Recall the governor's office statement: "It is in our best interest to help the cities work out their problems." Another area of state administration that potentially can aid smaller cities involves the bargaining aspect of grants. Political folklore and practice regarding HUD programs were addressed by one mayor who stated: "The way to get grants is to become known in the agency headquarters in Washington and to work with your congressman." To the extent that the state award process is objective and rational, jurisdictions will not be poltically disadvantaged in the grant competition.

Now that the process of SCCDBG transference to state control in Mississippi has been portrayed, a closer look at the outcomes of state administration is in order. The next section asks the question: did state control change the pattern of community development awards to small cities? A basic test of state control's impact would entail the comparison of the pattern of awards made by the state agency with the pattern of awards made by HUD. Although all of the issues raised by state control of the small cities program will not be answered by an inspection of the awards in one state, nevertheless, the experience with the first three years of state-administered SCCDBG in Mississippi is instructive about the effect of the program's devolution.

## THE "NEW" PATTERN OF SMALL CITIES AWARDS IN MISSISSIPPI

Mississippi's FY 1982 SCCDBG allocation was $34,010,899, or 3.3 percent, of the $1.019 billion national appropriation. Excluding state administrative costs and multi-year commitments, the balance of SCCDBG funds awarded equalled $21,508,399. A total of 237 applications was received by the govenor's office and 82 awards (excluding multi-year projects) were made, of which 57 (69.5 percent) went to cities and towns and the remainder went to counties.[52] Figure 11.1 demonstrates that FY 1982 state awards were more numerous than HUD FY 1981 awards (97 versus 43). Figure 11.1 also shows that FY 1982 state awards were smaller in dollar amount than were the previous FY 1981 HUD awards ($342,316 versus $720,875). This almost two-to-one difference between FY 1981 and FY 1982 in average award size perfectly reflects the opposing objectives of HUD versus Mississippi administration of SCCDBG. HUD area office personnel stated: "HUD gave larger awards based on its experience with the amount of money needed to do a job. Our experience came from (the many years of) urban renewal."[53] By contrast, the first guideline for awards developed out of the public hearings conducted by the GOFSP insisted that the state program would "provide access to these funds by small communities." Figure 11.1 also illustrates that these same trends toward more numerous, but smaller in dollar amount SCCDB awards continued in FY 1983 and FY 1984. Mississippi's governor's office, by awarding small cities CDBG projects to twice as many communities per year than HUD did, clearly has acted to meet the community development policy goals agreed upon by state and local representatives during the initial period of state program design.

In a similar fashion, state government control of the SCCDBG program in Mississippi also has produced a pattern of awards that fulfills the joint federal-state policy interest in directing CDBG assistance toward smaller cities. Figure 11.2 indicates that HUD concentrated its FY 1981 grants in the "larger" small cities of Mississippi (that is, about 5,000 population) by a factor of three-to-one. The state, in its first three years of CDBG management, reversed this concentration by increasing the number of awards to the smallest of jurisdictions (that is, under 2,500 population). Another way to express this shift of aid to the smallest cities is the change in the percentage of localities not receiving CDBG aid. During the period of HUD administration (FY 1975 to FY 1981), 77 percent of Mississippi communities under 1,000 population (48.9 percent of all incorporated areas) went unfunded; with state administration, the FY 1983 percentage of non-recipients among cities under 1,000 population dropped to 47 percent.[54]

Some comparison of Mississippi's first year award outcomes with the awards made by other states can be obtained from the 1983 U.S. General Accounting Office (GAO) report on the small cities program.[55] Figure 11.3 juxtaposes the SCCDBG awards for Mississippi with the awards granted by states listed in the GAO report. The changes promulgated by state "take over" are quite similar for all eight states. First, GAO observed "all seven states (in the report) awarded, on average, smaller grants than HUD, and five states awarded more grants with the funds they controlled."[56] Second, GAO found "in five of the seven states, the amount of housing rehabilitation decreased as a percentage of the total funds awarded."[57] Although the exact percentages for different types of HUD-funded projects in Mississippi are unavailable, all participants in the small cities program (HUD area office, governor's office, and local officials) agreed that HUD directed its money almost exclusively to housing; therefore, Mississippi's FY 1982 pattern of SCCDBG awards to public facilities (65 percent) fits with the five states listed in the 1983 GAO report that reduced the percentage of CDBG funds targeted to housing. For these eight states the overall average percentage of FY 1982 SCCDBG awards for housing equaled 20.3 percent in contrast with 46 percent of the awards devoted to public facilities. This shift in funding priorities away from housing and towards public facilities clearly indicates that the states and the localities (depending on the state award process) have very different objectives from those that HUD pursued. GAO's multi-state comparison also found that "in six of the seven states grants were supplemented by $281 million more... than grants funded under the HUD-administered program."[58] Mississippi's experience with leveraging other funds compares favorably with these other states. One of the most important findings of the GAO report is the FY 1981 to FY 1982 decrease in the percent-age of targeted low and moderate income beneficiaries that appeared in six of the seven states. The FY 1982 average percentage of targeted beneficiaries in the seven states is 77.1 percent compared to Mississippi's FY 1982 figure of 84 percent. GAO explains the drop may be due to "the shift in funding from housing activities to public facilities and economic development."[59] Again, this shift reflects the debate over the most appropriate strategy to achieve community development—slum elimination, income enhancement, or physical facilities to make a community livable.

On the policy outcome dimension of small cities management by the state of Mississippi, the evidence suggests that the state diversified its SCCDBG awards among many more of its smallest communities than HUD did. Second, the state's award system provided more choice for local officials to pursue local needs and development plans. The principal result of these expanded choices has been a signficiant shift of projects away from housing rehabilitation (HUD's prime activity) to public infrastructure construction. Given the previously mentioned physical needs of the state, this shift is understandable. A third consequence of state administration in Mississippi is the modest decline (from 91 to 84) in the percentage of low and moderate income persons who benefited from SCCDBG aid. In assessing this change from HUD administration, one must take into account that many public infrastructure projects in small cities are neces-sary to further comprehensive community development. Although a community-wide physical facility built with SCCDBG funds will lower (in a statistical sense) the percentage of low and moderate income beneficiaries served by the grant, nevertheless, the goal of improvement toward a more "viable community" for low and moderate income persons is attained. Although a modest shift occurred in social targeting of the SCCDBG projects in Mississippi, the state's award process attracted more funds to community development projects when compared to previous HUD experience. By encouraging localities to "leverage" other funds, the Mississippi award system significantly augments the money available for community development.[60] When one considers that a serious obstacle to community development is the lack of capital, this "leveraging" of additional dollars is an important accomplishment of state control of the Small Cities program.[61]

CONCLUSION

The small cities CDBG program represents one of the few deliberate efforts to test a functional reassignment of the responsibility for a federal assistance program. Of the nine "New Federalism" block grants created in the 1981 Budget Reconciliation Act, only the small cities program embodied an innovative approach to intergovernmental relations. Because the states had no previous experience with SCCDBG, its transfer to state control raised critical questions about the program's implementation and impact, particularly questions about the management capacity of the states and the degree to which state administration would be guided by congressionally mandated objectives. Analyses of state "take over" that explore program design, award processes, and the distribution of small cities CDBG funds are necessary to answer these questions.[62]

From the material presented based on the case of Mississippi, the fears raised by the National League of Cities officials about state inability to administer the small cities program as well as HUD did (from 1975 to 1981) appear to be unfounded. The establishment and operation of a small cities program by the Mississippi Governor's Office of Federal-State Programs within the first fiscal year (FY 1982) is, of course, the principal evidence on managment capacity. GOFSP staff in conjunction with representatives from local jurisdictions produced a set of state community development goals and then operationalized these goals into an objective award process that differed from the previous HUD system in three specific ways: (1) the Mississippi award process permitted local officials more choice than HUD did in terms of the types of CDBG projects that would be funded, (2) the Mississippi award process was designed to insure that the smallest cities (under 2,500 population) would not be at a competitive disadvantage as they were under the old HUD system, and (3) the Mississippi award process encouraged local officials to seek additional funds as part of the community's CDBG proposal, thus increasing the dollars applied to community development projects. Also, the GOFSP promulgated program rules designed to assure local project completion within a stated time frame. At the same time, GOFSP technical services were provided to local officials to educate and guide them through the state award process.

On the second issue of state take over the evidence from Mississippi (and from the seven states in the 1983 GAO report) suggests that states are willing and able to direct SCCDBG funds in a way that enhances progress toward the creation of viable urban communities as defined by state and local officials. In comparing awards made by the state of Mississippi to those made by the states in the GAO report, all eight states have engaged in a modest tradeoff between housing and public works projects. One of the consequences of this change in programmatic emphasis is a modest decline in the percentage of low and moderate income persons who benefit from SCCDBG projects (please note: the eight-state average of target beneficiaries for FY 1982 is 84 percent). In assessing this tradeoff, one must take into account that many public works projects in small cities yield important quality of life improvements to all citizens in the locality, even though from a technical standpoint the project aids a lower percentage of low and moderate income persons.

Another result of state control has been an increase in
the number of awards in contrast to the number granted by
HUD. Because the annual appropriation has not increased
dramatically, more numerous awards means that, on average,
state agencies provide fewer dollars to each recipient-
jurisdiction than HUD provided. This produces another
tradeoff; fewer dollars per project may lengthen the time
necessary to complete comprehensive projects, but smaller
awards also means projects of a size more manageable by
the smallest jurisdictions. Recall that the typical HUD
award to small cities could be a sum easily double or
triple the annual budget of many small communities.
Consequently, more modest awards more appropriately match
the management capacity of many small cities. An increase
in funds leveraged from other sources has accompanied the
transfer to state control. The fiscal distress that many
states currently suffer has been translated into state
decision processes that award localities for seeking other
"partners" (public and/or private) in the local community
development campaign.

Mississippi's track record to date is positive when
examined against the pessimistic predictions of the
opponents of SCCDBG's transfer to state administration.
Problems do exist in Mississippi (and other states) and
these problems will require close scrutiny before a
definitive judgment can be rendered on the reassignment of
SCCDBG to the states. For example, it still is too early
to determine the capacity of the states to monitor
mismanagement by small city CDBG recipients. Can state
agencies discover local malfeasance (deliberate or
inadvertent) and act to correct it? Second, will state
agencies in charge of CDBG funds be able to insulate
themselves from political pressures to award projects to
the favorite jurisdictions of powerful executive and
legislative authorities? And third, will state agencies
avoid the natural tendency to become bogged down in
process-burdens as happened to HUD? If a state such as
Mississippi that still retains a heritage of traditonal
political-administrative practices can "take over" the
small cities CDBG program with seeming ease and success,
then it would appear that intergovernmental reassignment
of program responsibilities from national to state
governments not only is possible, but it also may be
beneficial. Such arguments, however, will be less
decisive in all probability for the future of state "take
over" of federal aid programs than will be the base of
political support among state and local officials who
favor state administration over national administration.

NOTES

1. Parris N. Glendening and Mavis Mann Reeves, Pragmatic Federalism, 2nd ed (Pacific Palisades, CA: Palisades Publishers, 1984), p. 244.
2. Advisory Commission on Intergovernmental Relations (ACIR), Intergovernmental Perspective. vol. 8, no. 4/vol. 9, no. 1 (Winter, 1983), p. 33.
3. For a more detailed review of the legislative debates on the proposed transfer of the small cities CDBG program from HUD to state administration, see B. J. Reed and Roy E. Green, "Serendipity?: 1981 Budget Reconciliation Act and the Small Cities Community Development Block Grant Program." Paper presented at the 1982 annual meeting of the Southern Political Science Association.
4. The seven categorical grants amalgamated into the CDBG program were: (1) Urban Renewal, (2) Model Cities, (3) Sec. 702 Water and Sewer, (4) Sec. 703 Neighborhood Facilities, (5) Title II Public Facilities, (6) Title IV Open Space Land, and (7) Sec. 312 Housing Rehabilitation.
5. Richard Nathan, et al., Block Grants For Community Development (Washington, D.C.: The Brookings Institution, January 1977), p. 84. U.S. Department of Housing and Urban Development Contract H-2323R.
6. HUD created a formula consisting of three elements: (1) population, (2) housing overcrowding, and (3) the extent of poverty. The poverty factor was double-weighted in the formula and in 1977 "age of housing stock" (that is, percentage of community housing built prior to 1940) was substituted for "housing overcrowding." To dispense CDBG money, HUD staff merely fed the necessary census data into agency computers, which applied the operationalized "needs" formula to produce the list of eligible jurisdictions that would receive an entitlement. For more details on the CDBG formula, see (1) ACIR, Community Development: The Workings of a Federal-Local Block Grant (Washington, D.C.: March 1977, Document A-57) and (2) Paul R. Dommel, "Social Targeting in Community Development," Political Science Quarterly, vol. 95, no. 3 (Fall, 1980), pp. 465-478.
7. ACIR, Community Development Washington, D.C., 1977, p. 46.
8. Raymond Shapek, Managing Federalism: Evolution and Development of the Grant-in-Aid System (Charlottesville, VA: Community Collaborators, 1981), pp. 195-201.
9. ACIR, Community Development Washington, D.C., 1977, p. 46.

10. Walter Williams, Government By Agency: Lessons From The Social Program Grants-in-Aid Experience (New York: Academic Press, 1980), p. 105.

11. Carl Van Horn, Policy Implementation in the Federal System (Lexington, MA: Lexington Books, D. C. Heath, 1979), Ch. 4.

12. Michael Reagan and John Sanzone, The New Federalism, 2nd ed (New York: Oxford University Press, 1981), p. 141.

13. Paul R. Dommel, et al., Decentralizing Community Development (Washington, D.C.: The Brookings Institution, June 2, 1978), pp. 19-21. U.S. Department of Housing and Urban Development Contract H-2323R.

14. George E. Hale and Marian Lief Palley, The Politics of Federal Grants (Washington, D.C.: Congressional Quarterly Press, 1981), p. 54.

15. Reed and Green, "Serendipity?"

16. ACIR, Information Bulletin, No. 84-1 (Washington, D.C.: January 1984), p. 1.

17. ACIR, Intergovernmental Perspective, vol. 8, no. 4/vol. 9, no. 1 (Winter 1983), p. 33.

18. U.S. General Accounting Office, States Are Making Good Progress In Implementing The Small Cities Community Development Block Grant Program (Washington, D.C.: GAO/RCED-83-186, Sept. 8, 1983), p.3.

19. Eugene Bardach, The Implementation Game: What Happens After A Bill Becomes A Law (Cambridge, MA: The MIT Press, 1977), p. 36.

20. Donald S. VanMeter and Carl Van Horn, "The Policy Implementation Process: A Conceptual Framework," Administration and Society, vol. 6 (Summer, 1975), pp. 531-566.

21. Paul Sabatier and Daniel Mazmanian, "The Implementation of Public Policy: A Framework of Analysis," Policy Studies Journal, vol. 8, (special issue no. 2, 1980), p. 541.

22. Interview with Harvey Johnson, Director, Mississippi Institute for Small Towns, as quoted in Dale Krane, "The New 'New Federalism"--A Practitioner's Perspective," Intergovernmental News, vol. 5, no. 3 (Washington, D.C.: American Society for Public Administration, 1981).

23. D. Landry and Joseph Parker, Mississippi Government and Politics In Transition (Dubuque, IA: Kendall/Hunt Publishing Co., 1976), pp. 89-102.

24. Thad Beyle, "Governors," in Virginia Gray, Herbert Jacob, and Kenneth Vines (eds.), Politics in the American States, 4th ed (Boston, MA: Little, Brown, 1983), Ch. 6.

25. Lee Sigelman, "The Quality of Administration: An Exploration in the American States," Administration and Society, vol. 8 (1976), pp. 107-144.

26. Interview with J. Wilson, Program Manager, Community Planning Division, Jackson, MS. Area Office, US Department of Housing and Urban Development (1982).

27. Ibid.

28. T. Bolding, Director of Community Resources Management, Shelby, TN. Comments made at the Roundtable on Small City Policy Issues, 1984 annual meeting of the Southeastern Conferece of the American Society of Public Administration.

29. Governor's Office of Federal-State Programs, 1982 Community Development Block Grant Annual Performance Report (Jackson, MS: State of Mississippi, 1983), p. 1-4.

30. Federal Register, vol. 47, no. 68 (April 8, 1982), p. 15297.

31. Kenneth Bleakly et al., The State Community Development Block Grant Program: The First Year's Experience (Cambridge, MA: Urban Systems Research and Engineering, Inc., May, 1983), pp. 62-63. U.S. Department of Housing and Urban Development Contract HC-5546.

32. Interview with J. Kaat, Program Manager, Program Design and Technical Assistance Division, Office of Community Development, Governor's Office of Federal-State Programs, State of Mississippi (Jackson, MS: 1983).

33. GOFSP, 1982 Community Development.

34. Ibid.

35. Ibid., p. 3.

36. GAO, States Are Making Good Progress.

37. Interview with A. H. Cook, Executive Director, Governor's Office of Federal-State Programs, State of Mississippi (Jackson, MS: 1983).

38. Jeffrey Pressman and Aaron Wildavsky, Implementation, 2nd ed (Berkeley, CA: University of California Press, 1979).

39. Interview with G. Parsons, former director, Department of Policy and Planning, Governor's Office of Federal-State Programs, State of Mississippi (Mississippi State, MS: 1985).

40. Interview with A. H. Cook.

41. GOFSP, 1982 Community Development.

42. Helen Ingram, "Policy Implementation Through Bargaining: The Case of Federal Grants-in-Aid," Public Policy, vol. 25 (Fall, 1977).

43. Harrell Rodgers, Jr. and Charles S. Bullock, III, Coercion To Compliance (Lexington, MA: Lexington Books, D.C. Heath, 1976).

44. Charles E. Lindblom, Politics and Markets: The World's Political-Economic Systems (New York: Basic Books, 1977), pp. 52-62.

45. Interview with A. H. Cook.

46. Howard Ball, Dale Krane, and Thomas P. Lauth, Jr., Compromised Compliance: The Implementation of the 1965 Voting Rights Act (Westport, CN: Greenwood Press, 1982), p. 198.

47. Deil S. Wright, "New Federalism: Recent Varieties of an Older Species," American Review of Public Administration, vol. 16, no. 1 (Spring, 1982), pp. 56-74.

48. Dale Krane, "I Think I Can, I Think I Can: City Officials' Perception of Their Ability to Implement the 'New Federalism'," Paper presented at the 1983 national conference of the American Society for Public Administration.

49. Interview with A. H. Cook.

50. Ibid.

51. Walter Williams, Government by Agency, p. 228.

52. GOFSP, 1982 Community Development...

53. Interview with J. Wilson.

54. Governor's Office of Federal-State Programs, State of Mississippi Community Development Block Grant Program 1984 Final Statement (Jackson, MS: 1984).

55. GAO, States Are Making Good Progress.

56. Ibid., p. 15.

57. Ibid.

58. Ibid.

59. Ibid., p. 16.

60. John Sidor raises a similar point in his criticism of Morgan and England's assessment of recent changes in the small cities CDBG program. See David Morgan and Robert England, "The Small Cities Block Grant Program: An Assessment of Programmatic Change Under State Control," Public Administration Review, vol. 44, no. 6 (Nov./Dec., 1984), pp. 477-482 and John Sidor, "Communications," Public Administration Review, vol. 45, no. 3 (May/June, 1985).

61. For an in-depth statistical comparison of HUD versus state administration of the small cities CDBG program in Mississippi, see Dale Krane, "Does the 'New Federalism' Strategy of Devolution Make A Difference?: An Analysis of HUD's Small Cities Program in Mississippi, 1975-1983," Publius: The Journal of Federalism (forthcoming 1986).

62. See Edward T. Jennings, Dale Krane, Alex Pattakos, and B. J. Reed, "Community Development State Style: The Small Cities Community Development Block Grant Program," paper presented at the 1985 annual meeting of the American Political Science Association for a multi-state assessment of the changes in the implementation and impact of the small cities CDBG program since 1982.

# 12

# Using Federal Budget Cuts for Administrative Reform: CDBG Cutbacks in a City Marginally Dependent upon Federal Funds (Houston, Texas)

*Susan A. MacManus*

Federal budget cuts, the most focused-upon component of Reagan's New Federalism program, are generally assumed to have had negative fiscal and programmatic impacts on recipient governments. Consequently, most research on the New Federalism has concentrated on detailing the defensive strategies adopted by governments in response to the cutbacks. There are, however, some instances where local governments have perceived the cutbacks as potentially useful reorganizational devices. In such instances local governments' use of the cutbacks along with federal deregulation has resembled the federal government's: as an offensive weapon against governmental bureaucracies viewed as being "out of control."

In this chapter, a contrast is made of the city of Houston's Community Development Block Grant (CDBG) program through its expansionary (FY 1976-FY 1981) and contractionary (FY 1982-FY 1984) years. The contrast will show that contraction due to federal cutbacks actually helped the mayor mold the program into a more manageable size and shape and put it into a more logical organizational location. Federal budget cuts ("the feds made us do it") afforded a new mayor the opportunity to reduce the size of the community development (CD) division's staff, restructure citizen participation mechanisms, establish new subcontractor performance monitoring and evaluation procedures, and semi-privatize the housing rehabilitation program. Obviously, the use of contraction as a device to effect organizational change was a luxury that only a city with a relatively low level of federal aid dependency could afford.[1]

At the peak of federal aid to cities (FY 1978), the

city of Houston was only marginally dependent upon federal funds compared with other large U.S. cities, such as Detroit, New York, and Cleveland. In FY 1978 federal grants for operating programs ($84.7 million) were equal to 16 percent of total local revenues. Federal funds available for capital projects in 1978 (including carry-overs of unspent funds from previous years) amounted to $332 million, or about one-quarter of the city's bonding capacity. By 1982 only $141 million of Houston's $937 million expenditures--12.9 percent--were federal funds. The Community Development Block Grant program was one of the largest single components of this aid total. In the period examined (FY 1976-FY 1984), the program experienced rapid expansion, then contraction.

## CDBG DURING THE EXPANSIONARY ERA: TOO MUCH, TOO FAST?

The CDBG program expanded rapidly during its first six years of existence. Houston's allocation jumped from $10.4 million (year 1 allocation) to $28.3 million (year 6 allocation)--a 172 percent increase (see Table 12.1).

According to local analysts, the city's rapid expansion and its lack of experience with large-scale federal programs may have created a need to play "catch-up" from the very start of the CDBG program. Unlike other CDBG entitlement cities, Houston had no prior experience with development-oriented federal grants programs, such as the urban renewal program of the late 1960s. (The city's lack of zoning ordinances had made it ineligible for urban renewal grants.) In fact, the city's brief experience with a Model Cities grant from HUD in the early 1970s was its only significant experience with large-scale federal programs. Unfortunately, the Model Cities program quickly "garnered a reputation for inefficiency and mismanagement, characterized by a high turnover of department heads and a backlog of unspent funds."[2]

It did not take long for the newly formed CDBG division to gain the same "bad" reputation, perhaps because many of the "new" CDBG administrators and citizen-activists were the "old" Model Cities program actors. But there was another, more structural, reason. Like the Model Cities program (part of which became the Human Resources Department), the CD program was designed to be adminis-tered separately from regular city departments. Placing federally funded programs in separate divisions or depart-ments was viewed as a compromise between the mayor (Fred Hofheinz) and his business supporters who opposed heavy reliance upon federal aid, and his minority supporters, who demanded heavy input in the administration and design of these programs. Thus, from the start, the CD division and the CETA division as well were "viewed by regular city personnel as minority programs best run by minorities and best not absorbed into the city's general fund ..." or regular city operations.[3] This separatism was one of the leading causes of a CDBG spending problem: It tended to discourage cooperation between regular line departments and the CD division, although the division was technically a part of the Mayor's office. (In reality, it was housed outside City Hall.)

## The Spending Problem

In each of the first four years of the program the major problem plaguing the CDBG program was the city's inability to spend its allocations. In August 1979 Houston's expenditure rate was only 39 percent compared to a national average of 68 percent.[4] As a condition to the award of fifth- and sixth-year grants, HUD placed the city under a "spend it or lose it" directive: The city had to spend $8.7 million every four months or about $2.2 million per month. Such severe actions on the part of HUD were but one technique used to stimulate spending. HUD also took back $435,765 in unspent monies--nationally the first and only such action HUD took during the expansionary period.

In response to HUD "spend it or lose it" mandates, the mayor (James McConn) ordered each regular city department to supply the CD Division with a list of "regular" city projects that would meet HUD CD eligibility criteria and were "ready-to-go." Capital improvement projects on which a lot of money could be expended fast (for example, storm and sanitary sewers, water mains, street improvements) became more popular than projects whose design, bidding, contracting, and construction took much longer (parks, fire stations, social service facilities). McConn's directive reversed his predecessor's policy of not using CDBG funds for conventional capital improvements. It also recognized the consequences of the lack of cooperation between "mainstream" city departments and the CD division. Organizational separatism was regarded by some observers as the major cause of the spending problem. Others saw political separatism as equally problemmatic.

## Politics During the Expansionary Period

During this period, CD division officials made most of the decisions about allocational priorities, selection of subcontractors, and other implementational issues, following consultation (or confrontation) with HUD officials, administrative personnel in other city departments, and occasionally the Houston Residents Citizens Participation Commission (HRCPC). In general, the politics of expansion rarely involved the city council. Usually, the mayor intervened when HUD intervened or when there was negative local publicity about the CD program's management, which was increasingly the case.

The Mayor's Role. The mayor's role strengthened in the fifth and sixth years as a result of HUD's imposition of expenditure rate quotas and an uproar following the release of performance audits of the city's federal programs to the press. To combat these problems, the mayor (McConn) forced various city departments (Public Works, Parks and Recreation, Real Estate, Solid Waste, Health, Legal) to cooperate with CD officials to expedite processing CD projects.

One of the ways of expediting CD expenditures was to appoint personnel in each line department to serve as a liaison between the department and the CD Division. Out of an explosive meeting called by the mayor to get things moving came his order for departments to supply the CD Division with a list of regular city projects that would meet HUD eligibility criteria. The overall effect of both these directives was to strengthen the line departments' influence on CD program design and implementation, while weakening the influence of the CD staff.

In retrospect, the rapid expansion of the program and the city's inability to keep up the pace led to stronger intervention by the city's chief elected official. The mayor recognized the need to shape up the program or face the electoral consequences: a negative vote from the business community for poor monitoring of the program and from the minority communities for failing to deliver needed facilities and services. Council members faced the same problem.

The Role of City Council. Council members played a low-key role in CD decisionmaking during the expansionary period and were very much influenced by the mayors' recommendations. These recommendations were usually limited to annual approval of the CD application, various

subcontracts, and, occasionally, personnel ordinances
affecting the division.

In general, the council lacked familiarity with the
operations of the CD division because of the long-standing
"hands-off" attitude toward federally funded programs.
Few council members ever set foot inside the CD division
office or had any direct contact with the CD staff except
for an occasional phone call to check on the progress of a
project at the request of a constituent.

There were signs near the end of the expansionary
period, however, that council's involvement in CD
decisionmaking was increasing, though only slightly,
because of several factors:  One was a change in the size
and structure of city council.  In 1979, the city adopted
a mixed council-electoral system:  nine council mebers are
elected from single-member districts; five are elected at
large.[5]  Not unexpectedly, district council members became
interested in a program which, on its face, had the
potential to make noticeable improvements in deteriorating
areas of their districts.  Still, it took a while for them
to understand the program and its problems.  Like the
mayor's, their understanding increased significantly when
the program and its director were raked over the coals by
the local media.

The Role of Citizens.  The strength of the formal
citizen participation body, the Houston Residents Citizens
Participation Commission, declined when other citizen
groups became active.  In general, the role of the formal
citizens participation group was to react to spending
recommendations that the CD division staff submitted to
them.  Most often the reaction was negative, stemming from
the informal political agenda of individual HRCPC members.
At other times, their reaction resulted from an inadequate
technical understanding of the city's construction
process.  The CD staff was particularly frustrated.  On
the one hand, HUD wanted them to keep things moving, while
on the other, HUD mandated the division to seek citizen
input.

By the middle of the expansionary period, it had
become obvious that the old-style, 1960s adversarial
politics of the HRCPC leadership was unsuitable and
unacceptable for a rapidly expanding program under the gun
to spend money fast.  Ultimately, the negativism of the
group's leadership got to HUD and to a number of elected
officials.  HRCPC's rejection of a newly revised Citizen
Participation Plan[6] drawn up by the CD staff upon direct
recommendation of HUD finally alienated HUD. The revisions

had been designed to broaden citizen involvement, which had declined under the old structure. Each election to select target area commissioners had fewer candidates and a lower turnout. Not only did the HRCPC reject the proposed revisions, but they offered their own, which were in direct violation of the federal regulations. HUD saw this defiance as further evidence that HRCPC leaders cared more about developing and maintaining their own political power bases than promoting the CD program.

When the strength of the formal citizen participation group declined, that of other citizen groups increased. As the CD program became more visible, more groups became aware that CD monies could fund certain projects in their neighborhoods. More neighborhood civic clubs asked for CD funds to pay for needed capital improvement projects that the city, with its low taxing and spending policies, had not yet constructed. Even though many of these proposed projects were not included in the fifth- or sixth-year CD application, either because of technical shortcomings or astronomical costs, they were evidence of the increased visibility of the CD program.

Church groups and nonprofit organizations also became more involved when CD funds for social services to individuals living outside Neighborhood Strategy Areas were cut to comply with HUD regulations. These groups actively pressured the city and CD staff members to continue the services, particularly those affecting the elderly. In some cases, the city continued the services out of its general fund.

Other broad-based groups, such as the League of Women Voters, the Metropolitan Organization—a coalition of churches, and ACORN—Association of Community Organizations for Reform Now, began to monitor the progress of the CD program. Their interest picked up considerably after the adverse publicity had called attention to the city's poor expenditure rate. They were upset particularly with the slow progress of the housing rehab program because they knew that housing needs were among the most crucial for CD target-area residents. Some of these groups ended up contacting the HUD area office for information they could not get from the CD division itself.

The Role of HUD. HUD's influence over the city's CDBG program increased during the expansionary period, pri-marily through its imposition of expenditure rate quotas, its trimester monitoring procedures, and its actual removal of unspent funds from the city. From HUD's perspective, imposing expenditure rate quotas got the city to move its CD program off the planning board and into the targeted neighborhoods. From the city's perspective, especially that of the CD staff, the spending quotas improved interdepartmental cooperation, which then helped the city improve its implementation rate. The improvement in performance statistics also helped reduce the amount of negative news about the CD program reported by the local press.

In summary, the politics of expansion primarily involved administrative personnel (HUD, CD, regular city departments). Elected officials became involved only when failure to intervene would have meant undesirable ramifications at the polls. With a program out of control from the start, city officials hesitated to intervene until the problem became a crisis. This hesitancy derived from the traditional hands-off attitude toward federally funded divisions and departments. Citizen group influence was minimal, although it changed in character. The formal citizen participation group, HRCPC, continued to "politic" itself out of any major input as it failed repeatedly to heed HUD-mandated recommendations, changes in HUD regulations, (for example, reduction in social service funding levels), and changes in the local political climate. On the other hand, neighborhood civic groups became more involved as the program gained visibility, and citizen "watchdog" groups became active.

In spite of improved expenditure rates during the fifth and sixth years, the overall expenditure rate of CDBG funds over the course of the expansionary period (July 1975-July 1981) was only 74 percent. When the federal government first began cutting back the program (year 7), some CD personnel privately expressed support for contraction, hoping it would afford the opportunity to restructure what had been an unmanageable program. The basic assumption was that the politics of contraction would be a different game.

THE CONTRACTION FOR CDBG: OPPORTUNITY FOR REFORM

The Setting for Contraction

When the CDBG program began to contract, the city's political scene was changing dramatically. In November 1981 the city elected a new mayor, the former city controller, Kathryn J. Whitmire. Whitmire ran on a platform that promised better city management, improvement in city services, revitalization of the inner city, and revision of the civil service system.

The new mayor was elected by a constituency somewhat different from the one that elected her immediate predecessors, James McConn and Fred Hofheinz. Specifically, the new mayor was far less indebted to the traditional minority community "powerbrokers," even though she had substantial grass-roots support in those communities. Consequently, CD observers anticipated that she would feel less obligated to use the CD program for political patronage to the black and brown communities. One initial indication of this possibility was her selection of the new CD director.

While following the tradition of appointing a minority to head the CD division (the new director, like the previous one, was black), the mayor selected a different type of individual. She chose as her new CD director an auditor who had worked for her in the controller's office. The new director's mandate from the mayor was to clean up the operations of the CD division. She was to submit a plan for the complete reorganization of the division by the fall of 1982. Many observers viewed her fiscal background as a sign that the mayor would try to depoliticize the operations of the division; they believed that its activities would be integrated into a broader revitalization plan, designed by the new administration. Changes in the fiscal climate caused others also to believe that this scenario would come to pass.

Federal cutbacks in social service programs, the result of the Omnibus Budget Reconciliation Act of 1981, promised to increase pressure on the mayor and city council to replace at least some of the lost federal funds with the city's locally raised revenues. Expectations were that a number of nonprofit social service agencies providing training, employment, health, and day care services through federally funded subcontracts with the city would soon begin to lobby City Hall to continue these services. Likewise, federal cutbacks in capital programs when interest rates were skyrocketing would mean that city officials had to delay construction of much-needed capital projects. Many community leaders saw these capital improvements as the key to Houston's continued growth and prosperity. The nature of the CDBG program (a social service component and large capital component) naturally led some to think that as the impacts of the federal budget cuts became more intense, pressures to use CDBG funds for regular city activities would increase. Others speculated that the CD division would finally be incorporated into the mainstream of city government, fiscally and programmatically.

## Attempts to Restructure the CD Division:

The easing of application requirements and procedures, changes in the review process designed to limit HUD's influence over program content, elimination of the Neighborhood Strategy Area (NSA) targeting require-ment, and changes in citizen participation requirements began when President Ronald Reagan took office. The decentralization and deregulation of the CDBG program were viewed positively by the new mayor, CD director, and upper-level CD staff, who hoped that Houston's CD program would be reshaped in a more manageable form.

In quite a reversal from the previous administration, the new mayor and her CD director actively <u>solicited</u> input from the HUD area office at a time when such intervention was declining elsewhere. Because of their accounting backgrounds, they recognized the advantage of using "objective" external audits (financial and performance) as justifications, or mandates, for restructuring politically sensitive programs. In other words, the new mayor actively solicited HUD involvement as a politically neutral way of "cleaning house."

An examination of HUD's past audits of Houston's CD program during the expansionary years revealed four major shortcomings that still plagued the program when the new mayor inherited it. These four problems were (1) the slow expenditure rate in the city's housing rehabilitation program; (2) the failure to monitor and evaluate the performance of CDBG subconstractors and subgrantees; (3) excessive adminstrative costs associated with the rehab program and the HRCPC; and (4) the antagonistic relation-ship between the CD division administrators and the paid staff of the Houston Residents Citizen Participation Commission. It is important to note that the technical incompetency of CD staff-level personnel and the manage-ment inabilities of its administrators contributed to each of these problems. The proposed solutions tried in some way to alter personnel short-comings. In each case, the justification was "the HUD audit" federal budget cuts, and/or federal deregulation. Improved program efficiency became the preeminent goal.

Restructuring the Housing Rehab Program.

The city's inability to spend its programmed rehab money continued into the period of contraction. Because of its failure to meet numerous HUD-imposed rehab spending quotas in the sixth year,[8] HUD insisted the city reprogram $4 million of the $5 million it had proposed to spend on housing rehab activities before it would approve Houston's seventh-year application. At the time, HUD advised the city to make its rehab expenditure goals more realistic, as they are the primary yardstick for HUD's annual performance evaluation. But HUD left the door open for "re-reprogramming" the $4 million back to rehab if during the seventh year, the rehab expenditure rate improved significantly. Due to the imminent restructuring of the CD housing section and the arrival of a new deputy director from Pittsburgh's successful Urban Redevelopment Authority to head this section in August 1981, HUD was able to return the $4 million to rehab.

The new deputy director quickly proposed a major reorganization of the entire CD housing section. This internal reorganization plan was implemented in November 1981. Unfortunately, the new deputy director soon learned first-hand about the division's reputation for internal personnel problems. His plan was not accepted by several members of the staff, some of whom had not been trained to implement a successful rehab program. Much of the work-force had been hired a few years earlier when the mayor (McConn) and city council had voted to increase the staff by nearly 100 to get the rehab program moving. Yet they had been there long enough to be covered by civil service. Indeed, the new deputy director saw quickly that the major obstacle confronting him was his inability to make staffing changes because of the city's civil service system. He soon began investigating alternative structural arrangments. At one point, when it appeared he might even be appointed director of the Housing Authority, he discussed with the mayor and HUD the possibility of moving the rehab program out of CD into the Housing Authority. But when the appointment fell through, the discussion turned toward the idea of creating a nonprofit organization outside CD to run the rehab program. This idea was also rejected, but the notion of privatizing the program was not abandoned. What the mayor did endorse was the CD director's reorganization plan, which called for a 42 percent reduction in the housing section staff. (The rationalization for the reduction was a HUD audit, urging the city to cut administrative costs of this program.)

In spite of these personnel difficulties, the deputy director made major procedural and structural changes in the rehab program. In the short run, he streamlined the application process and instituted regular meetings with representatives from two savings and loan associations that held contracts with the city to run the rehab loan program. (This arrangement had replaced the unsuccessful ten-commercial-bank Houston Clearing House Association structure in March 1981.) The deputy director also opened the lines of communication between the CD division and a number of city council members and neighborhood civic groups. As a result of these aggressive management activities, the rehab program spent more in eight months than in its entire history.

In terms of long-range changes, the deputy director proposed a new rehab plan called the Houston Housing Improvement Plan (HHIP). The name change (no reference to rehab) was designed to improve the public image of the program. Once he finally sold the idea to the mayor and city council, the deputy director submitted an RFP (Request for Proposal) to the banking community to implement the HHIP--a major effort to centralize administration of this program because the entire rehab program (grants and loans) would be administered by a single private-lending institution. (Prior to the HHIP, rehab loans were administered through two savings and loan institutions and rehab grants through the city itself. Grants necessitated city council approval, which often meant lengthy delays.) This new arrangement was finally approved by city council on March 30, 1983. The deputy director resigned soon thereafter.

At the time of the eighth year audit, the rehab program was once again faulted for expenditure rate shortcomings. Shortly thereafter a major scandal involving the housing rehab program emerged. An investigation revealed that contractors were being reimbursed for rehab work that was done poorly or not at all. This (along with other factors cited later in the chapter) eventually led to the mainstreaming of the CD division and the downfall of the CD director. The mayor (Whitmire) ultimately placed the CD division in the Planning and Economic Development Department. But the role of the federal government in effecting reform aimed at greater program efficiency is clear.

Monitoring Agency Subcontractors. The division's failure to monitor and evaluate the performance of its subcontractors had been a persistent shortcoming during the expansionary years. Specifically, HUD came down hard on CD's failure to conduct on-site inspections and to internally audit the financial records of its subcontractors and subgrantees. HUD ordered the city to submit a monitoring plan, one that would guarantee that all subgrantees were routinely and regularly monitored for performance and compliance with applicable requirements.

The new CD director responded by setting up a system that requires monthly performance reports from agencies, with fiscal penalties for noncompliance, monthly site visits by auditors and inspectors, as well as in-house performance evaluations by CD staff members assigned to that duty. The new director also used the HUD audit to justify stripping the Human Resources Department of its contract to administer the CD-funded public service contracts with nonprofit agencies. She was well aware of past audits that showed that "loose" management of that department had contributed to CD's inability to get "hard" performance figures from those agencies, making program evaluation somewhat difficult.

The CD director also used the reorganization of the subcontracting structure to increase slightly the number of subgrantees and opening up the system somewhat. As the number of nonprofit subgrantees was increased, the amount of CD funds allocated to each agency was reduced. Nonprofits were required to put up more of their funds, especially for administrative costs. This move represented the director's attempt to implement a "leveraging strategy"--a goal promoted by the Reagan administration. It was also a first step in the planned move away from lump-sum contracts toward unit-cost reimbursement in anticipation of the need to reduce overall levels of CD public service spending. (The new federal regulations limited public service expenditures to 10 percent of a jurisdiction's total grant by 1985.) Both of these moves got the city high marks in the next HUD performance audit.

While the CD division vastly improved its monitoring of subcontracts already negotiated, it began to get bad marks for its procedures for awarding contracts in the first place. Another "old" problem reemerged--an attempt to circumvent regular city bidding procedures (RFPs) when it was advantageous. Such attempts to take short cuts only caused lengthy delays, because they led invariably to the involvement of the city's Legal Department.

Reducing Administrative Costs. HUD audits throughout the expansionary period repeatedly identified overstaffing and excessive costs as shortcomings of Houston's CD program. In response to these criticisms, the new CD director was ordered by the mayor to develop a reorganization plan. This plan called for a 46 percent reduction in the entire CD staff. The justifications used by the CD director were "external mandates." Specifically, she mentioned cutbacks in HUD funding of the division (a 14 percent reduction from the previous year) and HUD's previous performance audits, which cited overstaffing and duplication of effort as significant problems.

Few inside City Hall disagreed with the staff reductions. The problems that emerged with the layoffs stemmed from the manner in which they were achieved. The timing of the announcement (3 1/2 weeks before Christmas) and the disorganized determination of persons to be laid off[9] resulted in criticism of the process from council members.

## Reshaping the Citizen Participation Structure.

An antagonistic relationship between the CD staff and the HRCPC had been cited as a problem by HUD for several years. Past audits also had criticized the high administrative cost associated with citizen participation activities. The audits--plus changes in federal citizen participation requirements that shifted the emphasis toward providing information to citizens rather than soliciting their input into programmatic design--offered the mayor and her CD director the perfect opportunity to reshape the citizen participation structure. What they had in mind was a structure that would promote cooperation rather than confrontation. The first step toward that goal was to eliminate the paid staff of the HRCPC--a group that had been abolished by the previous mayor in the sixth year but reinstated in the seventh as part of his last-gasp effort to win reelection. The new mayor and her CD director adamantly opposed renewing the HRCPC contract ($290,000) once it expired on October 31, 1982.

In October 1982 the mayor appeared before an HRCPC meeting with the bad news: the contract, which at the time was supporting nine full-time workers, would not be renewed. In the midst of a storm of protest, the mayor stood firm and argued that the money should go into services, not administration: "You (HRCPC) can be in an advisory role without having to spend $290,000 in funds that should be going into community services. We want to use CD money to provide services to citizens, not to support a bureaucracy."[10] The mayor also pointed out that funding for the group had never been automatic; some previous administrations had entered into a contract with HRCPC, while others had not. She noted as well that other programs (CETA) had successfully relied upon <u>volunteer</u> boards to offer input as to citizen needs and priorities. At one point, the mayor even considered the possibility of making the HRCPC an appointed body instead of an elective one but decided instead to redirect their input through a liaison staff to be relocated in the mayor's Citizens Assistance Office (CAO). This office was headed by an individual with a long history of friendship and cooperation with HRCPC activists and target-area residents, and the relocation occurred at the time of the layoffs.

It was announced that 16 of the laid-off CD division employees would transfer to the Citizens Assistance Office to staff seven neighborhood Citizens Assistance Centers, located in CD target areas. These individuals (still funded with CD monies through a subcontract with the CAO) were trained to assist target-area residents with CD as well as non-CD-related problems. They learned to work closely with the regular city departments in ombudsman-like roles to solve problems for the people in their neighborhoods. They were also instructed to cooperate with the neighborhood HRCPC commissioners and area council members in arranging, publicizing, and attending their meetings and activities.

This new structure was intended to move the location of citizen input to a less hostile organizational unit inside City Hall. It was also intended to broaden citizen participation by encouraging these liaison officials to communicate with various neighborhood civic clubs and organizations as well as the elected citizen participation groups. (Few candidates and a low turnout rate in the 1983 HRCPC election had further weakened HRCPC's claims to represent the community.)

No matter what the outcome of each of these attempts to restructure the organization of Houston's CD program, one thing is certain--federal cutbacks and deregulation were the means to an end that had been sought for quite some time. Federal retrenchment had more impact on organizational structure than on programmatic content.

## Minimal Programmatic Impacts.

By February 1983 the city had begun to experience serious fiscal pressures because of federal cutbacks, the recession, and several errors in calculating revenue estimates. In spite of the fiscal crunch city officials hesitated to use CD funds to replace lost funds. They recognized that CD funds were also being cut back, a fact somewhat hidden by the large pool of unspent money. They also believed that the long start-up time historically associated with CD contracts would not alleviate the immediate fiscal crisis by the time the economy began to improve.

In only a limited number of cases were CD funds obviously spent to replace funds lost from other sources. Most of these involved nonprofit agency appeals to the city to allocate CD funds to help replace lost federal funds. The most notable example was the appeal by the Gulf Coast Legal Aid Foundation for a $180,000 sub-contract to provide legal services to CD target-area residents interested in participating in the CD housing rehab program. This agency had lost over $300,000 in federal funds due to federal budget cutbacks. In addition, a few day-care centers successfully petitioned city council to allocate more CD funds to replace lost state (federal pass-through) funds.

CD observers were quick to recognize that any prolonged shadow over the city's financial picture might change the city's aversion to replacement, particularly if the CD Division continued to have a large pool of unspent reprogrammable monies and if program management improved.

## Politics in the Period of Contraction.

Because organizational-structural changes dominated this period, involvement by elected officials (mayor and city council), the CD director, and the formal citizen participation group leaders and staff members was heavier than that of mid-level bureaucratic personnel in the CD division and other city departments.

The Role of Mayor. Mayor Whitmire took the lead in reshaping the structure of the CD program, although she left the details and implementation up to the CD director. The new mayor's primary goal was, as stated earlier, to improve the management of the program by making major alterations in its organizational structure. Her primary interest, from a programmatic perspective that emerged late in her administration, was to use CD funds for economic redevelopment of the inner city.

By the ninth year, the mayor began relying more heavily on her new planning department director to coordinate the CD economic redevelopment-related activities with other city departments and the private sector. By this time, most of the planned organizational-structural changes had been accomplished. Ultimately, as noted earlier, the CD division was mainstreamed into the Planning and Economic Development Department and the CD director resigned.

The Role of City Council. Council's involvement in CD programmatic decisions increased during the contraction period. There was evidence that the loosening of federal regulations and HUD's removal of "spend it or lose it" conditions had something to do with this. Citizen groups, recognizing these changes, began bypassing the CD staff and lobbying city council members directly for projects and activites to be included in the annual CD application. This strategy was particularly obvious in council's consideration of the eighth-year application (when it added spending for Gulf Coast Legal Aid Foundation, HRCPC, and three park projects in Hispanic neighborhoods whose representatives charged they had been shortchanged in the original application.)

Council members also began monitoring the geographic thrust of the CD program more carefully.[11] District-based council members especially began demanding to see allocation figures by district to be sure they were getting their fair share of CD funds. (See Table 12.2.) Their concern for geographic equity at times exceeded their concern for the types of projects being funded.

Finally, there was evidence that council members had become more knowledgeable about this program and, therefore, less likely to rubberstamp recommendations from the mayor and CD director. In presenting the eighth- and ninth-year applications to city council, the CD director was questioned extensively on subjects ranging from administrative vs. service expenditure ratios, criteria for project selection, and types of projects to be financed with economic development monies (the application did not list any specific projects) to the extent of citizen involvement in establishing program priorities.

The Role of Citizens. The influence of the HRCPC diminished in the eighth and ninth years. This change was a direct consequence of the mayors' decision not to renew this group's large administrative contract and a change in the group's access point inside City Hall (from the CD division to the Citizens Assistance Office). The domination of the HRCPC over project proposals also diminished.

In preparing the eighth-year application, the CD

staff conducted its own neighborhood meetings in order to see first-hand what were citizen priorities in the various target areas. (There had been a growing concern on the part of the CD staff that the HRCPC staff's project proposals did not accurately reflect the priorities of neighborhood residents.) Out of these 99 neighborhood meetings, some 700 project requests emerged. Of the 300 eligible, feasible requests, only a small percentage were actually used up by the eighth-year application. (However, most of the projects selected for the eighth year were from this list.) The remaining eligible projects, especially those that met the city's revitalization and leveraging criteria, served as the project pool for the ninth-year application. Consequently, neighborhoods had a stronger influence in project selection than they had had in the past.

Similarly, the creation of the CD-funded liaison positions in the Citizens Assistance Centers mandated that all segments of the community (low- and moderate-income persons, minorities, elderly, handicapped, business and civic groups) be encouraged and given opportunities to participate in future project proposals. In summary, CD regulatory changes opened up the citizen participation process--letting other groups get into a previously closed game.

The Role of HUD. HUD influence over program content decreased during the contraction period for two reasons: (1) the city had proved its ability (at least momentarily) to spend money and had gotten out from under spending directives; and (2) regulatory changes gave HUD less veto power over project selection. But while HUD's influence over program content lessened, its role as a conduit for organizational-structural changes increased, as its past audits were cited as justifications for change. The real initiative to treat HUD's recommendations for change as mandates came from the mayor and the CD director. This strategy, while effective inside City Hall, came under some attack from the outside. In an editorial entitled "Why Aren't City Officials Handling These Problems?" one local newspaper made this statement:

The city has a history in recent years of federal audits finding all sorts of problems in agencies funded with federal money, but effective action being taken only after the U.S. government blows the whistle. Why must the federal government police city hall?"[12] (emphasis added)

The political history of the program was one part of the answer, specifically the history of hands-off treatment of these programs by local elected officials. Another was the difficulty with personnel and untrained staff. Only external federal mandates (spend-it-or-lose-it dictates, budget cuts, and/or regulatory reforms) could be invoked to "override" these enormous local political obstacles.

## THE POLITICS OF CONTRACTION IN RETROSPECT:
## MINIMAL FISCAL IMPACTS, MAJOR ORGANIZATIONAL IMPACTS

In looking back, one can see that the fiscal impacts of CDBG contraction, at least initially, were negligible. And there were several explanations: The first was the persistently large pool of unspent, reprogrammable funds that prevented any real sense of a fiscal crunch in the program. A second reason was the popularization of the leveraging strategy, particularly with regard to the nonprofit agencies holding contracts to deliver the social service component of CDBG. Normally, this would have been the source of major pushes for replacement, since many of these groups had held contracts since the old Model Cities program days.

In spite of intensifying fiscal pressures on the city, there were relatively few examples of any use of CDBG funds to replace lost federal, state, or local funds. Locally, people expected that the fiscal crisis would be short-lived and they believed that economic recovery would begin before CD contracts could be finalized.

The real impact of contraction was organizational. Contraction offered the new mayor and the CD director the opportunity to try to get the program under control--and it had gotten very much out of control during the expansionary years. A tremendous reduction in the size of the CD staff, a restructuring of citizen participation mechanisms, an establishment of new subcontractor performance monitoring and evaluation procedures, and the semi-privatization of the housing rehabilitation program were all possible because of cutbacks in CDBG funding levels, HUD regulatory changes, and HUD "mandates" to improve agency performance. To use contraction as a device to effect organizational change was undoubtedly a "luxury" that could not have existed if the city had been heavily dependent upon federal funds. The real issue in the days ahead will be whether these changes had any long-lasting impact on program effectiveness, particularly once the "Boom" returns to "Boomtown."

NOTES

1. The city's experience with federal grant programs like CDBG has been relatively short. Until the mid-1970s, Houston politicians regarded reliance upon federal aid as undesirable and irresponsible. But changes in the demographic and political makeup of the city due to rapid growth led them to see the economic and political benefits of accepting federal funds. For a history of the city of Houston's late entry into the federal aid game, see Susan A. MacManus, Federal Aid to Houston (Washington, D.C.: The Brookings Institution, 1983) and Chapter 6 in this book.

2. Victor E. Bach, "Houston, Texas," in Decentralizing Urban Policy: Case Studies in Community Development, ed. by Paul R. Dommel and Associates (Washington, D.C.: The Brookings Institution, 1982, p. 90).

3. MacManus, op. cit., p. 46.

4. HUD's use of drawdown, or expenditure, rates was never popular among Houston's CD officals. They maintained it was unfair to compare Houston's expenditure rate with that of other cities for several reasons. First, Houston had no significant prior experience with large federal programs. Second, the mere size of the city, the location, and the different types of CD target areas (some inner city; some on the city's rim and of a more rural nature) meant that a greater variety of CD activities had to be planned and implemented, which increased the likelihood of slower expenditure rates. Third, climate-related problems (rain, floods) negatively impacted construction of capital projects. Consequently, the city maintained that the amount of "obligated" funds was a much more accurate measure of progress than the amount of "expended" funds.

5. The previous arrangment had been 8 council members. Five of them were elected from district-based seats but voted upon citywide. Three ran for nongeographically-based positions but were also voted upon citywide.

6. The city's formal citizen participation plan called for an elected body of 29 commissioners and their alternates, called the Houston Residents Citizen Participation Commission (HRCPC), to serve as the program's communitywide advisory board. The plan also called for an elected nine-member Area Council in each of the 24 Community Development Target Areas to serve as neighborhood advisory boards. This plan was adopted in spite of HRCPC objections.

7. NSAs (Neighborhood Strategy Areas) were narrower concentrations of low income populations in the larger target areas. Theoretically the easing of HUD regulations regarding targeting of CD funds to NSAs under the Reagan administration rules made "spreading" of CD expenditures easier from a legal perspective. However, the city of Houston did not abandon its NSA targeting strategy primarily because of political pressures from the minority communities to maintain it.

8. HUD imposed some expenditure rate requirements on the city in September 1981. At that time, the sixth-year contract conditions were revised. These new conditions set expenditure quotas at $750,000 for loans and $1,188,640 for grants by December 31, 1981. The city was able to meet its grants quota but not its loan quota. (By December 31, 1981, the city had spent only $108,617, leaving a shortfall of $641,383.) However, after a meeting with HUD, the deadline was extended an additional three months to March 31, 1982. The city also failed to meet this deadline. (By this time, it had spent only $532,493, leaving a shortfall of $217,507.) HUD once again granted a three-month extension to June 30, 1982. The city failed to meet that deadline as well (it spent $741,813 on completed cases and $129,143 on cases under construction).

9. After a great deal of adverse publicity, the filing of a lawsuit by four of the dismissed employees, an investigation of the procedures used, and a public grilling of the CD director by a city council member, the CD director admitted that the wrong organizational chart had been used to determine who would get laid off. Layoffs had been based on a chart from a reorganization plan adopted unilaterally by the CD director on June 29, 1982, but never circulated to the staff. Under the new plan, workers had been assigned to newly created sections without being informed and without any change in their duties. As a consequence, the layoffs had to be recalculated using the organizational chart which existed prior to June 29. The revised layoff plan, approved by the Civil Service Commission June 20, 1983, reinstated eight of the 54 employees originally targeted for layoffs and notified eight others not on the original list that they would lose their jobs.

10. Tony Freemantle, "Mayor Seeks to Cut CD Advisory Board Funds," Houston Chronicle, October 20, 1982.

11.    Contraction appeared to heighten the interest of council members in seeing precisely where CD funds were spent.    In the eight-year application process, several publicly alleged that CD funds were inequitably allocated across council districts.    In order to diffuse such allegations, the CD staff resorted to preparing detailed reports showing precisely how much had been spent in each council member's district (Table 12.2).    A comparison of these expenditures with district racial and CD target area composition figures confirmed that targeting continued to be an important part of the CD division's allocational strategy in spite of federal deregulation policies (see note 7).

12.    "Why Aren't City Officials Handling These Problems?" Houston Chronicle, December 7, 1982.

# PART FOUR

# Management Implications
# and Needed Reforms

Significant changes in the U.S. federal system inevitably produce defenders and critics of the new arrangement. Similarly, the debate surrounding the pros and cons of President Reagan's New Federalism has also produced supporters and detractors. The debate covers a wide variety of issues and subjects. Critics of the New Federalism frequently object to the lack of consistency among state controlled programs and the problems of resolving national problems with a highly decentralized, programmatic approach. Whereas, supporters often point to the opportunities for greater programmatic innovation and the return of essential decision-making to the states as important redeeming values of the New Federalism.

The final two chapters of this book examine the New Federalism from polar points of view. Agranoff and Rinkle present the view that the New Federalism is a unique opportunity for governments, at all levels, to adopt new strategies for planning programs and solving problems. Essentially, he argues that local and state governments will have to develop greater trust and cooperation in order to deal with the problems they mutually face. David Walker, however, argues that one of the major problems with the New Federalism has been the lack of attention given to programmatic implementation at the state and local levels. This failure has led to programs that only superficially attack the major domestic problems confronting the entire nation.

# 13

## The New Federalism and Intergovernmental Problem Solving

### Robert Agranoff
### and Valerie Lindsay Rinkle

This chapter explains how many routine, interjurisdictional issues are handled in the intergovernmental
system. The focus is on a widely used but little
recognized approach to intergovernmental management--
problem-solving, which is gaining in prominence as
officials recognize that a number of approaches may be
used to cope with the conditions that President Reagan's
New Federalism addresses. The discussion of managerial
problem-solving is based on an empirical examination of
metropolitan-based, public-private intergovernmental
organizations dedicated to the solving of human services
problems.[1]

Trends set in motion before the Reagan era have
brought on the need for intergovernmental management
(IGM). Growth and complexity in the federal grants
system, and then decline and resource scarcity amidst
steady demand for government services in health,
education, housing, income maintenance, employment and
training, and social services has caused governments at
all levels to become more interdependent. Many social
issues facing communities have proved to be beyond the
responsibility and capability of a single level or type of
government, or the private sector. Thus, governmental and
private sector agents found they had to combine and work
together to manage their way through community problems by
adjusting federal and state programs to their needs.

Then, at a national level, a new intergovernmental
administrative environment during the Reagan era began
addressing growth and complexity from a different but
complementary perspective. As is discussed in this
volume, the Reagan federalism program has included

proposals for sweeping changes in the grant-in-aid system, including consolidation of programs into block grants, elimination of some categorical programs, more flexible categorical programs, reduction in grant conditions and regulations, and shifting of program operation and administrative responsibility to the states. Other changes involve reduction in aid to state and local governments, elimination of the cost and regulatory burden placed on subnational governments, and devolution of intergovernmental programs by placing greater responsibility on the states and less on the federal government.

Admittedly, the Reagan policy of fiscal austerity has meant that federal control and supervision over some large programs, such as AFDC and Medicaid, has actually increased. In spite of these centralizing moves, there is no doubt that the balance point of intergovernmental relationships has turned in new directions.[2] This New Federalism context, with its emphasis on shifting the burden of making programs work at state and local operating levels, supports the need for IGM.

Expansion of the federal system has generated a myriad of intergovernmental relationships and has inevitably turned attention at working levels to management. IGM is considered to involve daily purposive transactional relationships between component governments in a federal system. The IGM, according to Wright,[3] emphasizes the goal-achievement dimension of intergovernmental relations (IGR).

These actions constitute managerial activities because management is a process by which cooperating officials direct action toward some goal.[4] Wright also suggests that IGM may well be the newest phase in intergovernmental relationships, representing a sharp and distinct departure from previous eras in federalism and IGR. He identifies IGM with three special qualities:[5] 1) a problem-solving focus, that is, "an action oriented process that allows administrators at all levels the wherewithall to do something constructive";[6] 2) a means of understanding and coping with the system as it is, including perspectives on how and why interjurisdictional changes occur and guidance on how to cope with the system; and 3) an emphasis on contacts and communication networks. Similarly, Agranoff and Lindsay conclude that IGM involves a complex of actions between officials brought together around a common task, recognizing and making jurisdictional-legal, political, and technical accommodations that bear on the task.[7] Rosenthal refers to IGM as an indirect form of management, because service production or program compliance occurs through different organizations--under conditions of partial accountability, differing program objectives, exchanges across organizational boundaries--on an ongoing basis.[8] To sum up, IGM can be construed as a complex activity involving the solution of interjurisdictional problems by parties on an ongoing basis, clothed within the need to understand and communicate over law, politics and the substantive components of the problem at hand.

## APPROACHES TO IGM

The literature suggests six additional ways to approach IGM. First, is the planning or "top down" approach to management and coordination. This approach was articulated by James Sundquist in Making Federalism Work, which was written as the "creative federalism" of the Great Society was in full bloom. The basic dilemma was said to be "how to achieve goals and objectives that are established by the national government, through the actions of other governments, state and local, that are legally independent and politically may even be hostile."[9] This problem was compounded because there was no overall national strategy, but a series of individual legislative enactments that were said to have led to confusion, overlapping program authority, uncertain responsibility, and duplication of effort. As a result of the hue and cry of state and local officials over this state of affairs, the federal government chose enforced or required coordination as a means of growth management.

Many pieces of grant legislation mandated interagency linkages, comprehensive plans, joint boards and councils, special planning areas, and quasi-governmental planning units. As Sundquist maintains, the government "designated coordination," but chose to "rely almost wholly upon systems of mutual adjustment."[10] While this approach was probably never very successful, critics of the growing power of the national government seized upon the requirements contained in this strategy as evidence that Washington was attempting to "manage" the federal system from its vantage point.[11] Some of the Reagan New Federalism initiatives are geared to reducing the centralizing effects of this approach.

A second approach is structural-legal reform of the federal system. The best known example of this approach is that of the Advisory Commission on Intergovernmental

Relations (ACIR) program. For some years ACIR has proposed a reform agenda that includes (1) standardizing and reducing federal grant requirements, (2) converting categorical grants into block grants and broader categorical programs, (3) assessing the regulatory impact of grant programs, and (4) re-examining the functional responsibilities of the levels of government in the interest of sorting out responsibilities by levels of government.[12] Again, the Reagan New Federalism has embraced portions of this agenda. Although some would question whether this is actually a managerial approach, there is no doubt that such structural-legal revisions directly affect the way daily business is conducted in IGM.

Third are the attempts to smooth the managerial processes of intergovernmental assistance without necessarily changing the structure of the grants program. These activities have been most prominent at the federal level. Shapek's thorough account of the development of the grant-in-aid system reveals many such tactics: mandatory notification of state and local chief executives, a series of Office of Management and Budget (OMB) circulars that attempt to make federal grants management easier, experiments at joint federal agency grant review and funding, authorization to waive program requirements that impede operations, decentralization of federal decisionmaking and regionalization, and Federal Regional Councils.[13] The Reagan administration de-emphasizes this approach in favor of legal-structural reform nevertheless; it remains alive in some form. For example, the Medicaid waiver program allows states to fund a number of home health and social services for the frail elderly, as alternatives to nursing homecare. These services are otherwise not allowable.

A fourth IGM approach develops governmental capacity to manage programs. Honadle identifies capacity as governmental ability to (1) anticipate and influence change; (2) make informed and intelligent policy decisions; (3) develop programs and implement policy; (4) attract, absorb and manage resources; and (5) evaluate current activities to guide future action.[14] How is capability an IGM tool? A government that has such capacity is presumed to be better able to manage or receive an intergovernmental program and make it suitable to a jurisdiction's purposes. For example, a city government that uses Community Development Block Grant funds to convert closed schools to senior centers may well be making a federal program work for local purposes. Likewise, a categorical program like a Developmental Disabilities grant may be used to support a state's own case management system by combining federal and state requirements into one program.

A number of the policy implementation studies point to agency capacity as a key element in program success.[15] States often pursue local government capacity-building as an IGM strategy, particularly in improving their ability to handle finances, personnel, and other areas of management and community and economic development.[16] Thus, for both the funder and the recipient of an intergovernmental grant, or for those regulated by government, possession of capacity that leads to successful program management can be an important strategy.

Policy management is a fifth approach to IGM. Policy management came into prominence nearly a decade ago when an OMB study committee defined it as "the identification of needs, analysis of options, selection of programs and allocation of resources on a jurisdiction-wide basis."[17]

Interest in policy management stems from the need for state and local officials to manage their jurisdictions as a whole by making conceptual and operational sense out of the maze of functional, vertically structured intergovernmental programs, and to assure that the programs are meeting community needs effectively and efficiently. An example of the policy management approach would be a city government's use of several federal and state programs-- Community Development Block Grants, Historic Preservation, Job Training Partnership funds, state enterprise zone and tax abatement programs, combined with private instruments to support a community development effort. Although not always formally identified as policy management, sub-national governments regularly engage in this IGM approach, and a number of managerial techniques have been developed to support this process.[18]

A sixth strategy involves the use of bargaining and its variations. Buntz and Radin describe the intergovernmental system as involving necessary conflict arising due to some structural condition (national vs. state goals) or process event (political changes), environmental events or conditions (fiscal changes or new national initiatives) or by events or conditions internal to the party (personnel changes or unique needs of states).[19] Bargaining then becomes a recognized means of managing this conflict. Ingram was one of the first to identify this approach in her study of water quality programs, concluding that federal grants do not necessarily buy compliance, because both grantor and recipient possess important resources, but create an opportunity for bargaining.[20] The use of bargaining in IGM has taken a number of different forms, most prominently through the use of the Negotiated Investment Strategy (NIS). Under the rubric of general community and economic development, three cities--Columbus, Ohio, Gary, Indiana, and St. Paul, Minnesota--initiated a set of intergovernmental program changes, that were bargained through by the three levels of government until package agreements were arrived at.[21] Although NIS represents a highly formalized use of bargaining, less formal bargaining is used in numerous transactions between officials representing governments, wherever conflicts between parties need to be worked through.

In addition to these six IGM approaches, problem-solving deserves consideration. It can be a major tool available to managers as they work within the intergovernmental system.

## THE PROBLEM-SOLVING PROCESS

Because problem-solving (PS) is a term that is loosely used as a "catch-all" label to identify a variety of managerial tasks (and is sometimes regarded as the essence of management), it is necessary to distinguish it as it is used here; as a technique that managers can select from a number of other working processes. It is neither a new approach nor is it exclusively an IGM tool. PS is a systematic process that can be used both inter- and intraorganizationally. Because the subject at hand is IGM, attention is focused exclusively between organizations. For the purposes of this research, the attention is on PS as a formal process, although it is obviously undertaken more frequently on an informal or ad hoc basis.

Formal interorganizational PS involves a systematic and pragmatic search for solutions in situations where oganizational representatives mutually recognize a discrepancy between a current state and a desired end, creatively explore options, and reach a solution that is beneficial to more than a single interest.[22] As L. David Brown has suggested, "Problem-solving involves clarifying common interests and differences, developing trust and communicating accurate information between parties, flexibly exploring alternatives and the potential for mutual benefit, and choosing alternatives that maximize gains for both parties."[23]

The use of PS in IGM is illustrated by the following case example:

A rural county health officer seeks a change in the way the federal-state Primary Care Program (community health centers) operates, to allow funding of nurse-midwives in remote areas where physician availability is non-existent. The service is not in the existing state plan but the use of nurse mid-wives is legal in the state and would be acceptable to federal officials if the state would agree. The state is initially reluctant to alter its plan because of the cost implications of allowing every county this option; it would drain fixed program resources from higher priority issues from the state's perspective. However, state health officials are sympathetic to the needs of the county. Although the county official does not disagree with the overall state priorities, she believes that conditions in her county are unique and the midwife option should be allowable.

Moreover, mild political pressure occurs from county commissioners and area state legislators. Without the program change county general funds would no doubt pay for the services. Pressure is also put on by the area congressional representatives who contacted the federal Regional Health Officer (RHO).

The RHO then instructs his staff to convene the parties and work out a solution. A "brainstorming" meeting, held in the state capital, begins with statements of agreement on program aims. Program cost and operational data are exchanged, then the group proceeds to agreement that the problem needs a solution other than approval or denial. It is also agreed that bargaining would lead to a compromise solution likely to make both state and local officials unhappy.

Continued processing and exploring leads to the emergence of a creative solution. The state agrees to seek a federal waiver, making the county a "demonstration site" for the use of midwives. The waiver request, jointly developed by county and state officials, which includes a plan of action that would involve shared minimal funding increases by state and local governments, is to be approved by the federal government for a three year period, after which the state will have to alter its plan or discontinue funding of nurse midwives.

This example is a fairly typical representation of PS. Parties to the issue recognize that a problem exists, the need for a type of primary care, and they wish to avoid high levels of conflict and seek solutions that will create the feeling of not having lost in a struggle. The issue focuses on overall program intent, program results, and the maintenance of a long-term relationship. The search for accommodation and a creative solution is central. The parties have chosen a management approach called problem solving and have applied it to IGM.

As most students of management know, there is a rich PS tradition in the literature. It is primarily grounded in two areas. First are works on creative leadership and decision-making, such as those of Kepner and Tregoe,[24] Koberg and Begnall,[25] DeBono,[26] and Simon,[27] which emphasize the importance of managers' defining problems, investigating situations and options, making choices and reviewing actions. PS is thus identified as an important process managers can use when facing difficult situations. Second, PS has been identified as a means of managing conflict. Walton and McKersie, for example, found that many unions and companies have been able to settle their differences through "integrative" solutions, or new ideas that transcend narrow bargaining issues, that are of benefit for both parties.[28]

The use of PS to solve interdepartmental conflicts was first identified in Lawrence and Lorsch's landmark study, Organization and Environment, where they found that managers openly exchanging information about the facts of a situation as they see them, and their feelings about these facts, and then working through their differences proved to be very successful in reaching solutions that were optimal for the organization.[29] This mode of difference resolution was identified as "confrontation" or problemsolving. Similarly, studies by Blake and Mouton,[30] Grenier,[31] Guest,[32] and Pondy[33] found that open processes by superiors and subordinates leading to mutual discussion and exploration of problems were important means of solving differences.

Problem-solving is, as one might suspect, closely related to bargaining. Distinguishing between the two is sometimes difficult. As is suggested in the conflict management literature, both PS and bargaining are considered "productive" interventions, and their use when differences between parties exist is considered superior[34] to escalating, supressing or withdrawing from conflict. In an interorganizational context, Brown identifies the differences between PS and bargaining:

Interorganizational bargaining involves the representatives' recognition of both conflicting and common interests, but focuses on issues in which one organization's gain is perceived to be tied to another's loss. Representatives recognize their differences, communicate information in guarded and selective terms, and act to control each other's options without escalating past shared limits.[35]

Interorganizational problem-solving, in contrast, brings together organizational representatives in circumstances dominated by issues of which common interests are perceived as more important than conflicting interests. Problem-solving involves perceptions of similarities of common concern, relatively open exchange of information, and search for alternatives that benefit both parties.[36]

Thus, combining creative leadership and decision-making with conflict management, PS involves open and shared difference management through some means of creative diagnosis and decision-making where two or more parties benefit from the solution.

Studies of public policy implementation suggest that PS-like processes are often used to help make intergovernmental programs work. Bardach refers to "fixing" as a type of PS in his study of California's state-county mental health programs, particularly when actors take "means adjusting certain elements of the system of games."[37] This type of fixing involved "lending a helping hand," "imposing a new set of priorities," "setting political forces in motion," and "trying to rewrite local zoning ordinances."[38] Meltsner and Bellavita's study of an educational proficiency "policy organization," that is, an inter-organizational network of activists involved in making a program work, avoided routine decision rules and operating procedures[39] by anticipating the future, encouraging participation, and helping people responsible for the program do their work.[40]

Radin and associates' evaluation of a federal experiment allowing twelve states to consolidate their state plans revealed that many of the changes desired by state officials did not necessarily require seeking formal waivers, as had been anticipated, or the need to bargain out differences. Numerous issues were resolved by development of mutually satisfactory solutions, or through joint administrative action or merely federal administrative interpretation that a desired practice could be

followed.[41]    Similarly, Williams' block grant study
concluded that in many cases bargaining between federal
and local officials was simply not enough to make programs
work; there is a need to develop additional capacity to
make program repairs and adjustments along the line.[42]
The need for this type of capacity emanates from a policy
implementation process that, as Elmore has suggested,
relies on a number of different organizations, with
veriegated loci of authority, expertise, skill, and
proximity to the task.   He concludes that "formal
authority, in the form of policy statements, is heavily
dependent on specialized problem-solving capabilities
farther down the chain of authority."[43]

The practice of PS is an important reinforcing
managerial strategy for the federalism of the 1980s.  In a
devolved intergovernmental system, in which fewer requirements and more flexible programs exist, it is important
that managers use all the options available to them.  One
important application of PS is enhancing the value of
federal programs at the local level.  The work of intergovernmental managers in the six metropolitan areas
explains how this PS process works.

RESEARCH SETTING AND FINDINGS

The research is based on the study of intergovernmental bodies (IGB) in six metropolitan areas.  In
each setting, local officials and private sector representatives, and in a number of cases state and federal
officials, voluntarily formed joint ventures to solve
intergovernmental problems impacting their area.  Chart
13.1 identifies the partner membership of each IGB, as
well as the general objectives and major working components of each structure.  As Chart 13.1 indicates, each
IGB involved the local general purpose government(s), as
well as special districts, such as school districts and
mental health authorities and private sector actors such
as United Ways and local foundations as linchpin partners.
Moreover, each developed a somewhat different set of
formal working components, although all developed some
distinct means for making basic decisions, and for doing
the actual work on problems.  Although the IGBs appear to
have somewhat different objectives, all share the common
characteristic of their working attention to planning,
management, and coordination related to human-service
delivery.
The operation of these IGBs was previously described

Chart I
IGB Structures and Objectives

| IGB Name | Partners | Working Components | Self-Described Objectives |
|---|---|---|---|
| Dayton-Montgomery County Human Services Partnership (HSP) | City of Dayton, Montgomery County, United Way, Miami Valley Regional Planning Council (MVRPC), Mental Health Board | Policy Council Director's Group Core Planning Group Hired Staff | Enhance analytical capability of planning and managing human services through IGM |
| Metropolitan Human Services Commission of Columbus/Franklin County (MHSC) | City of Columbus, Franklin County, Mental Health Board, Mental Retardation Board, United Way Community Action Organization, Chamber of Commerce, organized labor, two foundations, at-large representatives | Board of Trustees Cabinet of Executives Hired Staff Working Committees of shared staff | Provide a bridge between the various sectors to deal with planning, financing, and service delivery |
| Coalition for Human Services Planning in Indianapolis/Marion County (CHSP) | Mayor's Office, Governor's Office, City-County Council, religious community, two foundations, United Way, Indianapolis Public Schools | Steering Committee Screening Committee Staff support donated by Community Service Council | Voluntary effort of the public and private sectors to cooperate on funding coordination, information sharing, and joint planning of specifically identified needs |
| Baltimore Blueprint (Blueprint) | City, State, U.S. DHHS, Southwest Merchants Association, Greater Baltimore Committee, MD Department of Social Services, MD Department of Mental Health and Hygiene | Board of Directors 5 Policy Teams Hired Staff | Cooperative effort between the three governments, the community, and service providers to reform delivery of human services in a target neighborhood of 40,000 people |
| Pueblo Area Council of Governments (PACOG) Human Resources Commission (HRC) | City of Pueblo, County of Pueblo, two school districts, water district | PACOG Elected Officials Citizens' Group (HRC) Hired Staff | Intergovernmental planning and coordination of funding and program activities |
| Human Resources Coalition Seattle/King County (HRC) | County, City State, Region 4 Department of Social and Health Services, Region X DHHS, Pacific Northwest Grant-makers Forum, Region X Community Services Administration | Policy Body Task Forces | Address selected general problems of joint interest for planning and information purposes |

in a paper that attempted to define the components of
IGM. It was defined as a process in which actors make
three types of accommodations: 1) jurisdictional-legal,
2) political, and 3) technical. In other words, successful IGM involved emphasis on developing workable
solutions while recognizing and making accommodations
necessary to allow for law and jurisdiction, politics, and
the substantive details of the issue. These three types
of working accommodations converged on a fourth, a task
orientation or context, around which problem solutions
actually emerged.[44]

The processes by which IGBs solved their problems
were studied in the field through examination of the
development and operation of their structures, and through
the study of focused problem resolution. Seventeen "mini-
case studies" of problem resolution were developed.
Extensive documentation of each problem resolution process
is contained elsewhere.[45] Chart 13.2 provides a summary
listing of the PS projects. Each of the projects illustrated here contains a statement of the problem the IGB
was attempting to solve, the name of the PS project given
by the IGB, a summary of the major outcome(s) that
resulted from the problem-solving process, and a generic
descriptor of the intergovernmental routine represented by
the process. Each descriptor roughly corresponds to
similar work performed by all types of intergovernmental
managers.

As Chart II indicates, the IGBs worked on a variety
of different problems. They did not try to solve
community problems beyond their control nor did they
attempt to change the structure of the federal system.
The IGBs focused on "everyday problems" relating to
information, planning, management, and service delivery.
Moreover, the routines followed by the IGBs appear to be
relatively typical of the everyday issues followed by
other managers. Most managers who deal with intergovernmental issues are frequently called upon to adjust
categorical grants, understand the complexities of the
system, allocate discretionary funds, make state and
federal dollars and programs serve local purposes, adjust
regulatory positions to program intent, apply state codes
with local jurisdictions, and so on. Most solutions
involved taking such actions as local administrative
accommodations, joint venturing and coordination, improved
program management, improved capacity to manage multiple
programs, or some form of negotiated accommodation with
state and federal governments.

Chart II
IGB Projects, Outcomes and Intergovernmental Management Routines

| Location/IGB | Problem Addressed | Project | Outcome | Routine |
|---|---|---|---|---|
| Dayton/HSP | Inadequate Services access | Decentralization | New multi-service centers | Using combined funding sources |
| Dayton/HSP | Absence of funding criteria | Title XX Allocation | Needs based county process | Method for allocating dedicated block grant funds |
| Dayton/HSP | Guaging federal fund reductions | Impact Analysis | Program-by-program data | Providing policy-makers information on the local impact of federal funding patterns |
| Indianapolis/ CHSP | Inaccessibility and duplication of services | Access Services | New central management structure, mergers, extensions | Developing an interagency joint operations model |
| Indianapolis/ CHSP | Disparate information bases | Human Services Information System | Public-private common data base | Creating decision-making information for an inter-governmentalized local delivery system |
| Columbus/ MHSC | Grant funding and program requirements did not fit local needs | Negotiated Investment strategy | Rededicated funds, expanded services, local tax burden relieved | Reaching two or three level agreement on adjustments to categorical grants |
| Columbus/ MHSC | Conflicting pressure over proposed zoning ordinance | Deinstitutionalization/group homes | Study of non-effect of group homes on property values | Assisting local decision-makers apply a state code |
| Columbus/ MHSC | A community response to federal reductions | Contingency | Plan, funder commitments to meet priority needs, local fund raising, new referendum | Developing criteria based formulae for distribution of relatively unrestricted financial support |

Chart II (cont.)
IGB Projects, Outcomes and Intergovernmental Management Routines

| Location/IGB | Problem Addressed | Project | Outcome | Routine |
|---|---|---|---|---|
| Pueblo/HRC | Officials desire to manage funding | General Revenue Sharing Allocation | Planning model, review process, contracts management, technical assistance | A program for distributing and managing unrestricted financial assistance by local criteria |
| Pueblo/HRC | Lack of local coordination of federal grant applications | A-95 | Review process | Assessment of federal grant applications within local concerns |
| Pueblo/HRC | Lack of service provider linkages | Sector planning and coordination | Services planning system, functional service councils, joint agency practices, agency consolidations | Establishing linkages between disparate service providers in the same functional areas |
| Baltimore/ Blueprint | Inadequate school attendance verification | Welfare/School Enrollment | Changed regulation interpretation, computer tracking model | Reforming intergovernmental administrative practices and securing regulatory changes to achieve a program result |
| Baltimore/ Blueprint | Lack of standards | Foster care reform | Pilot projected to be model for statewide implementation | Changing administrative procedures and standards |
| Baltimore/ Blueprint | Disconnected agency responses | Adolescent pregnancy strategy | Joint agency program through policy interventions at three government levels | Developing a comprehensive strategy to meet a local concern through the actions of different government levels |
| Seattle/HRC | Insufficient community housing for the mentally ill | Housing/ Residential care | Model residential continuum, county government operation, state funding | Redirecting a major state program to fit changing state and local priorities |
| Seattle/HRC | Disparate planning processes | Common Data base | Joint taxonomy of service definitions, common reporting forms, reduction of financial reporting systems from five to two | Crafting new tools for joint planning |
| Seattle/HRC | Gaps in program availability | Energy Assistance | Extended coverage, reduced duplication, single county-wide information and referral agency | Implementing a complicated multi-recipient, federal-state program on a metropolitan-wide basis |

These solutions have led to a number of mutually beneficial outcomes: 1) tangible products, such as new housing units for the mentally ill, increased access to services, more equitable allocation of scarce grant dollars, easing the property tax burden, better information for decision-making, and joint management practices; and 2) decision-analytic processes, such as increased ability to coordinate, improved intergovernmental skills, better use of information, and better working relationships among officials at various levels of government.

The PS process itself was found to closely correspond to the problem-solving process found in the management literature. For example, Walton and McKersie examined interorganizational joint problem-solving and found the following sequence: problem recognition and definition, search for alternatives, search for consequences of alternatives, evaluate the alternatives against criteria, reach a mutually satisfactory solution, accept the best solution possible. Their process also suggests that parties continually redefine problems, alter criteria and search for better solutions.[46]

Since the IGB study also involved the process of bringing together intergovernmental parties and post-decision activities requiring independent parties to act, the IGM sequence was modified to incorporate these steps. The PS sequence that was investigated included: convening of decision-makers, identifying the problem, developing a course of action, implementing the decision, and monitoring the decision. Chart 13.3 attempts to illustrate this five-step process. It summarizes the PS sequence for one exemplary project from each IGB. Each of the five steps is identified along the left-hand side of the chart and the specific activity that parallels that step for each project has been entered into the appropriate cell. A horizontal reading of the chart reveals that, although the specifics were quite different, the activities were similar enough to fit under a common identifier. A vertical reading indicates that, in sequence, the steps make up a common PS format. Similar sequences were found to exist in the other eleven projects, although in some cases the pattern was altered slightly by previous work on projects outside of the IGB or procedures introduced by non-IGB partners. The sequence will now be explained.

First, pertinent actors and other parties to be involved were convened into decision-making bodies, in

Chart III  The Problem-Solving Sequence

| | Convening of Decision Makers | Identifying the problems | Developing a course of action | Implementing the decision | Monitoring the decision |
|---|---|---|---|---|---|
| Columbus/MHSC Negotiated Investment Strategy | MHSC Exec. Director made member of City team, preliminary discussions with mayor, other officials | MHSC cabinet framed set of human service issues where Federal and State requirements were unsuitable to local needs | Issues agreed on by local negotiating teams, forwarded to state and Federal teams. Teams synthesize issues. | Tripartite negotiations and agreement signed by officials at all three levels | Informal oversight of process by parties |
| Pueblo/HRC GRS Allocation Process | HRC staff bring elected officials into process | HRC staff needs assessment and resource inventory indentifies absence of priority-based funding for GRS allocations | HRC staff identify program needs and service gaps and elected officials review GRS procedures and priorities | HRC review applications for GRS funds and make recommendations to elected officials. Contracts between funder government and agency drawn by HRC | HRC monitor findings of agency reports and provides technical assistance where needed |
| Dayton/HSP Decentralization Strategy | HSP bring City and County officials together. Private sector also involved | City and County desire more multi-service centers to increase access to services | HSP study feasibility/develop plan for staffing, financing, facility options and social indicators | County Commission adopts a plan and HSP oversees implementation | Progress occasionally assessed, HSP becomes advocate as center development slowed |

Chart III cont.

| | Convening of Decision Makers | Identifying the problems | Developing a course of action | Implementing the decision | Monitoring the decision |
|---|---|---|---|---|---|
| Seattle/HRC Housing & Residential Care for the Mentally Ill | HRC places on agenda; loans staff to project | Shared staff investigate need for protected living environments, survey facilities and report to HRC on needs | Report presented as model residential care continuum and strategy for implementation | Review and acceptance by HRC. Implementation by City and County; use of state funds to construct 5 facilities | Verbal progress reports |
| Indianapolis/ CHSP Access Services Model | Coalition meets and recognizes the problem | Interagency staff group analyzed funding requirements | Model proposed by staff; adopted by coalition | Recognition of funding problem; joint funding of model | Executives group formed to oversee and develop long-term solutions |
| Baltimore/ Blueprint Welfare and School Enrollment | Policy Teams address school verification of AFDC children 16 and older | Research problems, regulations, standards and administrative practices | School and AFCD staff agree to track by coordinated computer data program | Agreement by federal-state officials to change support formula | Data program and policy teams review |

this case the IGBs. The fact that they are permanent bodies of decision-makers and administrators distinguishes them from normal "task forces," "study groups," or "blue ribbon committees." In every case, the groups were brought together over a problem, whether it was a sense of the need to coordinate for a given purpose or a specific issue such as an information system, grant allocations, or teenage pregnancies. Members understand the political implications of the problem areas, possess knowledge of human service programs, and, most importantly, have the authority to speak for their organization or jurisdiction. Considerable time was spent designing a structure and developing comfortable working relationships, but in each IGB these two functions were performed while approaching specific issues. Whether the original aim included the establishment of a broad-range program of coordination, a common information system, or a comprehensive planning program, in all cases continuity actually flowed from the initial consideration of a specific problem.

Second, the parameters of a specific problem were identified. Project staff and planning staff members from the "primary" or "sponsoring" jurisdiction, and perhaps key resourse persons who were not decision-makers, researched the problem area and presented the findings. In every case, actual coordination or planning began with the process of attempting to resolve a specific problem. Generally, the issue was discussed in detail by the decision-makers and agreement on the problem was forged. At this point, a specific issue became a "formal" part of the group's agenda with appropriate research tasks delegated to the staff. The staff usually presented their findings in the form of a staff report with a recommended course of action or a summary with conclusions, depending upon the particular style and operation of the locale.

Third, the decision body reviewed the reports submitted, discussed possible solutions, and ultimately developed or adopted a course of action. Because those adopting a course of action have authority to speak for their program or jurisdiction, securing the necessary support was less problematic than when actors not in authority attempt to coordinate. Through very different means, each of the six IGBs demonstrated repeatedly that once an issue passed the agenda and fact-finding thresholds, representative partners could usually "deliver" for their jurisdiction. However, support of a jurisdiction usually involved the process of "going back home," so to speak, and getting ratification or at least informal support from that jurisdiction. The entire process of investigating, ratifying, and then deciding, proved to be an extremely long process, but necessary for any hope of implementation.

Fourth, the course of action was translated from policy agreement into practice. Actually, the genesis of the action steps was almost always contained in the research or fact-finding process, which was modified as decisions were made. Many discussions and negotiations with service delivery agencies, funding bodies, and governmental jurisdictions were undertaken during the early stages to determine the willingness and commitment to carry forth a proposed course of action. In every case, the process was involved and somewhat cumbersome; however, this was necessary, given the interjurisdictional nature of the enterprise. Decisions were made by the IGB and ratified by the respective jurisdictions but almost always carried out by the respective jurisdictions and service delivery agencies. IGBs have little direct power to implement their decisions. Furthermore, they rely on several jurisdictions taking simultaneous action and/or the primary or project staff laying out the steps to be followed, parties to be involved, and resources required.

Fifth, the IGB or its staff attempted to monitor the course of action to provide an information base to be fed back to the decision body for assessment and modification of the course of action. Perhaps due to the difficulty of monitoring another partner's jurisdictional turf, or because of the need to attack new problems, or because of sheer exhaustion, the last step was not as closely followed as the others. As Chart 13.3 indicates, systematic attempts to follow what actually happened, or development of reporting mechanisms, or the use of internal program evaluations, were not regularly undertaken. Rather, information on the progress of joint decisions was informal and irregular, and evaluation tended to be post-mortem discussions or unstructured progress reports. Consequently, with a few exceptions, feedback to the IGB for assessment and modification of courses of action, while it did occur, tended to be limited and disjointed.

Some observations about this PS sequence might be useful for those interested in its utility. First, the process does not necessarily require a formal structure like an IGB. As the policy implementation studies mentioned earlier indicate, intergovernmental managers should be able to act on a more ad hoc basis when they agree a problem exists and choose to follow similar steps. Second, the observed sequence was occasionally modified in the light of real world circumstances. There had to be room for many decision "loops" throughout the process, and in some cases had to go back to earlier steps. Also, the IGBs often found it necessary to formally bypass steps, such as when a problem had already been researched or alternatives had been formulated. Rather than stand on procedure, they accepted what had been done to achieve results. Third, other considerations not systematically investigated, such as the willingness to reach agreement, put it on paper, and carry it out through relevant jurisdictions also appeared as important. These necessary conditions, along with the sequence of PS steps, proved to be a blueprint for focused or issue-based coordination between parties representing governments. Fourth, and finally, the sequence proved to be more exhaustive to execute than explain. It involved (1) a large time investment for process development and mutual understanding; (2) involvement of the real political and administrative decision-makers, leaving the fact finding and operational details to staff persons; (3) a focus on the problem itself and not tangential or extraneous issues; and (4) a constant testing and negotiating of solutions.

Because the six IGBs "naturally" participated in four expected steps, and the fifth to some extent, it seems reasonable to conclude that, while this may not be the only sequence of intergovernmental PS, it is one that is likely to serve others when they face similar situations. When faced with specific problems of importance to them, local jurisdictions can combine to solve them, bringing in the state and federal government, if necessary.

DISCUSSION:  PS IN MANAGING INTERGOVERNMENTAL AFFAIRS

In settings where it can best contribute to the facilitation of achieving process aims between governments, PS can be extremely useful and is perhaps most likely to be undertaken. The following discussion uses the IGB research presented above as a basis for a broader discussion of problemsolving in IGM.

The parties must agree that there is a discrepency between an actual situation and some desired state and be willing to face that situation together. In the IGB study, parties attempted to solve "middle-level problems" they had the capacity to deal with. Chart 13.2 has identified these problems, such as insufficient community housing for the mentally ill in Seattle, inadequate verification of school attendance in Baltimore, and the need to develop a strategy to deal with federal funding reductions in Columbus. These and other issues, such as those related to the allocation of discretionary funding, sector planning and coordination, or changing federal and state interpretations, involved issues where the IGB parties could get the relevant parties to agree that they would work on them.

Similar situations arise in other communities; a city manager and the director of a transit district find that a planned bus rerouting will disrupt city plans for some limited traffic areas; state finance department officials and town/village clerks are dissatisfied with the number of audit exceptions local officials receive for not performing according to state code; and a state education board adds a computer literacy requirement and a fiscally troubled school district has considered increasing its computer instruction but is hard pressed to find the funds to meet this mandate.

Of course, there are also numerous situations where such a problem agreement cannot be reached. Numerous grant regulations turn out to be detailed statutory presecriptions that administrators feel compelled to follow closely and can allow no exceptions. In the IGB study, issues where the state or federal government would not engage in resolution, or where local politicians wished to avoid major confrontations, or where there was fear that the independence of jurisdictions would be threatened were avoided. But in many other situations there was sufficient agreement that a problem existed and could be approached. These usually involved some minimal level of conflict conducive to a productive solution[47] that could be handled by the involved parties without outsider or third party intervention.[48]

In addition, the interests of the parties need to be common, but not identical. In the IGB study, local elected officials pressure to have a city-county strategy to allocate GRS funds in Pueblo, the agreed-upon perception by administrators in Dayton that there was inaccessibility to services, and Baltimore agency officials' concern for the absence of an adolescent pregnacy prevention strategy all constituted areas where parties had enough interest to be committed to doing something about the issue. Following the situations external to the study mentioned above, the city manager and the transit district manager want public transportation in the congested area of the city; state officials supervising local clerks' financial management prefer, along with the locals, that they do a competent job and not be subject to civil or criminal penalties; and, the school board agrees with the intent of a state mandated computer literary program even though it contests many details of the regulations.

In many other IGM situations, however, such commonality does not exist. The jurisdictional factor in intergovernmental relations, as well as the constitutional and legal arrangements surrounding federalism encourage the seeking and protecting of autonomy. Intergovernmental actors find the need to see their interests as distinct and protect their interests at all costs. But when commonality of interests can be recognized, the possibility of confronting the differences generated by representing different jurisdicitons is real. When discussing "picket fence federalism," for example, Wright suggests that implicit in the notion is "a sense of program purpose, or one or more strategies for coordination, and locus of responsibility."[49] Commonality of interest is perhaps what drives independent officials to work on the resolution of problems. In PS there is a minimal need for parties to come together and convene in some sort of forum. They must agree enough that there is a problem surrounding an area of mutual interest.

PS also requires that an open exhange of informtion related to the problem and its potential solution be revealed by the involved parties. IGB processes revealed such an open participative pattern. Budgets and funding sources were openly exchanged in order to study the impact of funding reductions in Columbus and Dayton. The availability of funds, per diem costs, and housing slots was revealed by all parties in Seattle. Fee and wage scales, service case load slack, and purchasing practices were shared in Pueblo. Federal, state, and local teams for Columbus did not hold back--they revealed what they could and could not do during the issue synthesizing stage (see Chart 13.3). The city manager and transit manager need to share their plans, funding sources, and funding requirements; local clerks must show state officials how they manage their books so problems can be discovered and improvements can be made; the school district must reveal available resources to meet the computer literacy requirement whereas the state must explain what might constitute acceptable compliance.

There are other intergovernmental situations where

such open exchange is not in the best interests of the parties. For example, when proposing grant objectives, potential recipients do not like to state anything that appears too jurisdictionally self-serving and not consistent with funder program aims. Recipient juris- diction intention in requests for grant dollars and actual dollar requests are often covert. A former state department head once related to the first author that he had two budgets, "one for the feds and a real one." But in PS, openess offers the benefits of bringing out out differences, contributing to understanding, clarifying the issues, building on ultimate acceptance, and suggesting procedures and ground rules for resolution.[50] In other words, the emphasis is placed on spontaneity and a more open participation pattern.[51] At a minimum, IGM parties need to focus on the issue in an open fashion, look deeply into the parameters of the problem using the shared information while exploring avenues of possible resolution.

There is also a need to look for and to develop the most creative solution possible. It begins with a search of the openly shared information, proceeds to clarifi- cation of issues, and then, most importantly, focuses on the actual working out of an alternative. It is through this process that the nonroutine, nonbureaucratic solution finally emerges. A number of policy implementation studies indicate how officials often have to go outside of normal bureaucratic routines to make things work: for example, by using a network of technical assistants, by allowing unconventional practices not in the regulations and guidelines but consistent with program aims, and by administratively approving practices that were thought to require formal approval.[52]

In the IGB study, solutions, such as a joint manage- ment model for multi-service centers in Dayton, a jointly financed and shared information system in Indianapolis, a common grants management process in Pueblo, and numerous joint or mutual administrative actions in Baltimore represent such creativity. Similarly, in our other examples, the city and the transit district agree to reroute to the immediate fringe of the limited traffic area; the state and local officials work out a plan for informal compliance review or a pre-audit; and the school board and state agency work out an interim agreement to contract with an area vocational school for computer training at school sites.

How are such creative solutions developed? Petrella

and Block's diagnostic work on creative conflict resolution offers important clues. After initial stages similar to those described in this study, parties must move to <u>confrontation</u> and <u>bonding</u>, that is, establishing a working contract.[53] They suggest that parties are ready to confront the issue when they can clearly identify (1) the important substantive issues, (2) the existence of mutual positive motivation, (3) the existence of a reasonable balance of power, (4) psychological readiness to confront differences, and (5) a belief, grounded in fact, that there is sufficient control to make a solution work.[54]

Readiness for bonding can be identified in one or more of the following ways: (1) pressure by the group to develop solutions; (2) recognition that critical issues have been explored; and (3) visible symmetry in the parties' perception of (a) injustices endured because of the problem, (b) competency and the kind of contributions parties have to offer, and (c) the interdependence or the need each has for the other.[55] While the IGB study did not empirically test each of these social-psychological states necessary for resolution, a similarity of process was suggested by informants. Investigation of the middle stages of our five step process--identifying the problem, developing a course of action, implementing the decision-- revealed consistent evidence that creative solutionmaking required these kinds of "states of mind" in confrontation and bonding.

Finally, solutions not only should be creative but also be as mutually beneficial as possible. In the IGB study, many benefits accrued as a result of the process: new sources of funding for agencies and reduced county property taxes in Columbus; a data base for all agencies and governments to use in Indianapolis; planning information for the state, new housing units for mentally ill clients, and relief of the overcrowded county jail in Seattle; and decreased federal, state, and local AFDC payments in Baltimore. In the three examples external to the IGB study: the city and the transit district end up with routes that minimize disruption and maximize ridership; state finance officials gain increased compliance and local clerks suffer fewer penalties, and both parties ultimately decrease their overall work load; the state education agency gains compliance while the local school district minimizes saff and equipment costs, and both parties launch a new program. Maximizing the benefits to all parties is not always possible in IGM. most regulatory requirements in grants put the cost burden on the grantee. Standards set in grants typically require many hours and dollars in compliance. The results of negotiations between a state and the federal government over a waiver may set standards at a level where the state is paying a far larger share of the costs than anticipated. In PS, however, intergovernmental actors need not assume that one party's gain is necessarily another's loss. The pursuit of a creative solution often leads to mutual gains.

## IGBs, PROBLEM-SOLVING AND THE NEW FEDERALISM

Although it is but one of a number of ways of mananging within the intergovernmental system, the PS approach is a potentially valuable means of making daily adjustments. IGB projects undertaken prior to the Reagan federalism changes, such as funding allocations, A-95 review, developing information systems, and new services for the community, can put the IGBs in a stance where they were better able to understand and cope with subsequent intergovernmental changes. The PS processes examined made it possible for these communities to develop and/or reorient the intergovernmental system prior to the Reagan generated changes. This enhanced their capacity to face a shifting federal agenda manifested by the New Federalism. Subsequent IGB efforts reveal the importance of a continuing need for managers to resolve routine problems.

There are numerous examples in which IGB work in understanding and planning for federal funding reductions, expanding services access and reducing duplication, and managing declining program dollars represent direct responses to the Reagan-generated federalism changes. Subsequent updating of IGB activity reveals continued work in response to the changes. In Dayton, for example, the Partnership has been instrumental in developing and staffing an Area Progress Council (APC), made up of corporate and business leaders. APC serves as a forum to educate the business community about the human services system, has been instrumental in developing community support for emergency funds, and provides management support for agencies. Also in Dayton, the IGB has developed an Emergency Planning Council to serve future shelter needs in the community, and was instrumental in providing research support for a combined human services levy. In Columbus, MHSC has been instrumental in developing new emergency services, getting the city and

county governments to cooperate with the private sector to
fund shelters for the homeless, and enacting a new
children's services levy. MHSC was also the prime mover
behind a successful effort to redirect state Social
Services Block Grant funds and to allow Ohio Mental Health
and Mental Retardation boards to use Medicaid dollars to
finance community services as long as they provide the
matching funds.

In Pueblo, the HRC has been the catalyst for seeking
new funds, both from within the local business community
and from outside sources, to support the efforts of its
Emergency Services Commission. HRC has also established a
Training and Technical Institute for nonprofit organizations, in cooperation with the United Way, the Pueblo
and Latino Chambers of Commerce, and the University of
Southern Colorado. In Seattle, the HRC has been instrumental in coalescing the three levels of government and
the private sector to establish an emergency fund for
agencies experiencing fund reductions; organize and
support metropolitan food banks and shelters for the
homeless; study youth employment; and develop a plan for
addressing the problem of street youths, including
counseling, medical services, and emergency shortterm
housing. IGBs have developed an ability through routine
problem solving to manage their way through the changing
intergovernmental system.

New and dramatic demands on intergovernmental
managers who reshape the system will, therefore, not
displace a corresponding need to deal with routine IGM
issues. Elected officials, public and private managers,
and private sector leaders will need to continue to tackle
the daily work of making redefined federal and state
programs work within their communities. Routines tend to
be neglected as intergovernmental attention is directed
toward the dramatic: a state declines to participate in a
health grant program, a local government refuses to comply
with a wages and hours regulation accompanied with an
announcement of a willingness to litigate, a $40 million
audit exception in a school district's federal aid is
announced, and a group of United Ways protest the way a
state is handling social services grant contracting.
While solutions to these issues represent significant
means of defining the workings of the intergovernmental
system, they mask thousands of routine transactions. The
need to redirect grant money from meals to transportation
in Columbus, or the need to streamline the means of
verification of welfare of children in school in

Baltimore, or the need to provide energy assistance in Seattle represent transactions that do not normally make the newspapers or come to the attention of mayors, governors, or presidents. They rarely involve confrontational contacts and decisions, threats of penalty, high level politcal pressure, or class-action litigation. Rather, as the PS process suggests, resolution occurs through protracted processes, leading to agreements made on the basis of administrative inter-pretations, single party or multiple accommodations, and other coordinated courses of action. Nevertheless, these PS routines make the system workable when small program adjustments are required.

PS is also a process that brings parties together in a spirit of long-term relationships. As in many types of coordinating activities, IGM involves a considerable amount of investment in actors' learning about each other, their style and approach, needs and agendas, and modes of operation. The longer IGB elected officials, adminis-trators, and private sector representatives worked together on problems, the easier subsequent PS became. Work on PS reinforces the recognition that problems cut across jurisdictions, mutual dependency, and the need to blend styles and operations. As a a result, the convening efforts made by managers in PS pays off as working relationships are established and maintained.

PS is also cumulative managerial activity. Few transactions prove to be one-time activities. Interaction tends to be continuous, over numerous activities sur-rounding different community issues and an over broadening list of grant programs. Work in Dayton and Columbus on understanding the impact of proposed federal funding reductions led to subsequent work in developing a range of emergency services. Thus, the investment in process and building understanding and trust pays off beyond the immediate problem being solved. The cumulative nature of IGM activity also suggests that potentially confron-tational approaches, such as bargaining and planning, are not always conducive to ongoing relationships.

PS also builds critical managerial capacity. Govern-ments' ability to anticipate and deal with potentially challenging situations was identified as an alternative IGM strategy. The research indicated that the process of problem resolution can contribute to such capability by providing officials with new abilities to understand and make adjustments in the system. In Columbus, for example, MHSC leaders learned very quickly that the leveraging that resulted from their intergovernmental advocacy efforts taught them how to play the game and who the players were. Experiences from the successful resolution of four essential federal-state grant changes brought in new services, dollars, and eased the local property tax burden. This led to an MHSC state leadership role in changing the state direction for one block grant. These newly found abilities to manage in response to environmental changes came as a direct result of the PS process.

The PS process is also a means by which the "top down" intergovernmental planning process can be reversed. Virtually all of the IGB projects studied involved adjustments that emanated from the local level. Projects like the Seattle effort to extend community and residential alternatives for the mentally ill began because the county govenment was concerned about the lack of treatment alternatives for mentally ill "street people." Through HRC, the issue was made a state-local issue, but the actual planning process involved a task force made up of federal, state, and local government staff people, as well as United Way representatives. The resulting residential continuum was a locally initiated plan that involved state financial participation. Many IGM projects demonstrate how planning can be interactive, locally initiated, and not federally driven.

A process like PS supports intergovernmental devolution as local elected officials and administrators work to adjust federal and state programs to their needs. While not the only means of developing responsibility, PS is a means by which management by jurisdiction instead of by program can be enhanced. For example, the Columbus Negotiated Investment Strategy (NIS) funding changes, Dayton's use of CDBG and Social Services funds to build and staff multi-service centers, the Pueblo General Revenue Sharing allocation and grants management process and the Indianapolis use of Social Services funds to support multi-service centers demonstrate how grant recipients make programs work for their own purposes. When local officals can make grants work while still complying with state and federal requirements, they play out their important part in a developing federal system.

CONCLUSION

The IGB study demonstrates how PS focuses on the daily execution of tasks within a "fixed" federal structure. That is, it is not a means of changing the system, but a means of living with it "as is" on a daily basis. As such, it is a mode that makes it possible to conduct a considerable amount of business in "the middle ground" between strict compliance and open defiance. As intergovernmental managers seek means to make adjustments in order to implement programs, they have more than two choices: (1) to insist on or to narrowly follow the statues, regulations and guidelines or (2) to openly ignore or resist such legal mandates. In practice there are vast grey areas of interpretation, priority, direction, substantial conformance, and the spirit of the law that are acceptable. To the IGBs, intergovernmental problem resolution becomes the process through which favorable interpretations, program waivers, redirected funds, coordinated plans, contingency allocations, joint efforts, model services, and pilot programs are effectuated.

Moreover, the PS results offer evidence that the system of intergovernmental relations as it is basically structured is perhaps more workable than rhetoric generally suggests. Many complaints have been registered that the system of categorical grants fosters too much federal control or, in the case of state grants, state control. They are said to unnecessarily restrict recipient initiatives to meet their own needs. The limited evidence presented from the six IGBs suggests that the grant system does leave room for local actors to meet needs by making adjustments in federal and state programs, if they are willing to manage for results through such means as PS. Moreover, it is assumed that on a less formal basis than that of the IGBs, literally thousands of such adjustments are made, under similar conditions, in order to smooth discrepancies between perceived needs and actual conditions.[56]

The PS mode may not constitute a dramatic approach to IGM, but it is inevitable, given the implementation structure of many public policies. So long as governments that enact programs eschew direct operations and choose a series of intermediaries--states, local general and special purpose governments, nonprofit organizations, and for-profit organizations (through categorical grants, block grants, GRS, procurement contracts and cooperative agreements), there will be substantial room and need for manuevering. Funder goals and recipient aims are inevitably field tested as programs are designed elsewhere and placed in a community.[57] As is well known, each side has its weapons; funders have legal intent and fiscal sanctions, recipients have daily program control and the power of execution. Both sides, moreover, have politics if they care to use it and the substantive technical know-how if they care to acquire and use it. What remains is the application of these issues to specific tasks as programs are put into place.

As new directions in intergovernmental relations are forged, PS will continue to play a significant, if not highly visible, role. Many categorical grants remain essentially intact. Block grants, legal reforms, and shifting responsibilities to state governments may smooth the way but will not lessen the need for daily adjustments. PS is a process that helps all parties meet the challenges of fewer resources, more flexible grants, and other new federalism dynamics. As the six IGBs demonstrate, PS is one means through which the work of policy implementors is carried out.

NOTES

1. The entire study is reported in Robert Agranoff, Intergovernmental Management: Human Services Problem-Solving in Six Metropolitan Areas (Albany: State University of New York Press, 1985).
2. Robert Agranoff and Alex N. Pattakos, "Intergovernmental Management: Federal Changes, State Responses, and New State Initiatives," PUBLIUS: The Journal of Federalism 14 (Summer, 1984), pp. 50-51.
3. Deil Wright, Understanding Intergovernmental Relations, 2nd ed (Monterey, CA: Brooks/Cole, 1982), p. 13.
4. Joseph L. Massie, Essentials of Management, 4th ed, (Englewood Cliffs, N.J.: Prentice-Hall, 1979), p. 4.
5. Deil Wright, "Managing the Intergovernmental Scene: The Changing Dramas of Federalism," The Handbook of Organization and Management, William B. Eddy, ed. (New York: Marcel Dekker, 1983), p. 431.
6. M. Mandell, "Intergovernmental Management," Public Administration Times 15 December 1979, pp. 2, 6.
7. Robert Agranoff and Valerie A. Lindsay, "Intergovernmental Management: Perspectives from Human Services Problem Solving at the Local Level," Public Administration Review 43 (May/June 1983), p. 228.
8. Stephen R. Rosenthal, "New Directions for Evaluating Intergovernmental Programs," Public Administration Review 44 (November/December, 1984), p. 470.
9. James L. Sundquist, Making Federalism Work (Washington, D.C.: The Brookings Institution, 1969), p. 12.
10. Ibid., p. 19.
11. Stephen L. Schecter, "On the Relationship Between Intergovernmental Relations and Management," paper prepared for 1974 Annual Meeting of the American Society for Public Administration, Syracuse, New York.
12. Wayne F. Anderson, "Foreword" in Raymond A. Shapek, Managing Federalism: Evolution and Development of the Grant-in-Aid System (Charlottesville, VA: Community Collaborators, 1981), pp. iv-v.
13. Shapek, op. cit., Ch. 2.
14. Beth Walter Honadle, "A Capacity-Building Framework: A Search for Concept and Purpose," Public Administration Review 41 (September/October 1981), p. 577.
15. Cf., Jeffrey L. Pressman, Federal Programs and City Politics, (Berkley, CA: U. of California Press, 1979).

326

16. Patricia S. Florestano and Vincent L. Marando, The States and the Metropolis (New York: Marcel Dekker, 1981), pp. 137-138.

17. Study Committee on Policy Management Assistance, "Executive Summary," Public Administration Review 35 (December, 1975), Special Issue, p. 701.

18. Robert Agranoff and Alex Pattakos, "Human Services Policy Management," Midwest Review of Public Administration 12 (December, 1978), pp. 261-262.

19. C. Gregory Buntz and Beryl A. Radin, "Managing Intergovernmental Conflict: The Case of Human Services," Manuscript, 1983.

20. Helen Ingram, "Policy Implementation Through Bargaining: The Case of Federal Grants-in-Aid," Public Policy, vol. 25 (Fall, 1977), p. 524.

21. James Kunde, "As in the Past, the Cities Propose: Under NIS They Help Dispose," Nation's Cities Weekly, November 26, 1979, pp. 4-9.

22. Ralph Brody, Problem Solving: Concepts and Methods for Community Organizations (New York: Human Sciences Press, 1982), p. 17; William B. Eddy, Public Organization Behavior and Development (Cambridge, MA: Winthrop, 1981), p. 64; Charles H. Kepner and Benjamin B. Tregoe, The Rational Manager: A Systematic Approach to Problem Solving and Decision Making (New York: McGraw-Hill, 1965); Richard E. Walton and Robert B. McKersie, A Behavioral Theory of Labor Negotiations (New York: McGraw-Hill, 1965), p. 128.

23. L. David Brown, Managing Conflict at Organizational Interfaces (Reading, MA: Addison-Wesley, 1983), p. 51.

24. Kepner and Tregoe, op. cit., p. 18.

25. Don Koberg and Jim Begnall, The Universal Traveler 6th ed. (Los Altos, CA: Wm. Kaufman, 1981).

26. Edward DeBono, "Information Processing and New Ideas--Lateral and Vertical Thinking," in Guide to Creative Action, eds. Sidney J. Parnes, et. al., (New York: Scribner's, 1977), pp. 195-200.

27. Herbert Simon, The New Science of Management Decision (Englewood Cliffs, NJ: Prentice-Hall, 1977), pp. 40-41.

28. Walton and McKersie, op. cit., pp. 128-29.

29. Paul R. Lawrence and Jay W. Lorsch, Organization and Environment (Boston: Graduate School of Business Administration, Harvard, 1967), p. 77.

30. Robert R. Blake and Jane S. Mouton, The Managerial Grid (Houston, TX: Gulf, 1964), p. 165.

31. Larry E. Grenier, "Patterns of Organizational Change," Harvard Business Review, 45 (May/June, 1967), p. 121.

32. Robert H. Guest, Organizational Change: The Effect of Successful Leadership (Homewood, IL: Dorsey, 1962), pp. 50-58.

33. Louis R. Pondy, "Organizational Conflict: Concepts and Models," Administrative Science Quarterly 12, no. 2 (Spring, 1967), p. 313.

34. Brown, op. cit., pp. 52-53.

35. Ibid., p. 223.

36. Ibid., p. 224.

37. Eugene Bardach, The Implementation Game: What Happens After a Bill Becomes a Law (Cambridge, MA: MIT Press, 1977), p. 274.

38. Ibid.

39. Arnold J. Meltsner and Christopher Bellavita, The Policy Organization (Beverly Hills, CA: SAGE, 1983), p. 213.

40. Ibid., 288

41. Beryl A. Radin, Robert Agranoff, C. Gregory Buntz, and Edward C. Baumheier, Planning Reform Demonstration Project Evaluation, report prepared for the Office of the Assistant Secretary for Planning and Evaluation, U.S. Department of Health and Human Services, October, 1981, Ch. 7.

42. Walter Williams, Government by Agency: Lessons from the Grants-in-Aid Experience (New York: Academic Press, 1980), pp. 235-37.

43. Richard F. Elmore, "Backward Mapping: Implementing Research and Policy Decisions," Walter Williams, et. al., Studying Implementation: Methodological and Administrative Issues (Chatham, NJ: Chatham House, 1982), p. 23.

44. Agranoff and Lindsay, "Intergovernmental Management," op. cit.

45. Agranoff, Intergovernmental Management, Chs. 3-8.

46. Walton and McKersie, op. cit., pp. 138-39.

47. Joe Kelly, "Make Conflict Work for You," Harvard Business Review 48 (July-August 1970), p. 104.

48. Kenneth W. Thomas and Louis R. Pondy, "Toward an 'Intent' Model of Conflict Management Among Principal Parties," Human Relations 30 (December, 1977), p. 1090.

49. Wright, op. cit., p. 65.

50. Warren H. Schmidt and Robert Tannenbaum, "Management of Differnces," Harvard Business Review 38 (November/December, 1960), pp. 112-13.

51. Richard W. Walton and Robert B. McKersie, "Behavioral Dilemmas in Mixed Motive Decision-Making," _Behavioral Sciences_ 11 (September, 1966), p. 380.

52. Bardach, _op. cit._, Ch. 7; Williams, _op. cit._, p. 188; Radin et. al., _op. cit._, Ch. 7; Williams, _op. cit._, 235-37.

53. Tony Petrella and Peter Block, "Diagnosing Conflict Between Groups in Organizations," in _Organization Diagnosis_ Marvin R. Weisbrod, ed. (Reading, MA: Addison-Wesley, 1978), p. 139.

54. Ibid., p. 140.

55. Ibid., p. 141.

56. Radin, et. al., Ch. 5.

57. Richard W. Walton and Robert B. McKersie, "Behavioral Dilemmas in Mixed Motive Decision-Making," _Behavioral Sciences_, vol. 11 (September, 1966), p. 380.

# 14

## The Condition and Course of the System

*David B. Walker*

Where stands our domestic system of governance in the fifth year of the Reagan era and in what direction(s) is it headed? These are the questions that will be explored in this brief assessment of recent and current inter-governmental developments.

THE CONTEXT AND ITS CONDITIONERS:

To arrive at balanced answers to these queries entails an awareness of five distinctive factors that in combination help to place Reagan domestic initiatives in their proper historical context.

The first factor involves the required mode of analysis. For at least a decade and a half, any effort to gain a full picture of the dynamics and functioning of our federal system inevitably required a multi-factored approach to capture the growing complexity of domestic governance in this country. Assessments of intergovern-mental fiscal transfers, grants, their conditions, their administration, and their impact--in short, the prime, if not the exclusive focus of intergovernmental research in the 1960s and most of the 1970s--was and is no longer adequate. Fast moving political party, pressure group, and media changes and the mounting number of court cases, regulations, and preemptions relating to diverse aspects of intergovernmental relations also have to be considered to gain a comprehensive overview of the many facets of contemporary American federalism. Such an approach, of course, led many to conclude by the mid- and late 1970s that the system had become a highly centralized one in policy, political, representational, and media-attention

329

terms, but still highly decentralized in its administrative and implementary approaches. All this was a basic backdrop to the emergence of Reagan federalism.

The second factor in gauging the direction and internal dynamics of a federal system is to compare and contrast it with roughly comparable federal policies abroad--such as Australia, Canada, and West Germany. This comparative analytic approach indicates that all of these systems exhibit--to a greater or lesser degree--certain attributes of post-industrial societies (secular societies with strong preference for a wide range of public services and high levels of economic, technological, professional, and functional specialization and interdependence). Modernizing factors and forces thus come into play that generally have exerted a centralizing effect.

Yet, the degree of functional and economic specialization and interdependence varies from country to country and more traditional social, cultural, constitutional, and formal governmental factors must also be considered. These after all are key factors shaping the extent, nature, and subnational governmental effects of centripetal dynamics and policies.[1] From this comparative vantage point, then, comes the broad finding that the constitutent governments in our system and their localities are still strong operationally but weak in political/representational and constitutional/legal terms--unlike the subnational constituent governments in Canada, Australia, West Germany, and Switzerland.[2] This perspective places recent American intergovernmental developments in a broader, less parochial perspective that underscores basic conditioners of the nature and extent of a territorial power balance within the system.

A third factor that must be considered in any assessment of the Reagan record is the recent history of our intergovernmental relations. Much of the Reagan effort, after all, is explicable in terms of the dramatic centralizing developments that occurred between 1964 and 1978-1980. During this period, the net growth (after mergers and block grant consolidations) in the number of funded grant programs amounted to at least 300 with a total of 537 as of the end of 1980[3] and in dollar terms grant outlays experienced a more than ninefold increase (and a doubling in constant dollars during the seventies). The traditional federal-state partnership approach was significantly altered to include federal-local, federal-nonprofit, and federal-state-local, as well. (Witness the rise in the proportion of total federal aid "bypassing"

state governments--from 8 percent in 1960 to 12 percent by
1968 up to 25 percent by 1978 back to about 23 percent by
the end of the decade.) The percentage relationship of
federal aid to state and local receipts from own sources
rose from 17.9 percent to 30.7 percent between 1964 and
1980.

Programmatically, significant expansions occurred in
such broad functional areas as health, social services,
education, manpower, and community and regional development, while the natural resource, agricultural, and
especially transportation aid programs experienced
proportionate declines. In terms of the scope of national
policy concerns, a wide range of governmental functions
were included that previously were considered to be of
state, local, or even private concern (libraries, fire
protection, policemen's pensions, bikeways, rat control,
potholes, and the like). In addition, a new era of
"social regulation" was ushered in during these years with
historic enactments in the equal rights and access,
environmental, conservation, health and safety, and
energy, producing the novel situation of state and local
governments serving as both the objects of and frequently
the implementors of federal regulations.[4]    Administratively, the tone and style of intergovernmental management
in many of the new program areas assumed a cooptive,
intrusive, and sometimes arbitrary tone on the part of
federal grant and regulatory administrators and a confron-
tational, if not conniving, behavior on the part of many
of the involved subnational recipient governmental
personnel.

By the late 1970s the system had become highly
centralized in terms of policy-making, yet still largely
non-centralized in terms of actual implementation. The
latter made an impression in the minds of many that no
basic change had occurred in the system. Yet, crucial
changes had occurred, probably the most drastic in this
century. Critics of these developments focused on the
national policy process, its nearly exclusively interest-
group undergirding in the 1970s, its prolific and
ultimately costly policy outputs, its panoramic pattern of
implementation involving at least sixty of the 82,000
units of subnational governments and countless thousands
of nonprofits.[5]    Questions of systemic overload, administrative efficacy, economic efficiency, basic equity, and
accountability--both politically and administratively--
were raised by most conservatives and many liberals.

At the same time, between 1960 and 1980, the poverty

percentage was cut in half and the gap between the economically stronger and weaker did not widen (as it might well have, given the massive influx of new "baby boom" generation job applicants). Thirty million members were added to the national work force, in part because of the federally-stimulated expansion of the state/local governmental sector, social security amendments encouraging early retirement, and some, but not all, of the federal jobs programs and expanded educational opportunities.[6] Longer life expectancy and lower child mortality rates were achieved and a necessary revolution was achieved in civil rights and civil liberties.

The Reagan election in 1980, in part, was a reaction to many of these earlier expansionist policy developments at the national level. The advent of an interest group-dominated national policy process, of an ever centralizing national judiciary, and of a near collapse of the national political parties, especially the ostensibly majority Democratic Party, as an effective broker, mediator, and conciliator of factions in national conventions and in Congress (thanks to populist reforms in both in the early 1970s) had given rise to a broad national sentiment that the overall system was overloaded, ineffective administratively, inefficient economically, not sufficiently targeted on equity goals, and basically unaccountable politically. Reaganism, in essence, was opposed to all of these results, save for the equity issue.

A more immediate conditioner of the past four years has been the fourth factor, the constellation of concepts--not always complementary--that comprise the Reagan creed.[7] Alongside his undoubted commitment to a more balanced federalism are a cluster of other ideas and values--some dating back to GE Theater days and others of more recent vintage--that conflict with his federalist concerns. Business and private sector favoritism, "moral majority" goals, retrenchment concerns, as well as his political pragmatism, can (and have) undercut his federalist beliefs, in that all of these can (and have) produce centralizing policies and processes. Some of the gaps between presidential rhetoric and the reality of his policies are explicable in terms of the conflict between and among the values composing the presidential creed.

The final factor demands a close examination of the Carter years, especially the last two, and suggests that some Reaganism preceded Reagan. Put differently, Reagan continued some of the broad outlines of Carterism as it emerged in 1979-1980. The turning point in the downward spiral of defense outlays and the soaring rate of grant-in-aid grants in the 1970s after all, ended by 1978. Moreover, deregulation, a curbing of the regulatory burden, and even block grants were all focal points of Carter administration efforts--though without the fanfare or success that accompanied the Reagan initiatives in these same areas.

REAGAN FEDERALISM:  ITS BASIC GOALS:

At least a half dozen separate objectives combine to comprise the Reagan federalist creed.  Most of these have been and are clear and explicit Administration goals.  A couple have been and are more implicit and inferential from policy proposals and actions.

--A drastic reduction in the federal intergovernmental role clearly is at the heart of his philosophic view and central to this is the need to reduce the number of and dollars for federal grant programs.

--Clearly related to the above is the belief in a devolution of program responsibilities (and the sometimes cited concomitant need to devolve the needed financial resources) to state and local governments; in 1982, this basic goal was modified by the great "sorting out" proposal and its call for a federalization of Medicaid, which tacitly conceded the need for a simultaneous process involving centralization and devolution.

--Deregulation was and is a third component theme in Reagan federalism; this involves curbing federal regulation of both the private sector and state and local governments.

--A return to the traditional dualistic partnership involving the states and the national government was and is a clear, though less trumpeted, feature of the president's federalism.

--A determined effort to abandon federal participation in multi-state and substate regional institutions and programs (deinstitutionalization) is a much heralded, but persistent objective of the administration.

--Finally, Reagan federalism in its broadest strokes calls for a reduction in the activism of all governments, not just the national.

## THE RECORD

Reagan's "New Federalism" achievements are less than what he wanted, but more than what most close students of national politics and policies as of 1980 would have believed was possible. This will become more apparent in the brief probe of the record that follows.

In its drive to reduce the Federal intergovernmental role, the administration succeeded in achieving an absolute reduction of $8 billion (from the Carter figure) for grant programs for fiscal year (FY) 1982, but projected further slashing of federal aid over the next three years did not materialize. Instead, the president himself requested amounts in excess of what was anticipated in the Omnibus Reconciliation Act of 1981 and Congress in all three years gave him more than he asked for. The result was a gradual rise in real dollar terms in aid to states and localities for FY 1984 and FY 1985 (of 1.5 percent and 5.3 percent, respectively) with the aggregate figure for the latter year surpassing the $107 billion mark. At the same time, the overall effect of these various actions was to achieve a net reduction of over $31 billion in constant dollars from what would have prevailed had grant outlays been held stationary at the 1980 level for each of succeeding five fiscal years. Moreover, as a percentage of state and local receipts (from own sources) total federal aid declined from 31.7 percent in 1980 to 24.3 percent five years later. And as a proportion of the gross national product (GNP) it slipped from 3.6 percent to 2.8 percent over the same time span.[8]

A related dimension of this drive to reduce the Federal role in the federal system was the cut in the number of separate grant programs from 539 in 1980 to 405 by January of 1984, largely through actions taken in 1981 (though more on that subsequently).[9] Not to be overlooked here, however, was the gradual increase in the number of new programs enacted in 1983 and especially 1984, suggesting that the dynamics of program proliferation that characterized the 1970s have not been totally eclipsed by the retrenchment concerns of the Reagan years.[10]

Turning to moves to devolve program and other responsibilities to the state and local levels, the administration scored its greatest successes in 1981. Some sixty odd aid programs were scrapped by the Reconciliation Act and seventy-seven were merged into nine new block grants. Congressional enactment of four more over the next three years plus the continuance of the older entitlement Community Development Block Grant, (but minus one of the 1981 cluster that has proved inoperative) brought the total of these less conditional and much more discretionary aid programs in terms of recipient project priorities to thirteen by the end of 1984. The renewal of general revenue sharing for local general governments in 1983, with White House support, marked another phase of this devolutionary drive.

Yet, these achievements must be placed in their broader context. The major Reagan effort to effect a massive devolution of program responsibilities with fiscal resources as well as some nationalization (Medicaid) reached a total impasse by the fall of 1982, despite six months of tough and sometimes fruitful bargaining between administration spokesmen and the four lead governors representing the states. Subsequent presidential proposals in 1983 and 1984 for merging 34 programs into four mega-block grants fared no better with the Congress or with state and local officials.[11] In addition, none of the newer block grants has proven to be a transitional vehicle to total devolution. Congressional renewals and increased funding for some of these would suggest just the opposite. Above all, perhaps, is the fact that in FY 1984 all federal outlays for block grants and for general revenue sharing amounted to less than 20 percent of the total, almost identical with the counterpart figure for the last year of the Carter administration.

In the complicated field of intergovernmental deregulation, the Reagan administration has curbed and softened the process, but deregulation as such has not been the focus of administration efforts in this area. The softening strategy involved a combination of Reagan loyalists appointed to key regulatory posts; personnel cuts in their agencies; relaxed, if not permissive, agency procedures; and a highly centralized review of proposed new, or modifications of existing, regulations.[12] As a result, the number of revised and new regulations was reduced, some intergovernmental regulations were muted in their impact; and delegations of greater authority to the states, authorized under some programs, picked up.[13] Additionally, the new block grants have been administered--at the behest of the Office of Management and Budget (OMB) and the Office of Policy Development spokespersons--in a heavily "hands off" fashion. In a few instances, regulatory relief took the form of revising internally previous administrative decisions as to how a regulation would be applied--as with Davis-Bacon--which, in turn, produced court battles and an ultimate victory for the administration.

Yet, no legislative initiative--other than the block grant proposals--has accompanied these efforts and the Clean Air and Clean Water acts have been awaiting full reauthorization since 1981. Moreover, Congress' propensity to preempt and to regulate has not slackened off and in some cases has been supported by the administration (that is, trailer truck and teenage drinking regulations and mandated procedures for responding to reports of medical neglect of handicapped infants). Moreover, new conditions and constraints in various of the large categorical grants (most notably Medicaid, Aid for Families with Dependent Children (AFDC), and food stamps) were sought by the Administration itself, in part for retrenchment reasons.

The primacy of the federal state partnership has been given some substantive and considerable rhetorical support by the administration. All of the new block grants are federal-state ventures, and the states were the focal point of the dialogue triggered by the president's 1982 state of the union "big swap" proposal. Moreover, there has been some decline in the proportion of federal aid channeled directly to the nation's localities, thanks in part to the state preference in the block grants. And in the realm of intergovernmental regulation, some federal agencies have assumed a more cooperative approach in the implementation of some of the environmental and health and safety programs.

Explicit in the administration's New Federalism is a larger role for the states in the system. This role, of course, already had assumed a crucial importance during the late 1960s and 1970s. In broad operational terms, the states had become the prime subnational governmental administrators of most of the national government's environmental, highway, welfare, and social programs. As planners, partial funders, and basic implementors of these programs as well as many of their own policy initiations (especially in primary and secondary education, economic development, and aid to their localities generally), the states entered the Reagan era occupying a more pivotal operational role than ever before, even though their political and representational roles in the system had become weaker and their constitutional/legal status more uncertain.

Yet, from the states' vantage point, the aggregate federal actions over the past four years hardly reflects the trust, collaboration, mutual give-and-take of the genuine partnership that Reagan federalism initially implied. Too many of the administration's intergovern-mental policy and fiscal initiatives have been of a unilaterial, if not preemptory, nature. Witness the large intergovernmental transfer programs that are federal-state joint efforts and that involve heavy state cost-sharing in the cases of Medicaid and AFDC. These now have more conditions (most notably relating to eligibility) attached to them than ever before. Moreover, preemptive Congres-sional actions (sometimes supported by the administration) and several recent Supreme Court decisions (most notably Garcia v. San Antonio Metropolitan Transit Authority--No. 82-1913), along with the above and other administrative actions, constitute cooptive and unnecessarily centralizing national behavior in the states' view.

Over the past four years, the administration (with some assistance from Congress) engineered a fairly sizeable withdrawal from its support for regional institutional building. Both the Title V (economic development) and Title II (river basin) federal multi-state commissions were scrapped with the Reconciliation Act of 1981, leaving the Appalachian Regional Commission as the last of the economic development and the Delaware and Susquehanna Commissions as the last of the river basin commissions. At the substate regional level, twelve of the thirty-nine federal programs (as of 1980) have been terminated, eleven experienced major budget cuts, nine lost their regional features, six were revised, and one was left intact.[14]

At the same time, several of the multi-state ventures (six of the economic development and five of the river basin commissions) have been continued or merged with other bodies as examples of "horizontal federalism" (states joining collaboratively without national partici-pation). State, and especially local, support for substate regional bodies helped fill some of the void left by federal policy and fiscal withdrawals. Regional councils encountered a less than expected mortality rate (only a little over 100 passed away). Moreover, federal support has by no means evaporated. Department of Transportation's (DOT's) Metropolitan Planning Organi-zation (MPO) requirements, the Area-wide Agency for the Aged (AAA) program of Department of Health and Human Services (DHHS), and even the "back-up" role of the federal government under Executive Order 12372 (the successor to A-95), which delegated major responsibility for the review and comment required clearinghouse function to the states, indicate--among other efforts--a continuing, though curbed, Federal substate regional role.

The administration's general philosophic goal of reducing governmental activism at all levels has not met with much success. Overall, federal spending rose from 23.5 percent to 24.1 percent of the GNP between FY 1981 and FY 1985 and the national debt nearly doubled over the same period. During the difficult recession-conditioned FY 1982, most states tried to cope without raising taxes: twenty-five made selective program cuts, seventeen made across-the-board cuts, eight shifted balances or expenditure among funds, thirty-seven set hiring limits, and twenty laid off employees.[15] And much of this would conform, in at least superficial terms, to the New Federalism goal of reduced government. But in FY 1983, thirty-eight raised at least one tax and twenty-two hiked sales or personal income taxes or both.[16] These actions, when combined produced an increase in state receipts of between $7 and $8 billion. In FY 1984, roughly half of the states made no significant tax changes and fifteen actually reduced taxes, frequently by allowing earlier temporary hikes to expire.

The net effect of these various actions from FY 1981 to FY 1985 was a rise in federal spending from $983.6 billion; to $1,258.1 billion, in state outlays (from own sources) from $175.6 billion to $220.4 billion; and in local expenditures (again from own sources) from $118.9 billion to $157.8 billion.[17] When combined, these outlays rose from 33.3 percent of the GNP to 34.4 percent over this four year period and on a per capita, constant (1972) dollar basis from $2,186 to $2,380. While the growth rate here is less rapid than that of the 1966-1977 period, the 1978-1980 Carter years compare favorably. In short, since 1978 governmental activism, as reflected in expenditures, has been tamed somewhat but it has not been reduced in absolute dollar terms.

Any assessment of the Reagan intergovernmental record would be remiss if its attitudinal impact were overlooked. State and local officials no longer seek out Washington as the prime, if not the sole, solver of their respective problems as many of them did in the late 1960s and in the 1970s. This is not to say the national government is being ignored. Far from it--too many legal, regulatory, preemptive, as well as fiscal actions are taken there to permit that kind of luxury. But the image of "Uncle Sam as the problem solver" has faded from the minds of subnational governmental officials and even of many within the electorate and the interest group complexes. This, perhaps, is the area wherein Reagan federalism has effected a real revolution. The rest of the record, thus far and with the exception of the deinstitution drive, suggests more of an incremental reaction to the heavy expansions of the Nixon-Ford years (aided and abetted by Democratic Congresses and a plethora of pressure groups) with some special Reagan flourishes, rather than a systemic revolution.

## THE DYNAMICS OF THE FIRST REAGAN ADMINISTRATION:

Why should the record of the past four years essentially add up to a victory for incrementalism and some decrementalism, and a defeat for radical surgery? At the outset, everything certainly seemed to point toward a successful strategy of drastic surgery!

More than any president in recent history, Ronald Reagan projected a coherent, forceful view of his goals for the nation to the electorate (notwithstanding the subtle and not-so-subtle conflicts in his cluster of core values) and he demonstrated masterfully his capacity to use the media as a means of communicating these views.

More than any other recent president, Reagan succeeded in drastically changing the focus of the nation and the national agenda to two items: the budget and the economy.[18] The fractured focii of the 1970s was replaced with a few overriding issues that subsumed--one way or another--nearly all of the panoramic policy thrusts of the previous decade and a half--including previous attempts at intergovernmental reforms.

More than some recent presidents, Reagan had a public that seemed ready, and certainly the newly-elected Republican Senate was clearly ready, for major changes, and like a few of his earlier predecessors, he legitimately could claim that the prescriptions he unambiguously offered during his successful 1980 campaign (and previously for many years) provided the needed and accepted "blueprint" for a fundamental governmental transformation.

More than any president in living memory, Ronald Reagan took command of the executive branch's central management institutions (the Office of Management and Budget, the Office of Personnel Management, and the lesser units in the Executive Office of the President) and

established highly centralized policy management and
regulatory implementation processes as a result. Through
his initially slow but ultimately generally successful
(from his viewpoint) political appointments process, heads
and subheads of federal departments, agencies, commissions, and boards hewed at the almost monolithic Reagan
creed. Only a few "closet gypsy moths" slipped through
the stringent screening procedures and few of the presidential appointments subsequently showed any overt sign of
"going native"--a rare personnel achievement in any
administration. This process and its budgetary companion
(with all its programmatic, fiscal, number of personnel,
and salary implications) provided the basic means of
rendering an already traumatized bureaucracy even more
sullen but almost totally subservient.

All of these factors would certainly suggest the
likelihood of some significant surgical successes. Moreover, many of them were sustained throughout the four-year
period, including the president's philosophy and
communicational skills, a Republican Senate, a public
concerned about the budget and the economy, and White
House control of the executive branch and its policy
processes. Why then should this part of an apparently
presidential government have produced a basically
incrementalist--albeit of a muscular variety--domestic
(and intergovernmental) record? The essential answer lies
in the fact that the dynamics of these four years--in
terms of policy actors, actions, reactions, issues, and
impacts--combined in a way that divided the period into
two unequal parts: 1981 and early 1982 and the remaining
two and a half or more years.

During the first part of the period, an authentic era
of presidential government prevailed. During the second,
the Congress, and especially its Republican Senate leadership with House assists, assumed a lead domestic policy
role with supporting parts played by various pressure
groups, including business and the inter-governmental
lobby. The White House and executive branch agency heads
assumed a secondary role more times than not.

In 1981 the president won his two biggest legislative
victories: the Reconciliation Act (that included his only
really significant intergovernmental enactments) and the
Economic Recovery Tax Act (ERTA). With a Republican and
fairly conservative Senate and an ideological majority in
the Democratic House, the administration moved
concertedly, promptly, and boldly to lower federal
domestic spending, to boost defense, and to cut taxes

through this pair of congressional actions. In the process, several choices were made: tax cuts and defense build-up won out over a balanced budget by FY 1984; fairly steep cuts in programs for state and local government and for the working poor were achieved, but Social Security, Medicare, and employee pension recipients were spared; and tax cuts that benefited disproportionately the more well-to-do and corporations were enacted.[19] All of this seemed to signify a rise in presidential authoritativeness (and a rise in the polls in public esteem for the office and government generally seemed to confirm this), a collapse of the "interest group state" and of congressional assertiveness and hyperresponsiveness, and the emergence of more cohesive parties in Congress (at least on the Republican side of the aisle).

These presidentially-sponsored actions also seemed to portend a drastic reformulation of intergovernmental relations, given the cuts, the new array of block grants, the severing of several direct federal links to the nation's localities and nonprofit agencies, and the draconian aid cuts slated for FY 1983--FY 1985. Neither this future federalism scenario nor the somewhat different, though still heavily devolutionary one projected in the president's 1982 state of the union message, however, were to be realized. The growing awareness of the implications of the 1981 choices, the slide into the deepest recession since the 1930s, the failure of centralizing interest groups to disband or to disperse, the projected deficit for FY 1983, the continuing high interest rates, the tacit reliance on heavy foreign investments to cushion the scramble for private sector savings, and an uneasy Wall Street--all combined to stiffen the opposition of various groups that opposed the New Federalism. Congress in 1982 clearly was not the Congress of 1981. Moreover, in some instances Reagan pragmatism replaced Reagan conservatism. Witness his endorsement of a new Job Training Partnership Act, his reluctant signing of a revenue enhancement bill (Tax Equity and Fiscal Responsibility Act of 1982 - TEFRA), and his late session approval of the landmark Surface Transportation Act of 1982. All of these actions ran counter to one or more of the core concepts in the president's conservative philosophy. Overall, the president's efforts to substantially reduce federal aid flow for FY 1983 were checked by Congress and funds for health, and human service programs were actually increased. Authorized funding levels came to $88 billion or nearly $23 billion above the president's initial FY 1983 budget request.

With a less conservative, but still Republican Senate and a House firmly in liberal Democratic hands (thanks to the mid-term elections), the 98th Congress pursued its own agenda even more vigorously than its predecessor in 1982. A $4.6 billion emergency jobs bill, the renewal of general revenue sharing, a $15.6 billion omnibus housing and community development authorization, and total federal aid authorizations of an estimated $98.7 billion for FY 1984 (or 8 percent more than the FY 1982 figure) suggest some of the key intergovernmental enactments during its first session. The first new housing bill in four years; a new criminal justice grant program; a major revision of the bilingual education program; reauthorization of nine other education grants, including education of adults, Indians, women, and immigrants; a new two year, billion dollar grant to improve science and mathematics education; scholarship grants to attract able students into teaching; a five year extension and significant overhaul of the venerable vocational education program; establishment of a U. S. Institute for Peace; reauthorization of the libraries grant; passage of more wilderness bills than at any time since the initial 1964 enactment; establishment of a new American Conservation Corps geared to putting unemployed youngsters to work on public or Indian lands; passage of an omnibus social services measure that included renewal of energy aid, the Head Start program, and VISTA; and the launching of a new government program to help states provide shelter for battered wives and other victims of domestic violence all provide some indication of the extent of congressional[20] and interest group intergovernmental activism in 1984. All this and a total federal aid authorization of an estimated $107 billion for FY 1985 may not signify a return to the exuberant congressional expansiveness of the 1970s. But they do indicate a significant level of programmatic activism and institutional independence, and they often run counter to the philosophy inherent in the New Federalism.

Not to be overlooked here is that Congress in its total spending kept well within the overall figures the president initially proposed. The increased domestic outlays, as it turned out, were largely funded--in effect--from the cuts that were made in the president's proposed military budgets and Reagan ultimately acquiesced in this congressional reordering of budget priorities.

To claim that the nation has experienced a version of "congressional government" in domestic affairs over the past two and a half years may be some exaggeration. But to describe the period as one of presidential ascendancy would be far off the mark. What the recent record does suggest the following. (1) There has been no wholesale withdrawal from its intergovernmental role of the 1970s, though aggressive programmatic expansionism clearly has been constrained by the deficit. (2) Centralizing tendencies have by no means disappeared or even significantly slackened off (given the new conditions for big categoricals, the pick-up in preemptions, and key court decisions). (3) State behaviour generally over the past four years has been remarkably resourceful (fiscally and otherwise), reliable (in administering the new block grants and in supplementing some of the federal aid cuts), and imaginative (that is, their new policy initiatives in the educational, economic development, and fiscal managerial areas). However, their legal and representational political status nationally still places them on a par with almost any other major interest group. (4) Localities have experienced fewer aid cuts than local representational spokesmen would have none believe, though they now are subject to the double jeopardy of federal and state regulation, conditions, and a concomitant erosion of old style "home rule." (5) The working poor and a cluster of nonprofit organizations have suffered from the 1981 budget cuts and the proportion of those below the poverty line did increase during the Reagan years and this has had a fall-out effect on state and local governments.[21] (6) The national agenda has been reoriented with the budgetary and deficit politics transcending old style programmatic politics, but this is as much a product of congressional as of presidential concern.

As for the second Reagan administration and the overriding concern with reducing the Federal budget deficit, the dynamics of the past two and a half years will not disappear. The April 4 presidential-senate GOP agreement indicates major presidential concessions as does his acquiescence in later Senate actions prior to the May 9th vote on the first budget resolution. Yet, in balancing the need for spending reductions with the federal government's intergovernmental responsibilities, the latter will probably encounter further cuts and more condiitons. Moreover, in the yet-to-be-probed tax reform realm, the crucial issues of the exempt status of state and local bonds and the deductibility of state and local taxes raise elemental questions about the time-honored intergovernmental principle of comity as it has operated in the state-local revenue area. These tax issues are as significant to state and local officials as the intergovernental fiscal transfer questions.

To conclude, the presidential role in the system has been reasserted as has popular trust in government. Yet the heavily pluralistic, polyarchic, democratic system of the 1970s persists. Moreover, within the wide array of interest group complexes, "issues networks," and iron triangles that constitute this system, the combination of big economic, technological and professional; programmatic and even populist; moralistic and religious; and the intergovernmental groups on balance still tip the scales in favor of centripetalism. The goals, after all, of many of these groups--whether of the right or left--combine to produce expanded federal regulation, preemptions, and a continued programmatic presence.

Put differently, the systemic position of state and local governments while operationally powerful is weak constitutionally and politically. And this is not to denigrate their representational efforts in the nation's capital. What it does mean is that before the Supreme Court (and this could change with a prospective Reagan ideological Supreme Court majority and a majority of the rest of federal judges being Reagan appointees by 1988), the state and local governments generally have fared poorly. And, in the political realm, national conventions, changed congressional attitudes, and the thrust of most Washington-based interest groups have produced a situation where the intergovernmental lobby, whether united or divided (as it is all too frequently of late) has difficulty exercising the authoritative role they did in 1960 or even 1964 at the national level. In comparative federal terms, local governments in the United States still have more discretion than those in the sister systems of Australia, Canada, and West Germany. Yet, the basic constitutent subnational governments in these polities, (the states, provinces, and lander, respectively), occupy a more powerful role at their respective national levels, thanks to the operations of a parliamentary system at both levels, the high court, and the functioning of the national bicameral legislative system (in all but Canada).

Reagan federalism, thus far, has done little to trigger developments that would place the American states on a par with their counterparts in these other federal systems.     This overall systemic conclusion must be considered in any appraisal of Reaganism and the future course of American federalism.

NOTES

1.  Cf, Milton J. Esman, "Federalism and Modernization: Canada and the United States, Publius, Winter 1984, p. 37; and Donald V. Smiley, "Federal States and Federal Societies, With Special Reference to Canada," Pluralism and Federalism, International Political Science Review, volume 5, number 4 (Sage Publications, 1984), pp. 443-454.

2.  Cf, David B. Walker, "The Contemporary Condition of American Federalism:  A Comparative and Chronological Assessment," MMS, 1985.

3.  Advisory Commission on Intergovernmental Relations, A Catalog of Federal Grants-in-Aid Programs to State and Local Governments:  Grants Funded FY 1984, Report M-139, Washington, D.C., December 1984, p. 2.

4.  Cf, Advisory Commission on Intergovernmental Relations, Regulatory Federalism:  Policy Process, Impact and Reform, Report A-95, Washington, D.C., February 1984.

5.  Cf, Advisory Commission on Intergovernmental Relations, The Federal Role in the Federal System:  An Agenda for American Federalism:  Restoring Confidence and Competence, Report A-86, Washington, D.C.; National Academy of Public Administration, A Presidency for the 1980's, (Washington, D.C., 1980); James A Sundquist, "The Crisis of Competence in Government," in Jos. Pechman (edit.), Setting National Priorities:  An Agenda for 1980's (Washington, D.C.:  The Brookings Institution, 1980), pp. 531-563; and Anthony King, "The American Polity in the Late 1970's:  Building Coalitions in Sand" in Anthony King (edit.), The New American Political System (Washington, D.C., The American Enterprise Institute, 1978).

6.  Cf, John E. Schwarz, America's Hidden Success (New York:  W. W. Norton and Co., 1983).

7.  Timothy Conlan, "Federalism and Competing Values in the Reagan Administration," Publius, The Journal of Federalism, Spring 1985 (forthcoming).

8.  Advisory Commission on Intergovernmental Relations, Significant Features of Fiscal Federalism - 1984 edition, Report M-141, Washington, D.C.,) March 1985, p. 21.

9.  Ibid.

10. Cf, Congressional Quarterly, vol. 42, no. 42, October 20, 1984; pp. 2701-2719.

11. Cf, Advisory Commission on Intergovernmental Relations, Intergovernmental Perspective, (Washington, D.C.), Winter 1984, vol. 10, no. 1, pp. 24-25.

12. Cf, Catherine H. Lovell, "'Deregulation' of Intergovernmental Programs: Early Results of the Reagan Policies," Public Affairs Report, (University of California, Berkeley), vol. 25, April 1984, no. 2, pp. 1-11.

13. Cf, George C. Eads and Michael Fix, Relief or Reform? Reagan's Regulatory Dilemma, (Baltimore, Md.: The Urban Institute Press, 1984).

14. Bruce D. McDowell, "Regions Under Reagan," Paper presented at the National Planning Conference, American Planning Association, Minneapolis-St. Paul, Minnesota, May 8, 1984.

15. National Governors' Association, State of the States, Report-1985, (Washington, D.C.), p. 23.

16. Ibid.

17. Advisory Commission on Intergovernmental Relations, "Significant Features of Fiscal Federalism - 1984 edition," op. cit., p. 8.

18. The Urban Institute, The Reagan Record, (Washington, D.C.) Policy and Research Report vol. 16, no. 1, August 1984, p. 5.

19. Ibid, pp. 2-3.

20. Cf, Congressional Quarterly, op. cit:

21. The Urban Institute, "The Reagan Record," op. cit., p. 29.

# About the Contributors

Robert Agranoff is professor and chairperson, Faculty of Policy and Administration, School of Public and Environmental Affairs at Indiana University-Bloomington. He specializes in human services administration, intergovernmental management, and public management.

Lewis G. Bender is director of the Center for Governmental Research at Central Michigan University. He has specialized and written extensively on regional policy and administration.

Beverly A. Cigler is professor of political science at North Carolina State University. She has written extensively on the topics of local policy and administration.

Timothy J. Conlan is currently a staff member of the U.S. Senate Subcommittee on Intergovernmental Relations and has previously worked with the Advisory Commission on Intergovernmental Relations. His current research interest is in national policy and its impact on federalism and intergovernmental relations.

Alan W. Frankle is professor of finance at the University of Tulsa. He has a research interest in the fiscal impacts of government policy and has published on this and other related topics.

George J. Gordon is professor of political science at Illinois State University. He is author of Public Administration in America as well as articles on intergovernmental relations and policy.

Dale Krane is professor of political science at Mississippi State University. He has written and published in the fields of community development and administration.

Susan A. MacManus is professor in the College of Urban Affairs at Cleveland State University. She has extensive research experience in state and local budgeting and policy.

Charles H. Moore is professor of political science at the University of Alabama. He has an ongoing interest in housing policy and administration and the relationships between federal, state, and local housing policy and practices.

Paul Posner is director of the Intergovernmental Relations Group at the U.S. General Accounting Office and is responsible for GAO's studies of intergovernmental change. Previously, he was director of Federal Program Review with New York City's Office of Management and Budget.

Valerie Lindsay Rinkle is currently a budget analyst with the Office of the Assistant Secretary for Management in the Department of Health and Human Services. Previously she was a policy analyst for the Veteran's Administration and for the Illinois Bureau of the Budget. She is a graduate of the School for Public and Environmental Affairs at Indiana University.

Raymond A. Rosenfeld is professor of political science at Eastern Michigan University. He has an ongoing research interest in urban policy and administration.

Irene Fraser Rothenberg is a senior staff specialist with the Office of Public Policy Analysis, American Hospital Association. She is author of numerous journal articles on intergovernmental relations.

V. Howard Savage is professor of economics at Southwest Texas State University. One of his research interests is in the economic impact of federal policy on state and local government.

David W. Sink is professor of political science at the University of Alabama. He has an ongoing research interest in local and urban administration and has published in these areas.

Robert M. Stein is professor of political science at Rice University. He specializes in state and urban policy analysis and has published widely in these fields.

James A. Stever is director of the Graduate Program in Public Affairs at the University of Cincinnati. He is the author of books and articles in the field of subnational administration and policy.

David B. Walker is professor of political science at the University of Connecticut. Formerly with the Advisory Commission on Intergovernmental Relations, he has an ongoing research interest in federalism and intergovernmental relations.

Pinky S. Wassenberg is professor of political science at Central Michigan University. Her research and publishing interests are public policy, particularly environmental policy, and intergovernmental relations.

Richard S. Williamson served from 1981-1983 as President Ronald Reagan's assistant for intergovernmental affairs. As a member of the White House Senior Staff, he helped design President Reagan's federalism proposals. He is now a senior partner with the Chicago law firm of Mayer, Brown, and Platt.

# Index

353

358

ISBN 0-8133-7153-